SELLING
US THE
FORTRESS

T0349728

SELLING US THE FORTRESS

THE PROMOTION OF TECHNO-SECURITY EQUIPMENT FOR SCHOOLS

RONNIE CASELLA

Routledge
Taylor & Francis Group

New York   London

Published in 2006 by
Routledge
Taylor & Francis Group
270 Madison Avenue
New York, NY 10016

Published in Great Britain by
Routledge
Taylor & Francis Group
2 Park Square
Milton Park, Abingdon
Oxon OX14 4RN

Printed in the United States of America on acid-free paper
10 9 8 7 6 5 4 3 2 1

International Standard Book Number-10: 0-415-95289-1 (Hardcover) 0-415-95290-5 (Softcover)
International Standard Book Number-13: 978-0-415-95289-7 (Hardcover) 978-0-415-95290-3 (Softcover)
Library of Congress Card Number 2005020079

Library of Congress Cataloging-in-Publication Data

Casella, Ronnie, 1963-
 Selling us the fortress : the promotion of techno-security equipment for schools / Ronnie Casella.
  p. cm.
 Includes bibliographical references and index.
 ISBN 0-415-95289-1 (hard : alk. paper) -- ISBN 0-415-95290-5 (pbk. : alk. paper)
 1. Public schools--Security measures--United States. 2. Security systems--United States--Marketing. I. Title.

LB3013.32.C373 2006
371.7'82--dc22   2005020079

Taylor & Francis Group
is the Academic Division of T&F Informa plc.

**Visit the Taylor & Francis Web site at
http://www.taylorandfrancis.com**

**and the Routledge Web site at
http://www.routledge-ny.com**

Dedication

This book is dedicated to Juliana, Quintin, and Sylvie

Contents

Acknowledgments

I wish to thank the individuals who helped me with this book, especially the security professionals I interviewed and observed for the last several years while I went about doing research on their work in the security industry. A number of vendors, sales representatives, engineers, and upper-management professionals were especially helpful, especially B. Caruthers, B. Snowden, K. Maynard, and J. Remson; they were sympathetic and understanding when I was first learning about the security business and had many "dumb" questions. Mary Green at Sandia National Laboratories was also very kind to share her knowledge and to help me make contact with individuals at schools and in the security business. Thanks as well to the countless individuals in advertising, sales, and distribution who sent me information about their companies' products and fielded my many phone calls and e-mail questions.

Several people read sections of the manuscript and gave excellent feedback. Thanks to Sari Biklen, who is always so willing to share her insights. Bob Bogdan gave the kind of suggestions any writer would be lucky to get. John Devine partly inspired me to write about security vendors and had comments that showed his deep knowledge on the subject. Catherine Bernard helped me to focus my conclusions and had a great sense for pointing out the significance of certain aspects of the subject. Thanks to you all.

Several people offered general comments and suggestions throughout the years. Thanks especially to Joan Burstyn, Ian Harris, Garrett Duncan, Mary Lee Morrison, Tianlong Yu, and Maureen Gilroy. I have worked with two great people for the last few years who have been especially influential—many thanks to Nan Stein and Johanna Wald. Emily Chasse is the best and most politically active librarian I know—special thanks. Farough

Abed helped with technology-related issues, and Daniel Mulcahy and Larry Klein are always an inspiration. And to my colleagues at Central Connecticut State University who keep conversations lively—much appreciation. A research grant from Central Connecticut State University also provided support and release time from teaching that helped me to complete the book.

Introduction

Getting Down to the Business of Being Safe

> *Schools have become a major market for these guys. The proliferation of security equipment for schools has taken off.*
>
> Peter Blouvelt, executive director of the National Alliance for
> Safe Schools, referring to security company vendors[1]

Who would have thought that schools in the United States would become the hot new market for the security industry? Not so long ago, in the 1970s, superintendents of schools in Boston, New York, California, and elsewhere bemoaned the use of random metal detector searches as a costly and unwieldy waste of taxpayer money and of time. Surveillance cameras were used mostly by the military, in prisons, and in some convenience stores, urban bodegas, and liquor stores; they were big and clunky and provided only grainy black and white images, and many did not record and archive images. Things began to change in the 1980s with the technology revolution, as new homes were built with motion detectors and access control devices, and buying a security system became affordable and common even for the middle classes.[2] By the 1990s techno-security devices, including surveillance cameras with pan–tilt–zoom capabilities, were becoming common in parking lots, on neighborhood streets and in downtown entertainment districts, in apartments, workplaces, and schools—creating what sociologist David Lyon described as a "surveillance society."[3] "Techno-security" refers to a type of safety measure that is highly technological, but it is also a way of demarcating a new era in security, one in which the technologies that were once reserved primarily for war are becoming a fixture even of schools.

1

While urban school district officials have often been the first buyers of techno-security equipment, suburban, rural, and wealthy school districts have all become part of the market, sometimes surpassing urban schools in their uses of the most advanced (and costly) security technologies. Consider, for example, the iris-scanning system that was implemented in three schools in New Egypt, New Jersey, in 2003 to monitor the entry and exit of teachers and parents. Plumsted Township, where the schools are located, is 95 percent White and its median household income ($61,357) is higher than the median income in both New Jersey ($55,146) and the United States ($41,994). The installation of the system, called T-PASS (Teacher-Parent Authorization Security System), was made possible through the partnering of several businesses and organizations, including the Plumsted Township Board of Education, the New Jersey Business Systems of Robbinsville, NJ (a state contract vendor), Iridian Technologies of Moorestown, NJ (a company providing the iris-scanning system), Biometric Solutions Group of Charleston, SC (a company providing the entry access control system that worked with the iris-scanning system), 21st Century Solutions, Inc. of Maryland (a consulting and research company that evaluated the system's use), and the U.S. Department of Justice, that provided $293,360 for the installation and evaluation of the system.[4]

During the last several years of studying violence and security in schools, I have seen school authorities in a variety of districts enter into deals with security businesses to purchase metal detectors, keypad locks on all classroom doors, surveillance cameras with pan–tilt–zoom capabilities, shoulder microphones for school police, and handheld mobile computers that are used, in part, to keep track of students in hallways. I have noticed police cruisers outfitted with computers attached to dashboards that provide instant access to a variety of databases and enable officers in their cars to operate and receive surveillance images from the cameras inside the school. Several years ago, I was surprised to see such equipment in schools; now it is becoming standard fare. And given the speed with which technology advances, this is only the beginning of the types of equipment we can expect to see.

The new standard fare has begun to change the way school guards, police, and administrators do their work. One of many examples is from a day when I was in a high school accompanying the school police officer and a school guard as they walked the halls between classes. The school had just invested in new security equipment that included about sixty surveillance cameras inside and outside the school; twenty-four were pan–tilt–zoom cameras "capable of reading a license number from across the parking lot," according to one school official. The system was networked to laptop computers in two police cruisers and at the police department, and could be controlled remotely by the police officers in the cruisers or at the police department. I was anxious to know from the police officer and guard how they felt about it. During our walk, however, the guard received a call on his shoulder microphone. It was a secretary alerting him to a disturbance in one wing of the school.

I had been with security personnel before when a call was made, and I knew standard procedure. I began walking rapidly to the wing, assuming that I would accompany both guard and police officer, but found myself with only one of them. I stopped and saw that the two had split up. I wondered if this was part of a plan—was there significance in the fact that the guard headed toward the scene while the police officer headed to the security office, where the monitors and controls for the security cameras were? I decided to go with the guard, and arrived at the scene a minute or two after him. By this time, the guard was talking to a student who had been making a lot of noise in the hallway. The student was compliant, though, and ready to go to class. But to make his point and to offer what he later called a "friendly reminder," the guard pointed out a nearby surveillance camera to the student, telling him, "We have an eye on people, you know." He did this in a good-humored way, with his hand lightly on the student's shoulder. All three of us looked up at the camera. By now, the police officer was watching us on the monitors. In case the student did not realize this, the guard told him, "Say hello to Officer Johnson." After the incident, I knew there was significance in what had transpired, but further, later in the day I discovered that the school guard had checked the archived images from the surveillance camera. He discovered that just before making noise in the hallway, the student had come in through a door that was supposed to be locked, and it appeared that he had arrived late to school or had been outside (sneaking a smoke?) in a courtyard that was off limits. Once this was discovered, the student was called out of class, questioned about the incident in the security office, and, though not suspended was threatened with suspension and told that a record of the incident was going to be put in his school file.

Part of me wanted to study such incidents and how techno-security equipment changed schools and relationships. But some time later, I was reading a popular security trade magazine and discovered by chance an article about the school I had been studying.[5] The article focused on the school's new security system. There was a photograph of the school police officer and guard sitting at the surveillance camera console, looking at the monitors on the wall. The article described the new system—how, as I noted earlier, it was networked to laptop computers in two police cruisers and at the police department, and how police and school authorities could control the surveillance cameras through remote control. The article also discussed the high-tech detector system that could activate the cameras. The system cost just over $300,000 for the initial setup, but the author of the article was clear that the system would save the school $200,000 per year in deterring vandalism.

The "disturbance in the hallway" incident was still on my mind, but I became more interested in what I knew the least about. How did the system get there, and where did this urban school in a rather poor district come up with the money to invest in the equipment? No doubt, the individuals who sold the equipment to the school scored big; they had outfitted one of the biggest schools in the state with a system that will need continual upgrades and upkeep, which means "reoccurring revenue" for years to come.[6] But who were they, and how did they get to the point where they were selling security equipment to schools? To answer these questions, I began communicating with sales representatives and vendors who sold school security equipment; many I interviewed. I began attending and studying security industry conferences, equipment trade shows, and training sessions dealing with particular kinds of equipment. I continued reading and studying the trade magazines and received thousands of pages of advertisements, e-mail postings, flyers, and news releases, which I also examined. I also began to study the federal policies and judicial rulings that helped to boost the use of security equipment and helped corporations to make inroads into the public school market.[7]

Naturally, the increased use of security equipment in U.S. schools is a response to incidents of horrific school shootings in Colorado, Minnesota, Kentucky, and other states, which served as ample evidence for school administrators that it was time to get serious about school violence, which meant investing in guards and security equipment. Threats of terrorism also pushed the use of security systems, especially when schools were identified by Tom Ridge, former director of the Department of Homeland Security, and Secretary of Defense Donald Rumsfeld as potential terrorist sites following the 2001 attacks on New York City and Washington, D.C. This made schools eligible for "homeland security" grants to purchase security equipment, coordinate with police departments and other authorities, and develop crisis management plans. Events overseas also spurred techno-security in the United States. When, in September 2004, Ingushis and Chechens attacked an elementary school in Beslan, Russia, torturing and killing over three hundred people (half of whom were children), President George W. Bush, in his address to the United Nations that year, reminded America of the threat of terrorism to our schools and children by referring to the massacre.

But there is more to school fortification than a wary America putting up its best defenses. The installation of security technologies in schools is also part of a larger trend involving the melding of two very powerful industries of the late twentieth century—technology and telecommunications—and the great capabilities for information gathering, observation, and digital communication that ensued. The result has been a windfall for businesses involved in all kinds of surveillance, detection, identification, and database technologies. The techno-security fortification of schools is also the result of the expanding international market for security equipment and the targeting of the public school sector by security businesses. Additionally, judicial rulings during the twentieth century have paved the way for techno-security fortification by establishing the legal use of random surveillance in public places. Support from federal agencies and corporations has made it possible for school administrators and school board members, including those strapped for resources, to allocate money to purchase security equipment. Security companies have also been successful in appealing to individuals who are already infatuated with technology. Whether we are talking about schools, gated communities, malls, homes, or gentrified city streets, fortification is also a way of selling a place to a customer base and fulfills certain middle-class expectations. Individuals enter into deals with vendors and take away a product produced to provide safety but geared to make customers want to buy more and better stuff as new devices come out, which keeps the security industry flush and contributes to a kind of consumer security. What is happening in the United States is part of a worldwide trend to create techno-security fortresses with devices that are so thoroughly a part of architecture, information gathering, telecommunications, urban renewal projects, military strategies, and policing techniques that to alter or advance them impacts worldwide organizations (the Department of Homeland Security in the United States, the Project Metropolit in Sweden, the British Department of Social Security, etc.) and matters both small (home construction) and big (military operations). Schools are a part of this. Using schools as a point of focus, this book shows how the techno-security fortification gets promoted through various political and judicial channels, and especially by businesspeople with safety for sale.

Here, Where Safety is Sold

The security industry has been very successful at tapping into the public school market. At their conferences and tradeshows, there is usually much

Figure I.1 School security makes the front pages of major security trade magazines. The biometrics device depicted at the bottom refers to a story about finger scanning in Philadelphia schools. *Access Control & Security Systems* (March 2003): front cover.

discussion about how security technologies can be applied in many contexts, including military, industrial, office, home, business, and school contexts. But some contexts get particular attention, which has become the case with schools. At conferences, schools both were referred to in passing and were sometimes specific topics of panel discussions and presentations; there were also training sessions by companies that specialize in schools. Additionally, major trade publications such as *Access Control & Security Systems*, *Security Management*, and *American School & University* have begun to include school-related articles, such as the one titled "Don't Let Them Hurt Our Children," the cover story of a 2003 issue of *Access Control & Security*

Systems that is accompanied by a prominent front-cover photograph of a schoolboy with a backpack walking down a shadowy school stairwell (Figure I.1). Direct mail and Internet advertisements by almost all of the major security businesses include references to school applications, and many companies advertise primarily to schools and include high-quality foldout brochures featuring school security technology—including surveillance cameras, which are advertised by Katatel Company under the header "School Video Surveillance in Action" (Figure I.2). For some companies, like Garrett Metal Detectors, the public school system is a major market.

Security devices have become a welcome presence for most people, and if not welcome, then ignored or tolerated, even in schools. Chapter 1 presents an overview of the security industry and its relationship with schools, and shows how it earned this welcomed presence. It provides basic facts about the businesses, trade literature, professional organizations, and hodgepodge of corporate, military, and federal contacts that make up the industry. According to security professionals I have interviewed, the buzz about schools has changed from "They never have any money" and "There is too much community resistance" to "They always find the money" and "People welcome it." The public school system has become a lucrative niche for the security industry, and the chapter begins to describe how this has happened.

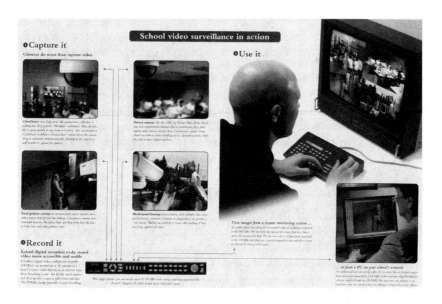

Figure I.2 "School video surveillance in action." Starting at left, viewing students from the perspectives of surveillance cameras, then male guard, then female administrator, stating, "Capture it, Record it, Use it." Katatel Company, advertisement (Katatel Company, 2004), inside spread.

Much of the book is based on three security conferences I attended, interviews with security professionals, and studies of security industry trade magazines, pamphlets, advertisements, and Internet postings that were sent to me. Information also came from telephone conversations and e-mail exchanges with security vendors and sales representatives. I also attended training programs with security professionals on using surveillance equipment and access control devices. These research experiences have given me an insider's view of the security industry, and Chapter 2 begins to take us into the world of this industry by exploring certain assumptions used by professionals in the business to sell their wares: that we all want a better world, that this better world is obtained through technological advancement, and that expert knowledge and the buying of things can help us to achieve this better world and free us from the worry and vulnerability we feel. The chapter points to a little-known side of the security industry—the way security professionals envision themselves as social reformers working to allay our fears and insecurities. They are the new guardians of our society, and their mission is nothing short of utopian, for they provide an essential component of life: safety. The chapter shows how progressive ideals of social reform and images of world betterment are used to sell equipment.

Technology is really at the heart of security equipment—its efficiency, allure, and cutting-edge sophistication are what make the sale. Chapter 3 discusses several key issues involving technology, including federal funding for technology research and development, and the way private businesses sell technology coming from research labs. Businesses contract with laboratories or develop their own versions of the technologies, package them in well-designed casings, and advertise them in particular ways to appeal to the general public and to social administrators (school boards, city planners, town councils, etc.). After discussing federal support for technology research and design, the chapter shows how the technology is marketed and sold not for its protective qualities, but rather for qualities such as efficiency, speed, and design, which relate more to consumer appeal than to security. The chapter also discusses one of the more advanced forms of security equipment at the beginning of the twenty-first century—facial recognition technology.

Building on the previous chapter, Chapter 4 discusses another factor that contributes to techno-security fortification. As a capitalist enterprise, the techno-security industry needs to appeal to middle- and upper-class professionals, who are the primary consumers of the equipment. In order to do this, security professionals tap into particular professional wants and make certain promises to their customers: that the equipment will not only provide safety but also grant its users professional clout, expertise, social and economic mobility, and personal power. The chapter explores these promises and demonstrates how they are used by security professionals to sell equipment. In doing this, the chapter shows how the security industry has been able to take equipment invented for war and national security purposes and turn it into an everyday "tool" for the on-the-go professional.

Another factor that has contributed to techno-fortification involves the way fear is used to drive an economic market. Chapter 5 demonstrates how many of the topics discussed thus far are based on a premise: that one must always consume in order to avoid a variety of dangers, including dangers of attack, dangers of social chaos, as well as those related to loss of personal power and status. The chapter examines how security corporations market danger, terror, and chaos to a wary public. It also demonstrates how fear is used in an agenda of privatization, by which individuals are convinced that the private sector is best able to take care of their social needs. The chapter also demonstrates how fear is used among security professionals to legitimize their work and to establish a sense of mission and purpose in the business.

In 2001, Visionics Corp. of New Jersey, a primary developer of facial recognition technology, along with the Security Industry Association of Alexandria, Virginia, an influential industry group, requested that the U.S. Congress regulate the use of surveillance technologies and create oversight and enforcement procedures. The case points out how the security industry tightropes the U.S. Constitution and looks to the courts and federal policy to define what is permissible. They also try to influence policy and laws. In Chapter 6, I examine the laws related to security and schooling, focusing primarily on cases that have involved metal detectors, surveillance equipment, and database information about youths. Most court cases have involved interpretations of the Fourth Amendment and have drawn on precedents involving search and seizure, the custodial roles of schools, and rights to privacy. The chapter shows how courts have generally ruled in favor of schools to have broad powers to use techno-security.

Having described the way techno-security is promoted by federal policies, laws, and corporations, Chapter 7 brings us to a central point of the book: the use of techno-security is not a logical response to danger, as is often assumed. It is a business response that benefits those involved in the transaction, each in their own ways. There are many types of transactions. There are transactions between businesspeople and customers, transactions between different groups in the security industry (between schools, police, and the military, for example), and transactions that occur between different businesses through subcontracting, as when architectural firms and construction companies team up with security companies to construct new schools outfitted with advanced security equipment. There are transactions of money, of equipment, of knowledge, and of ideologies. Transactions of one kind or another create the reality we call school security and make the business look natural. To some extent, techno-security fortification is another step in privatizing our social needs, of giving to companies another utility—another basic human need—to be dealt with at a bargaining table.

When trying to understand what is promoting techno-security fortification, it makes perfect sense to remind ourselves of real threats that we face: danger is a reality, and we cannot ignore the possibility that we can make life safer by using technologies. It also makes sense to see how we are convinced by media and political rhetoric to fear—how a culture of violence feeds our vulnerabilities and causes us to buy security. But, also, if you really want to know why security is the way it is and what we can look forward to in the future, look at the producers of the devices, those who get the equipment to those who pay for it, and, on top of that, look at those who benefit from it all. The conclusion of this book reviews these points involving business, governmental, and judicial support for techno-security, and highlights again how each has promoted the fortification of schools. There are no conspiracies here, no hidden agendas. What we see is not a surveillance society gone wild, but rather how a basic need is transformed into an item of trade—through what business processes, and with what kinds of federal and judicial support. This is a process that should not surprise us.

The Future of Being Safe

By the beginning of the twenty-first century, public controversies involving the installation of security technologies in schools began, especially as schools started installing cameras in classrooms, capturing hostile police raids on surveillance cameras that were then broadcast on national news, and using new forms of biometric technology, which have caused some people—adults and youths alike—to feel uncomfortable.[8] In 2003, the American Civil Liberties Union (ACLU) protested the use of facial recognition technology in a middle school in Phoenix, Arizona.[9] The school district had consulted with Maricopa County (i.e., the Phoenix metropolitan area) Sheriff Joe Arpaio, who helped to install the technology elsewhere and who also became, for a short while, nationally known as the person responsible for bringing back chain gangs to Arizona. In a letter to Tom Horne, the state superintendent of schools, and other officials, Eleanor Eisenberg, Executive Director of the Arizona Civil Liberties Union, and

Barry Steinhardt, Director of the Technology and Liberty Program of the ACLU, called on the superintendent to halt the installment of the technology by referring to cities, such as Tampa, Florida, as well as airports that have discovered that many "false positives" (mistaken identities and false arrests) resulted from the technology. However, officials from the school district maintained that the technology, which documents people's facial characteristics and then checks them against a database of collected identities, would alert officials to sex offenders and missing children, and that the technology can be used in a way to minimize false positives.

But what if we did perfect the technology? What if we were able to eliminate false positives? Would it then be okay for school district authorities to contract with security professionals to install facial recognition technology in schools—or in banks, stores, or public parks for that matter? How about random iris scanning on town and city streets? How about the use of technologies that can view through walls; how about technologies that have yet to be developed, a technology we can hardly even imagine now? To answer these questions, we would want to know if the technologies will actually make us safer or if they will just stomp on our constitutional rights, as many critics claim. I have no doubt—and I have seen this in my research—that security equipment can be used to prevent crime or violence. I also know that it can be ineffective and can be used in offensive and illegal ways. The surveillance camera that is used for voyeurism or to illegally track individuals undermines constitutional rights of privacy. But what about the surveillance camera that leads to the arrest of a rapist or is able to help solve an armed robbery?

When we battle over the good or bad of security technology, many topics central to the issue do not get discussed. Let us consider, for example, the fascination that humans have for technology and our faith in it to solve our problems. This faith in technology sustains the security industry, so rather than just talk about security we also need to talk about technology and what its advancement will mean for humans. Let us consider, as well, the monetary support for the development and installation of the technology. School districts lacking basic funds to support learning are able to spend hundreds of thousands of dollars on security technology—why? Let us also consider the big business that security has become not only for the security industry but also for technology businesses, construction companies, advertising firms, real estate agencies, and architectural firms. Imagine the number of jobs that are tied to the security industry, if not directly then indirectly through subcontracting and partnering with global networks of company divisions and affiliates. National security, once the domain of the federal government, has become increasingly the domain of companies. To what extent is techno-security another example of how the public good is put in the hands of the private sector? How successful can the private security sector be—whether it is protecting our schools, managing our money, or manning posts overseas in hostile lands? Should the future of safety be based on how many products one can buy and install; must it depend on a kind of self-fortification in gated communities and well-protected suburbs, where we send kids to techno-security schools and move around streets and in buildings overseen by surveillance cameras? What about the prevailing sense of risk and invasion that pervades modern society—that makes us submit to airport searches, school surveillance, and the use of lasers and scanners on our bodies? Is this something that is forced upon us in the Orwellian sense, or do we buy into it, not only psychologically but also financially?

The fortification of localities such as schools is a way of dealing with our troubled, embattled world in a way that promotes business. Children with guns? Buy metal detectors, the most sophisticated of which can also spot plastics used in bombs. Crime? Consider a camera surveillance system that runs twenty-four hours a day and is more powerful than the naked eye. We have greater faith in businesses and science to protect us than we have in our intellects to solve our problems. But this is nothing new. However, the extent of it is quite dramatic.

A Note about Tragedies and Carnivals

Early in the research, the seriousness of what I was studying struck me in an unexpected way. I had been communicating with sales reps and vendors who made me aware of an upcoming conference on security that would probably include sessions and presentations dealing with school security, and that many security professionals would be attending. I had yet to attend a security conference, so I registered for it. The conference was in early November 2001 in New York City. Several days after the September 2001 attacks in New York City, I received an e-mail from the conference promoters indicating that a special session on terrorism was being organized for the conference. When I went to the conference, I took a trip to where the World Trade Center had once stood, not far from where I had once lived. When I saw the smoking crater that was left behind, I had no idea that I would react with so much emotion. I went back to the conference. I interviewed some security vendors, asked questions during presentations by CEOs and presidents of security corporations, and met many in sales who were willing to talk about their jobs and educate me about the security industry. However, I passed through the day in a haze. Security was serious business, nothing to be dismissed, especially if you were in or near the World Trade Center on that day, or in Columbine High School on that spring day in 1999—or in any other place where tragedy has struck.

But conferences and security trade shows were not always so mournfully emotional, and at times the seriousness of the topic dropped off into something almost entertaining. Conferences were often places for happy socializing among security professionals, and security equipment trade shows could almost seem carnivalesque. There are sometimes hundreds of company booths, each with equipment that people meandering about can try out. There is plenty of glitz and eye-catching stuff, jars of candy, canvas bags being given away, and other incentives to get people to stay a while at the booths. Some companies haul in race cars that people can check out. One company set up a miniature golf course where security professionals and others in attendance could try their luck and possibly win a free gift; another company had a basketball hoop, and security professionals in suits stood in line taking free throws next to a table demonstrating facial recognition technology. One company had a snack table, and another was giving away soft drinks and sandwiches, but the longest line by far was at the booth with Budweiser on tap. The men and women attending the booths were mostly good-looking, thin, and professional looking. They handed out information about the equipment, as well as advertisements for cocktail parties sponsored by their companies. Walking around the trade show, past the hundreds of booths, one could feel like a flaneur taking in the sights of a happening little city or amusement park.

This book tries to capture this world without losing sight of that crater in the ground. The selling of security is serious business—it is also a big business. And the individuals who are a part of it are trying to protect us from tragedy; they are serious and professional—and they are also in line at the beer tap, stuffing their pockets with cocktail party invitations.

CHAPTER 1

The Security Industry and the Public School Market

School security is one of the fastest-growing areas in the security industry, and with good reason.

Alan R. Matchett, from the handbook *CCTV for Security Professionals*[1]

In the United States, a spree of school shootings in the 1990s and mounting threats of terrorism in the early twenty-first century prompted school authorities to respond, which they have done in several ways. Techno-security fortification has been just one response. There have also been crisis management drills and lockdowns that school authorities have begun to initiate, partly to deal with terrorism. To deal specifically with student-related violence, educational programs have been developed, including conflict resolution and character education. Like techno-security, some of these programs are supported by federal grants and involve businesses, which in this case produce curricula and conduct mediation and violence prevention trainings or act as consultants. There have also been policies related to zero tolerance, especially after the passing of the

Gun-Free Schools Act of 1994, as well as the hiring of school police officers and guards.

Another security tactic proposed for schools involved profiling strategies: checklists and software that enabled users to "profile" potentially dangerous youths. In some ways, this strategy was a form of techno-security, for the profiling equipment included identification software and databases, in and of themselves a kind of techno-security; additionally, the software could be networked into other kinds of techno-security devices, such as surveillance cameras. And yet, the student profiling strategy did not expand like the use of surveillance cameras, metal detectors, and biometric readers, primarily because these forms of security technology were hailed as more just and fair than student profiling. Though the Safe School Initiative did not initiate this thinking, it certainly promoted it and to date is the most prominent study to do so, and it is therefore worth discussing.

The Safe School Initiative

The Safe School Initiative, one of the most ambitious studies on school violence to date, was carried out from 1999 to 2000 by the National Threat Assessment Center of the U.S. Secret Service and by the U.S. Department of Education, with funding by the U.S. Department of Justice.[2] The researchers on the project—individuals from the National Violence Prevention and Study Council, the U.S. Secret Service, and the Safe and Drug-Free Schools Program of the U.S. Department of Education—studied thirty-seven lethal shootings in schools between 1974 and 2000. Each of the thirty-seven incidents was assigned a research team that studied court documents, school records, mental health records, and other material that shed light on the circumstances surrounding the attacks. In addition, the group interviewed ten perpetrators of the violence. In 2002, they released a document, *The Final Report and Findings of the Safe School Initiative: Implications for the Prevention of School Attacks in the United States*. There were ten major findings:

1. Incidents of targeted violence at school rarely are sudden, impulsive acts.
2. Prior to most incidents, other people knew about the attacker's idea and/or plan to attack.
3. Most attackers did not threaten their targets directly prior to advancing the attack.
4. There is no accurate or useful profile of students who engaged in targeted school violence.

5. Most attackers engaged in some behavior prior to the incident that caused others concern or indicated a need for help.
6. Most attackers had difficulty coping with significant losses or personal failures. Moreover, many had considered or attempted suicide.
7. Many attackers felt bullied, persecuted, or injured by others prior to the attack.
8. Most attackers had access to weapons and had used weapons prior to the attack.
9. In many cases, other students were involved in some capacity.
10. Despite prompt law enforcement responses, most shooting incidents were stopped by means other than law enforcement intervention.[3]

In its conclusion, the central recommendation of the Safe School Initiative was this: schools should conduct "threat assessments" that would enable them to intervene before an attack occurs. The idea of threat assessment is central to the mission of the U.S. Secret Service, which developed the technique and uses it to guard the U.S. president, vice president, and dignitaries, and their families. In general, U.S. Secret Service agents employ two methods in their national security work. One is the use of security measures (including techno-security), and the other is threat assessment. In threat assessment, they attempt to identify potentially dangerous individuals, conduct research to determine the level of risk of a situation, and then determine the best course of action based on the potential for danger. The Safe School Initiative suggested a very similar method when it urged school administrators to focus their energies in two main areas: "developing the capacity to pick up on and evaluate available or knowable information that might indicate that there is a risk of a targeted school attack; and, employing the results of these risk evaluations or 'threat assessments' in developing strategies to prevent potential school attacks from occurring."[4]

Threat assessments are an important part of any safety plan, but the problem with them is how individuals do their assessments. In the late 1990s, software was being fine-tuned that would enable school administrators to use profiling programs to determine the level of threat of students based on certain characteristics. Part of what spurred on the development of so-called student profiling software was the media attention given to the fact that the shooters at Columbine High School dressed in a particular way (they wore trench coats) and listened to particular kinds of music. It seemed that alienated, quiet, trench-coat-wearing students listening to Marilyn Manson were potential time bombs. It also seemed that we could gather these characteristics (and others) by using computers, and then hone in on students who met the criteria. The strategy was not really new, for the software was based on systems used by airlines, banks, real estate agencies, casinos, and hotels to collect and organize information about each of us, usually through surveillance cameras, swipe cards, purchase cards, and Internet activity. At the same time that profiling software was being considered for schools, though, techno-security was also being employed in schools, and sales were skyrocketing.

In general, it seemed that school techno-security strategies could go in two general directions—strategies to better profile students with the newer profiling systems, or strategies to better oversee them through the installment of surveillance, detection, access control, and biometric equipment. Ultimately, though, the uses of student profiling software lost steam while those of techno-security gained. Whether the Safe School Initiative had an impact on this trend is uncertain, but the report is very clear about profiling, again by hailing its own strategy: "Threat assessment, as developed by the Secret Service and applied in the context of targeted school violence, is a fact-based investigative and analytical approach that focuses on what a particular student is doing and saying, and not on whether the student 'looks like' those who have attacked schools in the past."[5] In the interim report of the Safe School Initiative, published in 2000, the U.S. Secret Service also cautioned against the use of student profiling software, especially one of the more popular packages (developed by a Hollywood celebrity bodyguard) called Mosiac 2000, which was supported by the Central Intelligence Agency (CIA) and the Bureau of Alcohol, Tobacco and Firearms.[6] In an even earlier report, *Protective Intelligence Threat Assessment Investigations*, the U.S. Secret Service again warned against the use of profiling software.[7] While the Federal Bureau of Investigation (FBI) has issued "checklists" of common traits among school shooters, the organization too has warned against overreliance on such checklists and is clear about its disapproval of student profiling software.[8]

There have been other cautionary notes about student profiling, sometimes coming from documents that offer profiling characteristics and checklists. The "Checklist of Characteristics of Youth Who Have Caused School-Associated Violent Deaths" was produced by the National School Safety Center and includes twenty characteristics. The checklist states that the National School Safety Center has "identified the following behaviors, which could indicate a youth's potential for harming him/herself or others," but also includes a disclaimer that states, "While there is no foolproof system for identifying potentially dangerous students, the list provides a starting point for educators seeking to prevent student initiated violence."[9] The other, *Early Warning, Timely Response: A Guide to Safe Schools*, was a collaboration among the U.S. Department of Education, the U.S. Department of Justice, the Center for Effective Collaboration and Practice of the American Institutes of Research, and the National Association of School Psychologists. It included sixteen characteristics (social withdrawal, drug and alcohol use, past history of violence and victimization, affiliation with gangs, among others) and a slightly stronger disclaimer stating that "such signs may or may not indicate a serious problem—they do not necessarily mean that a child is prone to violence"; that it is "important to avoid inappropriately labeling or stigmatizing individual students because they appear to fit a specific profile"; and, finally, that there is "a real danger that early warning signs will be misinterpreted."[10] At least two organizations— the National Association of Secondary School Principals and the Center for the Study and Prevention of Violence at the University of Colorado—have released statements discounting the effectiveness of student profiling, stating that profiling unfairly labels many nonviolent students and can lead to many "false positives" (mistaken identities and unfair accusations). The scholarly magazine *School Administrator*, one of the more popular magazines for school administrators, published in a special issue articles under the provocative titles "The Perils of Profiling" and "Profiling Bad Apples."[11]

The final report of the Safe School Initiative states in finding number 4 that there is no useful profile of students who engage in targeted school violence, yet, like other documents, the report provides some "profiles" by stating that many attackers were bullied, suicidal, and had difficulty coping with losses and personal failures. Consider this astonishing fact: of the forty-one attackers in the thirty-seven incidents of lethal violence, all were boys. Given this, who would claim that we should not watch boys more than girls when it comes to potential shootings? Still, the Safe School Initiative report noted that there are "no set traits that described all or even most of the attackers." This overstatement is understandable in light of the potential trouble that could result from student profiling. The presentation of characteristics and disclaimers in all of these documents tries to achieve a balance where we are able to recognize a potential time bomb without picking on students because of their clothes, attitude, disposition, or other "characteristics." How this is achieved is by getting back to the U.S. Secret Service's other mission, mentioned earlier. In addition to threat assessment, the organization employs the latest security technologies to handle threats.

There is something about the move toward techno-security that is a response against unfair student profiling systems. The rise in techno-security was partly prompted by a general consensus among prestigious groups and even newspaper writers that there was something potentially sinister about student profiling. While some forms of checklists that try to identify depressed and potentially violent students seemed okay, a formal system of profiling, with computer networks and databases, did not catch on (at least, not at this time). That it was referred to as "profiling" is an indication of our concerns about the practice, since the word is reminiscent of the racist "profiling" done by police officers and state troopers that was reported on repeatedly during the late 1990s, just as these student profiling software packages were hitting the shelves. Though there are concerns about techno-security raised in the media and by prestigious groups, in the late 1990s worries about Big Brother were more easily hurdled than the idea that we could build a system of profiling that created havoc in schools and would inevitably bring on accusations of prejudice and even Nazism. Techno-security had its problems, but they were nothing like this, for techno-security was seen as nonjudgmental. As any security professional will tell you, techno-security does not pick on particular people; it oversees everybody.

Techno-Security and Schools

Though their use is still relatively modest, the number of schools with forms of techno-security equipment is increasing. According to a National Center for Education Statistics study conducted in 1996–1997, about 4 percent of public schools conducted random metal detector checks on students and 1 percent of schools required that students pass through an upright metal detector each morning.[12] In a study conducted in 1999–2000, the use of random metal detector checks doubled, occurring in nearly 8 percent of schools, and the daily use of upright metal detectors increased to 1.7 percent of public schools.[13] In the 1996–1997 study, the use of video surveillance was not included, but in the 1999–2000 study, the category was included, and 15 percent of public schools reported that they used surveillance cameras in their buildings. The later study also included the presence of police in schools: nearly one in four schools reported that they used police or guards in their schools. If a kid goes to a city school, the chances are greater that they will have to pass through a security checkpoint. According to the 1999–2000 study, the random use of metal detectors is about three times higher in urban schools (about 14 percent of urban schools) than in suburban and rural schools, and the daily use of upright metal detectors is nearly five times higher in urban schools (about 5 percent of all urban public schools). However, the use of video surveillance is relatively the same in urban (15.5 percent), suburban (15 percent), and rural schools (14.1 percent), which may be an example of how individuals in the United States have become accustomed to random surveillance (but not random searches by metal detectors) in most areas of their lives.

The earlier 1996–1997 study included two categories related to security equipment (two categories about metal detectors), and the rest of the categories were related to actions or rules, including "visitors must sign in," "closed campus for most students during lunch," "controlled access to school buildings," "controlled access to school grounds," and "one or more drug sweeps." In the 1999–2000 study, there are three categories related to security equipment (the addition of "video surveillance") and another related to the presence of school police or guards. It is possible that future reports will continue a trend that began with these two reports, replacing old categories having to do with actions and rules with more categories relating to policing and security equipment. In other words, it is likely that categories such as "visitors must sign in" and "closed campus for most students during lunch" (which are in the 1999–2000 study) will be replaced with categories relating to the use of palm and iris scanners and facial recognition technology.

Given the historical role of schools to shape and mold the characters of youths, it makes sense that schools would use the most updated forms of technologies to better control behaviors and to provide a safe environment. But we may ask ourselves, How far are we willing to go with this technology? Some of the security technologies developed in the early twenty-first century include items that can be used to see through walls, sticky foam that can be sprayed on a street to stop a car, and flying surveillance cameras. What seemed like science fiction yesterday is reality today, and schools have a newfound place in testing and using the equipment. This puts schools in the same league as other groups (military, national security, and urban policing) that make increasing use of digital networking, lasers, and ultra-high-tech equipment that can be traced back to the Cold War production of spy and detection devices.

There is an easy argument that could be made that school security has become a branch of national security, and to some extent this is true, especially with the threat of terrorism. This makes it the job of the federal government to protect schools, which the federal government in the United States has done through various kinds of policies and funding programs. When the federal government is involved in the fortification process, though, one needs to be aware because it becomes easy and tempting for authorities to misuse techno-security and even simpler forms of information gathering. The United States has a long history of opposing government strategies to collect information and track citizens. This has been seen in continuing mistrust toward issuing national ID cards (most recently, after the New York City and Washington, D.C., attacks in September 2001), mistrust of the U.S. Census since its earliest uses, and even opposition to the 1935 Social Security Act, which started the issuing of Social Security numbers. In regard to Social Security numbers, many equated the federal program to a kind of Communist or Fascist tracking system, and claimed that individuals would have to start wearing metal ID tags. The word "security" was used instead of other possible names, such as "registration," in order to avoid any association with regimentation and the listing of identities. In spite of this, though, William Randolph Hearst's *New York Journal-American* described Social Security as a new way of "snooping and tagging." The *Boston American* newspaper warned that "your personal life will be laid bare, your religion and the church you attend will be listed. Your physical defects will go down in black and white, your union affiliation will be stated, even your divorce, if you have one, will be included." The United Mine Workers and the United Steelworkers unions worried that Social Security numbers would be used to blacklist union organizers and pressed Franklin D. Roosevelt to include a provision in the Social Security Act that would enable people to change their Social Security numbers. There was justification for concern: the Social Security Act, an unprecedented move that before the advent of computers took up six acres of storage space, gathered information that became beneficial to FBI Director J. Edgar Hoover, who pressed President Roosevelt to pass an executive order allowing FBI analysts access to Social Security Administration files for any federal criminal investigation.[14]

While there is reason to worry about governments' attempts to use their powers and access to technology in unjust ways, the fortification of schools is different from many previous fortification and information-gathering processes spearheaded by governments. Though the U.S. government (and other governments throughout the world) supports the fortification of schools, there is something about security equipment's sleekness and appealing designs (sometimes taken from Hollywood movies) that tells us another story. Techno-security in schools is not just an example of how federal and state authorities monitor individuals, but also shows how security businesses, marketing to you and me, manipulate the looks and names of devices to make them appear like toys for adults: even a surveillance camera advertised to a school can look like a fashionable gadget, something that would be fun to use. Security companies transform the looks of what is essentially military equipment to make it more appealing to a general public. The transformation is made easier because people are already used to—and even like—military fashions. Military colors, patterns, styles, and even names (compare the "Hummer" to the military "Hum-V") have been introduced by auto, sporting, and clothing companies especially. The trendiness of military styles has also helped to lay the groundwork for the acceptance of techno-security fortification, because the transformation of a military device into a consumer product is made easier when the public is already used to military styles. Who would have imagined that equipment first developed to fight wars could look so good?

The people who distribute the equipment also look good. They are not the scowling bureaucratic types imagined by those who worry that they will be tagged and spied on by black-booted government villains. They are businesspeople. What you see at security industry conferences, where much of the wheeling and dealing and information trading go on, are sporty men and chic women. They are company players, often young techies and salespeople who bring to the profession a sense of cutting-edge showmanship and youthful vitality. There are groups of men with ponytails who dress in black, others who act the part of the smooth operator, women who seem hip to the business world, and middle-aged guys still playing the part of the party boy. Some companies actually try to project an image of youthful trendiness. We see this even in the name of one company that advertises to schools, WizKid Opto Tech, located in British Columbia, Canada. I attended a training session given by the company in 2004, which began with a presentation by a young, handsome African American man. A young, pretty female assistant helped the man with his PowerPoint display. The duo seemed cosmopolitan, the perfect image of diversity and hipness. The security industry is composed of people like this because they are not there to impose their products, but rather to sell them to other professional people who want an image and look they like. Many security professionals had backgrounds in policing and the military, but these were usually people either in personnel services (guards, surveillance camera operators) or at the higher levels of a company (sometimes partners or founders of companies, or on boards of directors). The midlevel vendors most responsible for selling equipment to schools were a different group composed of people who had gotten degrees in business (and similar fields) and entered the security profession after college. There were also individuals who studied technology during the rise of personal computing and dotcoms, worked for technology companies, and had then entered the security profession as the technology revolution of the 1980s and 1990s began to fade and the security industry boomed. Many of these techies are involved in research and development (working for security companies that research and develop new devices) and in manufacturing (working for companies that do the hardware construction of security products). Increasingly, there are also professionals in training and consultation services. The distributors (sales reps and vendors), the consultation and training professionals, and to some extent the techies were the individuals among all security industry players most in contact with school authorities. The techno-security fortification of schools has been spearheaded by this rather new group of professionals who have found their home in the security industry.

Overview of the Security Industry

The school security market has been developing since the first uses of walkie-talkies and metal detectors accompanied the hiring of school police officers in the 1960s, often in urban districts. However, the public school system, especially when we take into account rural and suburban schools, is a relatively new market. It is also a lucrative one. Imagine the opportunity to outfit all public (and perhaps private) schools with security equipment that can cost several hundred thousands of dollars for the initial setup and more with ongoing upgrades and service. Include in this mix day care centers, colleges, and universities, and, for international companies, schools in Britain, Germany, France, and other countries that have begun to fortify schools—and the potential for profit is immense. The security industry, once dominated by military and government agencies and a few select businesses that received the bulk of government contracts, is now composed of these same groups, but also many thousands of businesses in various fields, including security design, research, training and education, distribution, manufacturing, and installation. This has occurred partly because security has become increasingly profitable with the opening up of the market beyond war and national security and into housing, community design, public transportation, and of course schools.

The security industry has capitalized on the school market, and businesses have flourished since the 1990s. Security companies range from small offices located in suburban office parks to worldwide, multibillion-dollar corporations such as Bosch, Honeywell, Siemens, Johnson Controls, and Diebold. There are also businesses that market to the U.S. military and federal government. These include Advance Paradigms, Inc., which provides equipment development and training to federal and commercial organizations; Pacific-Sierra Research Corp., an employee-owned company that markets information technology and software; Loyal Security, Inc., which markets videoscopes, infrared illuminators, belt packs, and other such equipment primarily to law enforcement agencies in the United States; and corporations such as Boeing, Northrop Grumman, and Lockheed Martin, which market heavily to governments throughout the world. There are also federal organizations that are part of the security industry, such as the Defense Security Service (which oversees the Personnel Security Investigations Program, the Industrial Security Program, and the Security Education and Training Program) and the Defense Technical Information Center (part of the Department of Defense that sponsors the exchange of technological and scientific information). There are also academic groups involved, such as the Federation of American Scientists (a distinguished, nonprofit group whose members analyze and try to influence global security issues) and the International Intelligence History Study Group (a group of historians, scientists, cryptologists, and others who research global relations and intelligence gathering). Groups that disseminate information about security are also a part of the security industry, including the International Centre for Security Analysis (based in London) and the National Security Institute (providing product news, events, and advisories for security professionals). There are also colleges that offer degrees and courses in security-related professions and that have created security-related libraries, such as Mercyhurst College. There are also organizations and lobbyists associated with security, including the 32,000-member American Society for Industrial Security (ASIS); smaller, regional organizations; divisions of larger organizations such as the International Association of Professional Security Consultants; as well as ancillary organizations that share interests in security, such as the National Association of School Resource Officers (NASRO) and National Association of School Safety and Law Enforcement Officers. Each of these organizations has lobbying power, professional conferences, and trade publications, and each is part of the world we call the security industry.

Trade literature is an important part of the security industry, for its magazines, newsletters, and Internet postings are crucial for communication among companies and among producers, distributors, and end users of the equipment. They also provide a window into the world of the security industry and how it has managed to connect with the public. There are at least four prominent security trade magazines (*Security Management, Security Magazine, Security Technology & Design*, and *Access Control & Security Systems*), one that addresses school security routinely (*American School & University*), several monthlies and newsletters such as *School Security Report* and *Security News*, and many more magazines, such as *Professional Equipment* and *Sound & Video*, that cater to those in the plant management, architecture, and communication professions and that include information about security. Many of these magazines are given out freely at conferences and trade shows, and are offered through websites; sometimes a subscription to a magazine is included in the annual dues to professional organizations. These magazines include information about security products, advertisements of security companies, and stories about particular security developments; they also facilitate communication among professionals and keep people informed about recent business developments and upcoming events.

Also facilitating communication among security professionals are conferences, training sessions, and trade shows. In addition to the usual presentations, businesses promote their wares and professionals network at these events. Security industry conferences usually include trade shows that sometimes host hundreds of security vendors who set up booths to advertise and demonstrate their latest equipment. Like other professional organizations, the security industry conferences also promote the industry itself by enabling meetings, discussions, contact making, and information exchanges about job opportunities, mergers between companies, and other kinds of news that are usually exchanged through person-to-person conversations. In less direct ways, and not always at these conferences, the industry also includes architects, scientists, engineers, and their associated professional organizations, which contribute to the production and installation of the equipment. While there is a dynamic core of the security industry, there is also a lot of overlap between the security industry and other organizations and individuals in science and technology, construction and architecture, and communications and media.

With other markets saturated, and with school funding available and court cases permitting the use of the equipment in schools, security businesses have begun marketing to schools in earnest. They include Wackenhut, one of the largest government security contractors and in 2001 the second-largest private contractor for state and federal prisons. In 1996, Wackenhut had yet to contract with schools, but by 1999 the Florida-based company had provided security technology for over one hundred schools and had created a separate school division of the company. A manufacturer of security identification card systems, DataCard Corp., initially developed its computerized cards for corporations and government agencies, but by 1999 the Minnesota-based company had contracted with hundreds of school districts directly and hundreds more indirectly through security vendors.[15] The Huntsville School District in Alabama was a typical district: in 1995, it installed a surveillance system in over forty schools that involved hundreds of cameras and an integrated digital network to deliver images from school locations to a central security office.[16] The system was developed and provided by Bell South Telecommunications. In addition to fewer incidents of vandalism and theft, the district's insurance premium yielded a $700,000 savings, according to a school spokesperson. Often, security measures involving technologies are installed after an incident prompts action. In Hartford, Connecticut, a high school purchased hand-held metal detectors and began random searches after three students had been stabbed outside the school; a school in Philadelphia installed a closed-circuit television (CCTV) system after a teacher was raped on school grounds; and WebEyeAlert, in conjunction with the Littleton Public School District and local police department, developed the SOS Littleton Initiative after the most tragic school shooting of the twentieth century in Littleton, Colorado.

The SOS Littleton Initiative was started by the Littleton Public School District, Congressman Tom Tancredo (R-CO), and Xybernaut Corporation, which contracted with WebEyeAlert, a subsidiary of Biscom (which started in the fax machine business).[17] WebEyeAlert, as its name indicates, specializes in surveillance cameras. It provided the CCTVs for the initiative, which first involved a Littleton elementary school but has since spread to other schools. WebEyeAlert installed a digital video recording (DVR) server in the elementary school and connected it through wireless networks to surveillance cameras that were already in the school. Law enforcement personnel were then able to conduct an emergency raid with Xybernaut's MA-5 wearable computer units and watch real-time (live) broadcasts of what the cameras recorded. They were also capable of controlling the pan-tilt-zoom cameras from their wearable computer units. Essentially, the new technology enables law enforcement officers or SWAT teams to storm a school while watching live streaming images on computer monitors attached to visors. Or, in less dramatic ways, emergency personnel are able to monitor events from outside the school, with zooming and panning capabilities.

School security technology is not confined to school buildings, and there are several businesses that have begun to hone in on a submarket: the school bus. Several districts in Connecticut, Florida, Ohio, Louisiana, Pennsylvania, and elsewhere use video surveillance cameras on their school buses. The fleet maintenance officer for the St. Lucie County, Florida, public schools stated that the installation of video cameras on the district's 280 buses began in 2003 due to problems of vandalism, which cost the district about $160,000 per year. The district contracted with GE Interlogix Video Systems Group. The equipment, which GE Interlogix calls the BusSecure system, is digital and records and stores information for up to four cameras mounted inside or outside the bus. The district has placed two cameras inside twenty-five buses (one at the front and one at the rear of each bus) and plans to continue installation as new buses are brought into service and as old equipment is updated.[18] The system also eliminates videotapes and increases download capabilities. With the old system, which used analog video cameras, there was a tape for each day of the week, and each week the tapes were copied over. The BusSecure system enables law enforcement and school district personnel to copy images to CD-ROM or remove the hard drive and connect it to another PC for viewing. They can also search and mark tapes. This enables school district employees or law enforcement personnel to save the information for later reviewing and investigations. Security businesses such as CameraWATCH, Inc., which specializes in school security equipment, and Gatekeeper-System Inc., which specializes in school bus surveillance, have also installed cameras that are accompanied by speakers that enable school administrators and bus drivers to speak to students while they are on camera or to remind students that the cameras are recording them.[19] Most of these systems also include Internet capabilities that enable school personnel as well as police officers to monitor the cameras even from their homes.

When security businesses initiate relationships with schools, usually they start with a preliminary needs assessment that is conducted by security industry representatives associated with particular companies or through the company's contracting with security consultants and architecture firms with their own school security divisions. IR Security & Safety, for example, offers schools a Safe Schools Site Survey to "evaluate your school's key control, access points, building security and maintenance practices, along with the suitability of your existing hardware."[20] Building Security by ESSEX provides schools a needs analysis by a building security team that include three groups: "ESSEX Total Openings (representatives who install door hardware and access control mechanisms); Diebold, Inc. (experts who advise on integrated electronic security solutions); and Safe School Solution consultants (who develop appropriate policies and procedures for each school). Almost all security corporations offer these types of services, which involve a preliminary fact-finding survey about the number of square feet of various parts of the school, the age of the buildings, current forms of security devices already installed, and needs. This will accompany a visit by security experts from the company or outside consultants hired by the company. A report is usually written and submitted within a specified number of days. If a school is accepting bids, the report may be accompanied by an estimate of charges for a security installation.

Crime Prevention through Environmental Design

While most security installations involve technology, there is a niche in the security industry of individuals, groups, and especially architectural firms that incorporate Crime Prevention through Environmental Design (CPTED) principles, whereby spaces are built to be conducive to supervision, community building, and orderliness. CPTED was started in the 1970s and was influenced by the idea of "defensible space," a term that Oscar Newman came up with to describe a new way of urban development based on designing parks, buildings, parking lots, streets, and other places in ways that inhibited crime.[21] Newman, an architect and city planner, was a consultant for government agencies, police departments, public housing authorities, and other groups, and his books have been distributed by the U.S. Department of Housing and Urban Development (HUD) and other agencies. He has won awards, including the 1976 Award of Excellence by the United Nations Conference on Human Habitat and the 1995 Man of the Year award by the John Jay College of Criminal Justice's *Law Enforcement News*. Newman began his research by studying public housing in St. Louis, Missouri. He noticed that although public housing (such as the 3,000-unit Pruitt-Igoe high-rises) was based on the planning principles of the architect Charles Le Corbusier and the International Congress of Modern Architects, and although it included public areas and communal rooms, people did not take care of the communal areas (outside grounds, laundry rooms, and bottom-floor community centers), and the buildings soon became overridden with trash, vandalism, violence, and other problems. Meanwhile, other public housing composed of similar people did not deteriorate—at least not as badly. One such housing unit, the Carr Square Village, was right across the street from the Pruitt-Igoe. Newman felt that it was the design of the buildings that made the difference. In his work in St. Louis and cities throughout the world, Newman advocated for the use of gated or clearly demarcated units (to increase a sense of ownership among a small number of people), aesthetically pleasing environments (to avoid stigma and to give people a sense of pride and ownership), and small, open spaces (for better observation). His idea of defensible space influenced city and suburban planning, municipal building construction, and ultimately, by the 1990s, school building planning.[22]

With Oscar Newman's principle of CPTED, schools are built with more windows and skylights (to have more soothing light but also to allow for better viewing and to cut down on darkened corridors), with straighter hallways for better viewing, and with security technologies that blend in with the architecture. Large window partitions around offices, one of the more distinctive traits of the CPTED concept, allow school office workers to see people coming in (Figure 1.1). An article in the School Security supplement of *American School & University* described the main concept of CPTED for schools:

> CPTED helps guide planners in creating a safe school environment [and] focuses on the behavior desired rather than

Figure 1.1 CPTED at work. Open areas and windows for better observation. Photograph in 2004 Calendar of Industry Events, featuring award-winning schools and universities. Campbell K-8 School, Ohio.

emphasizing behavior that is prohibited. Key elements include natural surveillance, natural access control and territoriality. These principles should be used in the pre-design phase. Gathering input from administrators, school board members, staff and the community is important during this pre-design phase.[23]

Architects have played a key role in promoting CPTED to schools. The 2002 Architectural Portfolio is a weighty 435-page issue of *American School & University* that highlights outstanding school facilities. The issue describes and displays some of the most beautiful, open, bright, and architecturally advanced schools in the United States—schools with patios and courtyards, vaulted ceilings, lecture halls, and gardens. One middle school in Minnesota, designed by Cuningham Group Architecture in Pennsylvania, was "modeled on an Italian hill town." Another school, listed under "Outstanding Buildings," is Charlotte Middle School in Michigan, whose "community design team" worked out a "uniquely zoned floor plan" to keep certain grades separated, but to allow access to shared areas and to keep all areas of the school visible.[24] The idea of CPTED was also picked up by security businesses, which began to mention design issues in their ads and to show images that would call to mind a control of spaces through open, orderly hallways where space is clearly demarcated, visible, and aesthetically pleasing.

Security professionals often talk about how their technologies "integrate" with school facilities. While CPTED is meant primarily for school construction, security professionals (sometimes partnered with architectural firms applying CPTED) will promise safety through not only what they call "product delivery" but also "product placement," which is a subtle reference to a version of CPTED. We can see this in Philips Communication, Security & Imaging advertisements that promise "Integrated Functionality."[25] Their advertisements provide blueprints for what a facility should look like and where cameras should be placed (Figure 1.2). The company's vision of a school is egg carton-like, where strategically placed cameras provide oversight over hallways, the entrance, the parking lot, and the cafeteria, and outside the bathrooms.[26] An IR Interflex brochure demonstrates a similar orderliness in a bright, airy school that is outfitted with stand-alone and computer-managed locks on exits and entryways (Figure 1.3). The company's description of a well-integrated access control system involves four levels of functionality: Level 1 includes securing exterior and interior doors, door hardware, mechanical locks, keying systems, and portable security; Level 2 involves electronic access control

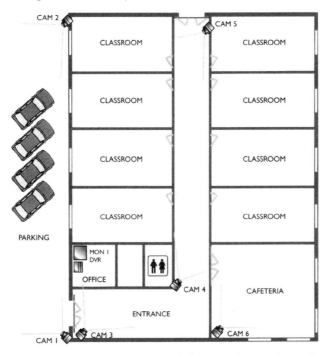

Figure 1.2 Mapping the placement of cameras and classrooms for optimal surveillance. Philips Communication, "Security & Imaging Easyline 2002/2003," advertisement booklet.

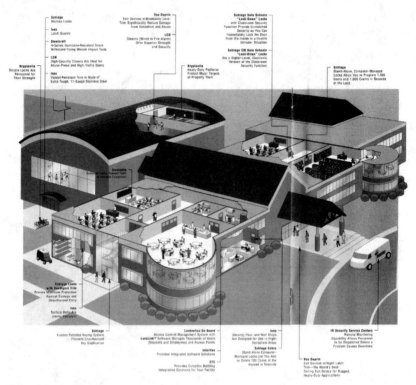

Figure 1.3 A well-planned techno-security school, with access control covering nearly every area. IR Security & Safety, foldout brochure (IR Security & Safety, 2002), inside spread.

and key management; Level 3 entails the management of perimeters and controlled public openings through the use of biometrics and electronic access control systems; and Level 4 involves the total integration of security with other forms of access control and time and attendance and personnel scheduling.[27] This is a highly integrated, efficient work of orderliness that integrates everything from biometrics—an iris-scanning system, let us say—to attendance sheets.

If the installment of techno-security is in part a reaction against student profiling software, as discussed earlier, CPTED is to some extent a reaction against techno-security, or rather the overreliance on technology. The principles applied in CPTED are not so different from those used to design gated communities, malls, as well as prisons and detention facilities. While the term "defensible space" goes back to the 1970s, the ideas associated with CPTED are much older. No doubt, medieval castle builders knew the importance of environmental design for fortification. Jeremy Bentham's eighteenth-century development of the Panopticon—the ultra-efficient prison—was also based on the manipulation of space and, as he stated, "the simple idea of architecture."[28] The modern use of CPTED combines elements of fortification, optimal surveillance, and environmental design and planning to create a space that hinders theft, vandalism, violence, and other crimes. Safety is built into the architecture; it is the motivating force behind the lighting system, the placement of areas (parking lots, restrooms, and stairwells), the layout of hallways, and almost everything else about the building. CPTED enthusiasts do not deny the effectiveness of techno-security when used correctly. But they will also point out how security is achieved with limited use of advanced technology, as when windows are added to a school, or offices and rooms are set up in particular ways. CPTED is a significant influence in the security industry, though it is sometimes overshadowed by the wow-power of technology equipment.

A Place for Better, Safer Living

All these aspects of the security industry—the different concepts, businesses, technologies, professional organizations, trade literature, conferences, marketing divisions, subgroups and niches, and more—are united in a mission to create a place for better, safer living and to profit along the way. This mission drives the techno-security fortification in schools and cities. It is also the driving force behind "planned communities," gated communities, some suburban communities, and many new housing developments.[29] Residential communities for the elderly have also bought into the trend. Bosch, for example, in 2004 completed work on a forty-three-acre residential community for seniors that uses what Bosch calls Security Escort. The Security Escort is a wireless detection device that works through a necklace or wristband transmitter worn by the residents. A map of the residential facility and grounds is on constant display on monitors and is updated every seven seconds as transmissions are delivered from the necklaces and wristbands to the monitor. Security Escort is equipped with Check-In-Monitoring (which informs staff when a resident has not moved from a specified area), Wander Alert (which notifies staff if a resident has left a designated area), and Acknowledgement Transmitters (handheld devices that staff use to get readings from the transmitters without having to be confined to a desktop). There is also a feature called Staff Tour, which keeps track of staff and provides a database listing staff locations and movements. An administrator at the residential community explained, "We monitor our assisted living residents routinely. If someone attempts to walk away from the area without advising us first, we are alerted by the system and able to track their location. We first check the system to see where they might be."[30]

To find out where they might be, a red circle on the display map shows the problem area. Automatically, information about the wearer of the transmitter is called up. The system can also be used to track and receive information about an individual without the sounding of an alarm. Security Escort and other security tracking devices are hailed as ways of making life better and safer. A news release from Bosch gets right to the point: "The comforting sense of personal security provided by Security Escort ... clearly enhances their residents' lives every day along with much greater peace of mind for their loved ones."[31]

In spite of their polished packaging, the devices are not very different from those that parolees are sometimes forced to wear by judges to keep track of their whereabouts. Youths and teachers in schools refer to these as "electronic ankle bracelets" and sometimes "electronic leashes." The device is sometimes used as an alternative to incarceration, and allows nonviolent offenders to stay in school or at work and then return either home or to a detention facility. The technology has recently taken a great step forward. The traditional ankle monitors were simple FM transmitters, but today's devices use technology developed by scientists who worked on President Ronald Reagan's Star Wars program in the 1980s, and now use geographic positioning systems so that authorities can track wearers of the devices in greater detail, get continuous information, even know how fast individuals are traveling.[32] The old devices only told authorities when a person stepped outside of a designated area (a house, for example) and gave information at particular intervals of time. Now the devices give real-time information about the movements of people and can be used to follow them.

When youths in schools wear the devices, it is because judges require it. But the items could also be issued by school administrators. If the devices are good enough for the elderly, why not for the young? Already, the devices—once reserved for nonviolent offenders—are being used to keep track of low-risk juveniles in New Jersey using a system called Com-Trak, which allows authorities to program into the devices very specific information, such as where a kid is allowed to go and at what time of the day.[33] In schools, such devices could be used as an alternative to expulsion or suspension—as a way of not only keeping students in school but also keeping track of them. How about for certain kids in special education programs, who like the seniors at the residential home may "wander off" or need assistance? It is not such a stretch to imagine a world where all students are tracked with electronic leashes. In fact, today's student ID cards are not so different from the ankle monitors. Students have quite easily learned to carry their school ID cards without complaint. Could they be as easily convinced to carry a detection device? How about inserting a device right into their ID cards? Who would object to this—and if there were objections, besides getting some good press perhaps and support from the ACLU, who is going to care?

When the Spring Independent School District in Texas equipped 28,000 ID cards with built-in tracking devices, there were very few complaints. The ID cards are based on radio frequency identification (RFID). RFID uses a computer chip that contains a microantenna that transmits information to central posts, in this case to the school district main office and police department. When students board and exit school buses, they must scan their cards, and in school and police centers an icon appears on a map showing the position of the cardholder. The technology is not new—a version of it has been used by companies to track livestock and inventory, and it is similar to the systems used to keep tabs on truckers. But the Spring Independent School District is one of the first to use it on children. It was first introduced in an elementary school and promoted as a way of keeping track of little children who could get lost or kidnapped. Other schools are also using the technology. A school in Phoenix in 2004 started using a biometric scanning device on buses to keep track of students getting on and off buses. In 2003, a school in Buffalo, New York, started keeping track of attendance with microchip-equipped ID cards. When students entered the school, they passed a scanner that registered their attendance in a main database.[34]

The future of techno-security will look a lot less ominous than many critics claim and will be more prevalent in our society than most proponents want us to believe. Consider the fact that in the 1990s, there were serious news and academic articles weighing the possible ramifications of random surveillance on city streets, and yet by the early 2000s, cities have virtually steamrolled over the critics and become technology fortresses without us even knowing it. Chicago's school system is one of the most fortified in the world, and the city itself has become an example of things to come. Chicago's security system was designed after city officials studied London's security system (built to ward off IRA terrorists), security systems in casinos in Las Vegas, and systems used by the U.S. military.[35] In addition to traditional monitoring, the system uses software that is capable of identifying particular kinds of behavior. Police will be alerted (as with the Security Escort, an area on a map will be highlighted to show the trouble area) when individuals wander aimlessly, drive erratically, linger outside a public building, or leave a package and walk away from it. There are about 2,400 surveillance cameras posted on the streets and other municipal areas, all of which are networked into the system. The cameras have pan–tilt–zoom capabilities, can magnify images up to four hundred times, and can keep track of individuals by having operators working several cameras at once, following a suspect as he or she moves from one camera area to another. The entire camera network includes not only police department cameras but also cameras mounted by the transit, housing, and aviation authorities. Private businesses will also be able to network with the cameras and have video images feed into the central control room, which is in a secret fortified building in the city. The security system was supported by a $5.1 million federal grant, and city officials have met criticism of the security system with further plans: to place surveillance cameras in commuter and rapid transit cars, and to install them on street-sweeper vehicles.[36]

Whether or not the city surveillance system will also include school cameras is yet to be seen, but it is likely that schools could be added to the mix. Mayor Richard Daley Jr. has responded to criticism of the system by stating, "We're not inside your home or your business. The city owns the sidewalks. We own the streets and we own the alleys."[37] He could make the case that the city owns the schools as well. Imagine a surveillance system that may observe an individual from the moment he or she leaves a house to the moment he or she comes home (and, if one lives in public housing, may also include surveillance at home). This describes a city that would have been unimaginable to the everyday dweller fifty years ago. And this is only the beginning, for the technology is just starting to develop.

Security—It's About the Economy

Part of the impetus for the security system in Chicago has to do with terrorism and crime, but it is also a central part of the city's revitalization program—it is a way of boosting business. Under the direction of Mayor Daley, city officials have been trying to turn Chicago into a global city—a host of major events and a city of international business, world-class entertainment, and tourism.[38] So-called global cities such as Chicago are being revitalized around entertainment districts, the creation of which has entailed gentrification and the creation of upscale neighborhoods, and the subsequent displacement of those who cannot benefit the new economy and are a detriment to the plans of developers.[39] The security system in Chicago was supported by businesses, and was installed to help business and to be part of this gentrification process. Even keeping schools safe is good business during a time when students have greater opportunities to switch out of schools, move to other districts, or take part in "school choice" programs.

Well-secured public schools (or private schools), fortified cities, and gated communities are examples of how places are manipulated and sold for their protective qualities and how the middle classes and wealthy are lured by assurances of carefree living. This is seen, as well, in the forti-fication of consumer places, such as malls or entertainment districts in gentrified sections of towns and cities. In 1994, Glasgow, Scotland, became one of the first cities to use random CCTVs on city streets (a practice that is becoming more common in the United States, as the case of Chicago points out). The Glasgow program involved the installment of thirty-two cameras in the downtown of the city. The installment of the cameras was prompted by a 1992 study by the Glasgow Development Agency that concluded that investment and tourism in the city were hampered by the perception that the city was dangerous. A steering committee called City-Watch was formed "as a crime prevention initiative which aimed to effect a reduction in the cost of crime to businesses, reduce the clean up costs of crime and vandalism, increase the opportunities for employment and improve the overall feel-good factor in the city center."[40] Essentially, the security initiatives were prompted by the business community so that business would improve.

No doubt, safety is a big seller. In the late 1990s, when a Baltimore-area mall was deteriorating and on the cusp of going out of business, it proved significant that improved sales were obtained through increased secu-rity. Paul Martin, a retired Baltimore County Police lieutenant who was security manager for Security Square Mall (the name refers to its location next to a Social Security office), explained how one of the first steps in the mall's makeover was to publicize the new security initiatives, including the placement of a prominent police station in a main corridor, bicycle patrols, more high-profile and aggressive vehicle patrols, more prominent security guards with new uniforms that resembled those worn by the Baltimore County Police Department, surveillance cameras, hotlines, and improved lighting. Marketing of the mall and improved sales at the stores were linked directly with greater security. The security manager pointed out,

> The immediate goal was to transform any negative perceptions about Security Square Mall into positive ones. Toward that end, new security measures and procedures were developed to provide visible proof of the mall's commitment to the safety of customers and employees. Security worked hand-in-hand with the marketing and public relations team to educate consumers about the mall's security initiatives. It also partnered with the mall's architect to upgrade and renovate the signage, food court, and mall amenities; and it forged cooperation among mall merchants, police, and out-side organizations. The results have been impressive.[41]

There is a pattern that turns up over and over again whether one is talking about city fortification, ultra-secure malls, or tracking devices on elderly people. The primary impetus for the changes in both the designs of places and the techno-security used in them is to create a place for better, safer living. But the security installments are also meant to increase business. Though schools are different than businesses, this becomes less true as a business ethos infuses public education. Schools have become a marketplace for food and soft drink, transportation, athletic gear, computer, curricula, as well as security businesses. Additionally, a free market approach to school reform (including charter schools, vouchers, merit pay, etc.) has been spearheaded by many business and educational groups, including the Business Roundtable; Educational Alternatives, Inc.; the New American Schools Development Corporation; and the Whittle Communications Corporation.[42] The security industry has ridden on the coattails of these business developments. In this competitive environment, school administrators and building managers will have to call on security professionals to provide them with the necessary equipment to boost the desirability of the school. An administrator at the elderly residential community discussed earlier was very clear about Security Escort when she stated, "It's a great marketing tool for us."[43] Likewise, the fortification of Chicago is part of the selling of the metropolis as a world-class city. Schools too will have to compete on the open market. And security professionals have stepped in to consummate the deals and to provide those items needed to compete. But before that, in order to make the sale, a world is presented to us, one where technology is so completely integrated in society that we do not even notice it—rather than ominousness, we get jewelry tracking devices and surveillance cameras imbedded in architecture. This is a new kind of security, one that is expected as part of owning a home, shopping, visiting cities, living in rather expensive residential communities, and going to school. It is a type of security sold to professionals by professionals and, as the next chapter points out, a type of security that depends on the buyers' and sellers' shared belief in social betterment. The selling of techno-security hinges on an image—in this case, an image of utopia—that is used by security professionals as a kind of unstated reference point for appealing to our intrinsic yearnings for peace and safety, which they provide, they will tell you, at a cost that is reasonable.

CHAPTER 2

Selling Social Betterment for One's Own Private Utopia

The value we gain in public safety far outweighs any perception by the community that this is Big Brother who's watching. The feedback we're getting is that people welcome this. It makes them feel safer.

Ron Huberman, executive director of Chicago's emergency management and communications office, remarking on Chicago's surveillance system[1]

Any security professional will tell you that school security is part of a movement to improve society. There is no shortage of utopian ideals in what security professionals say when they describe their jobs. They manage to get their wares into the hands of customers by convincing people that what they are doing—together, both security rep and customer—is a deal that will inevitably prove beneficial. If you really want to help kids in school, you will do all you can to keep them safe: I have had several security professionals tell me, "Children cannot learn in an unsafe environment." There is truth in this, but there is also an implicit message that says that security professionals are the individuals who provide the safe environment that enables our children to learn—they are, in a sense, our guardians and our saviors. Or perhaps "savior" is too strong a word? Perhaps their own descriptions are more appropriate, including "protectors," "helpers," "expert managers," and "a lifeline to safety"—all phrases that security professionals used when I asked them to describe themselves. In spite of criticism of techno-security fortification, security professionals feel quite good about what they do; recent events in the world (especially school violence and terrorism) only seem to prove their points. Where would we be without them? they ask. A security professional who consulted with schools told me that he was often greeted "with open arms" by people who had once been critics of security technology in schools: "Now they see that what we do is keep the world safe, keep our schools safe, keep our loved ones safe."

Again, we can ask the question, How is it that security equipment once reserved for fighting wars is now standard fare in many schools in the U.S. and elsewhere? This happens when salespeople convince buyers that what they are engaged in is for the betterment of society. Sure, we are talking about business, but we are also talking about a grand mission of improvement that occurs in different ways: we have betterment of a school environment; we also have betterment associated with better learning. Safety is hailed not only because it makes individuals safe but also because it enables them to learn and do better in schools. According to security professionals, there is always a secondary activity that is improved when safety is improved—when people feel safe, they work better, travel more, spend more money, and enjoy life to the fullest. Kids do better in school. Test scores go up. One security vendor put it this way: "If you are feeling safe—if you are safe—you are going to do those things that keep us succeeding in life—work, education, spending, being productive. If you are in danger, you will lock yourself in your room."

But in order to make the sale work, the rhetoric of social betterment has to be accompanied by general feelings that the world is undesirable in the first place. Why else would we lock ourselves in our rooms? To some extent, social betterment is based on the presumption that all is not well in the world, and therefore betterment is necessary; and this is where the security professional comes in. They make it seem natural that their equipment will make betterment possible. Security professionals view themselves as social reformers, working to improve society. They use this shared value as a starting point for their sales pitches and press releases: it becomes a theme underlying almost all the work they do. The ability to make this theme stick depends on people's own feelings of vulnerability; after all, who has a need for a security professional if they are feeling safe?

Of Social Reformers

Security professionals view themselves as underdogs battling a cruel and dangerous world. They like to highlight their companies' acts of charity, their goodwill, and what many security professionals view as their progressive ideals, such as when a company representative for ASSA ABLOY told me about his company's support for Habitat for Humanity. In 2001, the company signed a five-year contract with the charitable organization to supply locks for 25,000 homes that they expected to build in the United States and Canada. The security industry also includes companies that are members of federal, statewide, and nonprofit crime prevention groups, and that donate products such as bike locks to community groups. In an advertisement for ASSA ABLOY, under the title "Our Cornerstones" and subtitled "People Make a Difference," the security lock company lists their "cornerstones" around an illustration of a Roman pantheon: "Vision; Realism; Courage; Ethics," the brochure claims (Figure 2.1). Though the words are marketing techniques used because they sound good even if you cannot be sure what they refer to, they also call to mind a courageous mission

The ASSA ABLOY culture is based on four cornerstones that represent the main objectives and core vision of the organization – Courage, Ethics, Realism, and Vision. Each company is guided by these principles as they conduct business day-to-day.

Figure 2.1 "People make the difference." Security as a progressive and grand mission of social betterment. From ASSA ABLOY, *ESSEX 2002* catalog, 6.

of creating a better, more ethical world. It is an elevated mission, one to be compared to a Roman pantheon surrounded by good character traits.

Nearly anyone who has looked into company relationships with cities, towns, and schools knows that corporate benevolence can be a two-edged sword: some would say that corporate benevolence is an oxymoron since benevolence is often shrugged off by corporations when profit leads action. But for security industry professionals, the general feeling about benevolence is that the industry is founded on it: they do their jobs for the sake of other people; they are our "protectors" and "lifelines to safety." One vendor told me, "Good business and good deeds go hand in hand." They see their work as innately good and themselves as reformers who use all items at their disposal (technology, know-how, and skills) to improve the social circumstances in which we find ourselves.

Though connected to mostly conservative political, military, and corporate establishments, there is a progressive and sometimes even subversive side to the industry. At times, these progressive ideals border on the rebellious. Perhaps a sign that the security industry has clearly captured the government, police, and corporate markets (to the point where they no longer have to worry so much about coddling or offending people in these sectors), security industry professionals freely make reference to the possibility that security devices can be used by the general citizen to catch authorities abusing their power and acting illegally and immorally. This is also a sign that they are marketing to the general consumer, who is likely to see great power in using devices against authorities. In presentations and interviews, for example, salespeople made reference to the possibility of using the technology to catch corporate criminals and lawbreaking police officers. One vendor described this to me as the "Rodney King effect," referring to the well-publicized incident involving the videotaping by a citizen of Los Angeles police beating Rodney King, an incident that set off violent protests and riots. Melanie McGee, president of Evolution Software, Inc., also made reference to the notion that security equipment could be used by citizens on authorities when she remarked in a presentation to a conference gathering that her company's "wearable computer" with surveillance technology could record police interactions with citizens.

Security professionals do not view themselves as stuffy business types; they see themselves as cutting-edge, forward thinking, and even a little rebellious. Slightly subversive and progressive ideals abound in the industry, even when marketing to authorities. Frances Zelazny, who in 2001 was director of communications for Visionics, explained that the New York Police Department (NYPD) was using facial recognition technology to replace antiquated systems of "mug shots" so that "justice can be better served." What she meant by this had a progressive intent. She claimed that the technology was less likely to lead to false arrest and racial profiling, and would therefore be more just. Again, while some will criticize security professionals for spreading wares that will inevitably lead to racial and other forms of profiling, this security professional viewed it quite differently: the equipment she helped to sell actually made profiling less likely. It took what she called the "subjectiveness" out of surveillance, making it more automated and therefore more accurate.

In a discussion after her presentation, she explained that the "facial technology must reach the consumer level," and when I asked her if this included the school market, she nodded enthusiastically and said, "It already has." She viewed this development as a step forward for justice, emphasizing that if a digitalized facial feature finds no match in the database, "there is no memory." The software does not archive facial images (another database is needed for this). She insisted that the technology "is free of the prejudices that come with profiling. It surveys everybody"— another example, as well, of how techno-security is seen as the logical alternative to student profiling and profiling software. Other security professionals had similar sentiments. When I raised the issue of metal detectors being used to illegally search youths, one vendor responded with a question: "What do you want to do, go back to the days when people were patted down in back rooms?" Essentially, security professionals felt that advanced devices are fundamentally democratic since they avoid the pitfalls of human subjectivities and are without prejudices. A security professional explained about an iris scanner he sold, "The scanner doesn't pick on who to scan; it only gives us reliable, untainted information."

Security industry professionals share with progressives their disaffection with society and have a strong belief in perpetual betterment, which is accomplished through the ingenuity of knowledgeable people such as themselves. But behind their rhetoric about justice and social betterment are bleak presumptions about our world. Even ASSA ABLOY's often lofty language is tempered by other, grimmer, more foreboding tones. Peter Kott, director of ESSEX Building Security (a division of ASSA ABLOY), is described in a news release distributed by the company as a specialist in school security.[2] What he called "physical security" was an important aspect of his three-pronged security plan for schools.[3] He commented,

> Schools by and large have response plans, but plans that are not practiced will not be effective. For example, lockdowns in which teachers contain students in classrooms behind a locked door and take attendance are a common element in emergency response plans. In the best case, schools will drill until they are confident

they can achieve a complete lockdown in under two minutes. Unfortunately, denial is pervasive. Everyone thinks "that could never happen here" even though the demographics show violence can occur in any community. Leaders in the school systems that are addressing safety and security are also communicating about it in the classroom and in the community through letters, assemblies, the PTA and town meetings.[4]

The mention of lockdowns, of emergency response plans, and that "violence can occur in any community" is mixed with communitarian ideals of involvement, letter writing, and, of course, improving safety. The blending of utopia and dystopia, of good and bad, and of safety and danger all aid in selling the equipment. Security industry professionals use neither promises of safety nor fear to make the sale. They blend the two together, leaving us with a question to ponder. It is not a question about whether or not we want to be safer, but is a question about whose side we are on: those stuck in the old days, open to potential threats, or those who have embraced modernity and utilize human ingenuity to make the world better. Security professionals present us with this option. Naturally, they do all they can to convince us to buy, but their sales rhetoric and advertisements also make it seem like all decisions are in our hands: we, consumers of the world, possess the power to either buy or not buy, and what it means to buy—a meaning carefully crafted by security industry advertisers and repeated by vendors—is the difference between advancement and stagnation. Any security professional will tell you that in a rapidly changing world such as ours, only the ignorant are sitting still.

Security professionals describe themselves as helpers, protectors, and people who work so that others can be safe. And what do they ask of us? They need us to trust their decisions and to accept the development and distribution of products sold by the educated classes of service providers, of which they are a part. In no way do security industry professionals imagine themselves overwhelming schools with security technology or creating a culture of fear, and some security trade literature is very clear that professionals should seek buy-in from parents, students, and teachers before installing their wares. They easily dismiss the critics. What they see is the danger that is already there. "Schools can be worse than prisons," said one vendor who had put up installations in both. A consultant who did initial needs assessments said, "That's why the schools call me—they know I have what it takes to prevent another tragedy. I have the expert knowledge." Behind the marketing of the wares and the intention to make a sale, security professionals propose a return to certain progressive, sometimes utopian ideals. They try to connect with us by presenting a world of sure-fire expert knowledge and cutting-edge technology.

The Business of Social Improvement

At a security industry conference in 2002, Peter Bender, sales channel manager of Security Applications, Inc., who had at one time been involved in the installation of surveillance cameras in New York City public schools (funded by a federal Safe Schools Act grant), spoke about the purpose of his profession. In many ways, he sounded like a utopian expressing his yearning for a better future while denouncing the state of current conditions. But he also sounded like the businessperson that he was:

> Making money is a key thing of what I do, since we are a business. How I make money is by selling equipment that gives our customers greater oversight of facilities. Are we going to change things, shake things up? You bet. But wouldn't you agree that things need to be shaken up? Schools can be scary places; we do not want them to be scary. Students and teachers are assaulted; we want to end assaults in the classroom and hallways. You know that things will change, and we in the business will be part of that change. But the world has changed and we are making accessible to our investors the ability to roll with the changes.

The shaking up, rolling with the changes, and future talk that are so much a part of the industry are part utopian sounding, but they are expressed with the explicit intent to sell equipment, to improve profits, and to bolster one's position in the industry. White-collar workers such as this salesperson are the educated professional experts of an early twenty-first-century technical-information society. They represent certain levels of the service sector workforce that provide what one company referred to in their advertising as "one-stop shopping for a complete security program."[5]

The primary people facilitating this one-stop-shopping techno-security program are businesspeople who have behind them scientists and before them their potential customers. They are not the common image of the authoritarian henchman. Rather, sometimes they are in conflict with over-zealous police and government agencies who may use the equipment for ill purposes. Part of the reason for this is because business is not served when security equipment gets a bad rap. Also, security professionals are regular citizens and know that the equipment is used not only to benefit but also to watch over people such as themselves; security professionals are not blind and are indeed sometimes sensitive to the fact that the equipment can be used against them. Additionally, the security industry is composed of groups that are sometimes in competition with each other; sometimes the younger, trendier professionals are in competition with the business types with backgrounds in policing and the military. Additionally, sometimes security businesses want to "cut in" on the services that police and even the military provide. Private security professionals, for example, have been increasingly involved in policing domestically and even in war zones. For these reasons—and probably others—many security professionals view themselves as a friendly kind of authority, sometimes at odds with more brutish police and military types.

Business, police, and military groups rub elbows at security industry conferences and need to work together in spite of their occasional differences.[6] While police and the military have had their influence on techno-security fortification in schools, it has been the business sector, however, that has been most influential. Businesses have been integral to getting schools to make the initial investment in the equipment, thereby assuring a long-term arrangement of fortification where newer and more advanced equipment will be installed for decades to come. With techno-security— as with much technology—the initial investment is only the beginning of what will inevitably turn out to be a long-lasting security program of upgrades and integrated networks. It is a simple matter of business, and quite common, that all contracts have built into them reoccurring revenue. Security salespeople also know their customers. Their customers are often people just like them: professionals in the rank. So they offer what professionals expect from their products—and who better than security professionals to know what their professional customers want?

Keeping Your Professional Customers Satisfied

Security businesspeople appeal to the wants of professionals (and increasingly young people) who expect individualized attention (or at least the appearance of individualized attention) and the ability to take control of their technologies and to feel empowered by them. Though mass production was the engine for the industrialization and mass consumerism that fueled economic growth in countries throughout the world, today many individuals feel at odds with mass production and expect uniqueness even as items look and operate increasingly the same. They want one-of-a-kind items and individualized attention. They want expertise—and they are willing to pay for it. Security salespeople know about these wants and strike a balance between being experts without undermining the expertise of the buyer. They also balance a set of ironies: they attempt to give individualized attention while attempting to increase their sales base, making individualized attention less likely; they offer what are purported to be unique cutting-edge devices when in fact the devices resemble other companies' equipment and even other types of gear (such as entertainment equipment).

A common refrain among dealers is that "each customer, each facility is unique." Security professionals present themselves as expert professionals, but also, and equally important, hail the uniqueness and expertise of the person buying the equipment. This can be seen, for example, in ESSEX Building Security advertisements:

> ESSEX has focused the initial phase of the Building Security initiative on developing solutions for schools and commercial properties. In schools, there are complicated issues to deal with to ensure the safety of students and employees, while making sure buildings are accessible. Educational facilities have strong guidelines regarding fire and life safety, and ADA accessibility. There are high traffic and low traffic openings, as well as those that require high security such as computer rooms. Some schools are highly susceptible to vandalism. Yet, the entire environment must be conducive to learning.
>
> School administrators and office building owners are the experts in the needs of the people who use the facilities, as well as the community that surrounds the buildings. The Building Security team is a group of experts that is experienced in building security programs that combine the use of security products such as locks, alarms and cameras with policies and procedures that support the products.[7]

ESSEX subcontracts with companies, including Diebold, Sargent, and Securitron, so that school officials can have all of their access control needs met by one company (again, for "one-stop shopping"). They offer what they call their Safe School Solutions Total Management System, which involves a visit by ESSEX Industries security consultants, who do an evaluation of a school's current security system, a needs assessment, an outline of security goals that can be achieved, and an estimate of costs.[8] All of the members of the Safe School Solutions "team," which includes ESSEX, Diebold, and "You—employees, faculty, students, patients, medical staff, visitors," are considered experts in their own ways. But in the following excerpt, the company is a bit clearer about their own expertise:

> [We are] expert consultants in developing policies, plans and procedures for creating and maintaining a secure facility. Safe School Solutions Total Management process delivers measurable results to schools and peace of mind to teachers, students, and employees.

Consulting. Implementation. Continuous improvement. Their best practices approach to school safety coupled with robust technology solutions delivers a customized safety program that addresses the needs of America's schools.[9]

Here we have the ingredients for pleasing professional people: the "continuous improvement," the "robust technology," and the expertise of a group who promises "measurable results" and who oversees and ensures people's "peace of mind." We also have the business savvy, the delivering of individualized attention ("a customized safety program"), and the idea that professionals are meeting the "needs" of schools. Of course, schools need to be safe, but security professionals get another point across—that schools need equipment. Like all social reformers, they have big ideas for improvement and the expertise to make it work; they love their technology; and like all good businesspeople they aim to please by offering customized and individualized attention and products that are exactly what you need.

There are certain aspects of the professions—of white-collar work—that play a crucial role in selling security to schools. Right from the start, the security industry is composed almost entirely of professionals, and in most cases, they team up with other professionals (engineers with scientists and architects with salespeople) to get their products out to customers: they know too that their customers will be professional people with certain expectations typical of their professions, including profitability and efficiency. This is a world of suits and ties, of business meetings, networking, and "consultations," and to be a part of this world one must have the right professional cultural capital and know-how. Knowledge is a defining characteristic of being a good professional; to some extent, professionals are distinguishable by the fact that they possess advanced, complex, or esoteric knowledge; what Raymond Murphy described as "formally rational abstract utilitarian knowledge."[10] No doubt, for the security industry professional, a grasp of this kind of knowledge about their equipment is crucial. In addition, school security professionals need to have some familiarity with the jargon specific to education. This is recognizable when vendors talk about "meeting the needs of all learners" or "pedagogy [being] improved" when students feel safer. One vendor for Garret Metal Detectors paraphrased George W. Bush's No Child Left Behind law when he told me, "If we are genuinely serious about leaving no child behind, we know that we can only do this when students feel safe." And in a statement revealing the progressive nature of the industry, he added, "There is more to education than just tests and facts and figures, and everything else you hear about, even in my son's school. There is also the matter of being safe and not being worried that some person is going to bully you or worse."

In addition to this knowledge of education discourse, and the technical and credentialed knowledge that makes one a professional, security industry people need knowledge of manners and dispositions. They need to know how to conduct themselves in formal business settings and how to use language in other settings such as cocktail parties or conferences. They also need knowledge of sports, current events, and the dos and don'ts of making a deal. While I lacked some of this knowledge (and made some blunders because of it), I was able to study this topic partly because I could enter this world and talk to professionals as a professional, with some level of a shared language, unstated understandings between us, and a common well of middle-class knowledge. With the rise of the professions, activities such as the selling of security have become the purview of experts, and I understood what it meant to call on experts for what they had to offer.

Since this is a professional world, to some extent the security industry embodies what the professions have become in the twenty-first century. Several branches of writing in the social sciences point out some aspects of what it means to be a professional.[11] One branch focuses on how professionals function as part of a larger social system, providing the economic and moral backbone for society. In these studies, often based on the work of Émile Durkheim and Talcott Parsons (among others), we get to understand the roles that professionals serve in society.[12] Often, these studies are grounded in structural functionalism and are noteworthy for describing professionals within the larger social structure of society. Other writers, such as Howard Becker and Everett Hughes (among others), focused more on how professionals create their professional identities.[13] Grounded in qualitative research and phenomenology, this view looks at the way professionals do their "professing." Everett Hughes pointed out, for example, that "professionals profess. They profess to know better than others the nature of certain matters, and to know better than their clients what ails them or their affairs. This is the essence of the professional idea and the professional claim."[14] Security professionals act on their professional claim, they live a professional idea, and, as with all professing, they aim to convince us too of the professional claim and idea, and to know our place in it. They are the helpers, the expert providers, and we are the consumers, willing to put our trust in titled people with products for sale.

Each type of business in the security industry (manufacturing, development, sales, etc.) has its own set of knowledge, language, outlooks, culture, and loves (e.g., one loves the technology, while another loves working with people to install the technology). Without this knowledge—which is increasingly acquired through college classes and classes offered by businesses and organizations in the security industry—one's professional value is nil. While the British sociologist Keith McDonald has pointed out how within the professions knowledge is often shared, there is also an element of knowledge hording, where different groups, recognizing the value of their knowledge, keep it to themselves.[15] They sell their particular expertise by claiming that they have unique knowledge, and manage to move up in the business hierarchy by convincing contacts that their know-how and expertise can be valuable to a company. That security professionals will share expertise and knowledge with each other is not likely unless they are getting paid as consultants or trainers, and even when getting paid it is unlikely that they will share knowledge with customers. Customers might get the equipment, but will always need the expertise of others to keep it going. Just as customers are beginning to think of themselves as the experts ("You—the consumer, who knows best," as some advertisements proclaim), the expertise is actually being consolidated within the knowledge base of an industry separate from the consumer. In spite of the fact that Garrett Metal Detectors "makes everyone an effective security scanner," as their advertisements claim, school personnel do not have the knowledge to update, repair, and further integrate security technologies.[16] They depend on businesspeople, who, if they were to go away, would leave school administrators exposed and befuddled.

Professional Insecurities

There is another aspect of the professions that has had bearing on the selling of security. Professional insecurities—shared by both sellers and buyers of the equipment—keep the development and sale of equipment in overdrive. Some writers, in talking about professional insecurities, have made reference to the changing world economy and its effects on professionals. For example, the rise of expert professionals in the service sector accompanied what Scott Lash and John Urry referred to as the end of organized capitalism.[17] With disorganized capitalism, there occurred a "spatial scattering" of power and the means of production, distribution, and consumption into various segments of business, where each segment provides the expertise and services needed to create a commodity and to get it to consumers. If organized capitalism thrived on contracts and a steady job, disorganized capitalism thrives on subcontracting and temp work. "Disorganized capitalism" also refers to the spatial scattering of companies and divisions of companies that are less centered in urban areas. Work has moved out to the suburbs, and in many cases the urban industrial center has been replaced by the suburban office park. Once identified with a local site (a factory, plant, and/or office), work is now scattered across lands and even oceans, and in many cases the website has replaced the physical site. This, of course, is partly a by-product of globalization, which began ages ago but went into high gear with the passing of the North American Free Trade Agreement (NAFTA) in 1994 and with perks to overseas companies that soon followed NAFTA.[18]

Disorganized capitalism has helped to move along several developments in our society that have influenced the security industry and, by extension, promoted the use of techno-security equipment in schools. First, there is the creation of professionals who possess one bit of expert knowledge that is their hook for selling. The security industry is composed of unknown numbers of titled professionals with particular fields or expertise to share (and sometimes not share), who convince us—and they have the credentials and university knowledge to prove it—that they have the coveted know-how to bring about improvement. Along with this, work has become scattered across continents, which has helped to turn the security industry into a global network of business enterprises, thereby promoting the equipment throughout the world and enabling companies to profit from Asian factories, for example, that manufacture many of the parts for techno-security equipment.

At the same time, though, these changes make work for mid- and lower-level management, including many in the security industry, more insecure. Professionals in the twenty-first century are often easily replaced, are more likely to be independent contractors, and are often quick to change jobs, and their jobs change unexpectedly when corporate buyouts, divisions, and consolidations occur. John Urry made the point that while many critics of capitalism will decry the management system of nineteenth-century industrialization, capitalism until the early twentieth century actually depended a lot on the workers (who sometimes knew more than management about the machinery), the ethnic groups (that sometimes monopolized certain skills), and foremen (who could be very influential in labor disputes).[19] But professionals today, such as those in security, have expert knowledge that makes them valuable to consumers (or so consumers are led to believe), but not very valuable to business execs. Professionals who are trained at colleges and in business training seminars, who possess a certain knowledge that most in the profession have, are interchangeable. In general, the rise of the service sector, the accrediting of professionals, and the consolidation of expert knowledge into specific professions and subgroups within professions, along with the increased use of outside part-time workers, contractors, and consultants, created divisions between the various levels of production and consumption, and contributed to what

Barbara Ehrenreich called the middle class's "fear of falling" —fear of losing one's sense of social worth and falling lower in the economic and professional hierarchy of which many in the middle classes are a part.[20]

A regional sales manager for Mitsubishi Electric Security Products had this to say about his work:

> We strive to keep people safe by securing facilities and localities. That is clear. That's what I love doing—at least most the time. I'm also doing this for my job. I'm not fooling anybody saying that this is just about personal and institutional security, what I do. I hustle every day for my job. There is a lot of competition out there, and there are plenty of people who do what I do, and they're getting more all the time because this is becoming a big business. Don't we all feel this way?

To some extent, many of us do feel this way. We want to feel secure in our jobs, and security professionals know this, so what they offer may protect us not only from physical danger but also from economic and social downfall—helping to allay our insecurities. This can be obvious in the sales pitches of security professionals. A woman who worked the booth of Rainbow CCTV at a security conference brought up protection of my family as well as protection of my "assets" to make her sale. She wanted to know,

> How is it that people can leave themselves so vulnerable? Everybody needs a cutting edge, an in. You have kids? A family? Who would provide for them if something happened to you? We have to protect ourselves each and everyday. That's a basic fact. But what do most of us do—we don't think about our safety until it's too late. That's why we have to be always on guard, protecting ourselves and our assets. We shouldn't have to think of it, really, we are busy people—that's why we have complete surveillance programs for all your personal, business, and safety needs.

In an e-mail message from a sales representative for Extreme CCTV, I was told that "our products give you that specific upper hand in all your safety, work, and economic needs, a protective shield to keep you on top of the world." There is more going on here than protection from wrongdoers, though that is certainly part of it. Security professionals also know your work and economic needs, especially as they relate to taking care of your insecurities. One security vendor who I met at a trade show was quite up-front with what he intended to do: "I can make all your insecurities go away. You name it, I can fix it." Of course there is a certain amount of bravado in what he said. Salespeople like this one will overstate to make their points (and ultimately the sale), but when they overstate, they don't just point out physical dangers, hyping us up with threats of attack, but also in less overt ways they remind us of more subtle worries and insecurities we may have about our jobs and stature in society.

Of course, these professional insecurities are not new. C. Wright Mills saw them developing decades ago in the white-collar worker of the 1950s, whose antiseptic and routine life was carried out for the purpose of trying to establish some sense of physical, social, and economic security, often in suburban and fenced-in homes with clear property lines that were, for all practical purposes, meant to be one's own private utopia.[21] Suburbanization was in part a movement motivated by security, for the suburban enclave was a sign of safety and personal and economic security.[22] As several writers have pointed out, insecurities have also been spread by the media and politicians, which also propelled people out to the suburbs, and ultimately, into meetings with security professionals.[23] Insecurities were also the result of scientific advancement. Anthony Giddens pointed out how increased insecurities accompanied nuclearization and technology-based wars: suddenly, all that technology that was supposed to make life better was creating havoc and the potential for self-annihilation.[24] Insecurities are also linked to the ways that technology and telecommunications have undermined old notions about space, seeming to bring us closer to plights and disasters, and the way that digitalized and "up-to-the-minute" news programming brings to us detailed and all-too-real images of terrorist attacks, school shootings, and other tragedies. Security vendors do not have a monopoly on spreading insecurities, though they of course play their part.

Whether physical or economic, real or imagined, insecurities impel people to search for something better. And security professionals have very clear ideas about what this "something better" is—they will be happy to demonstrate their wares or send you any number of advertisements, Internet postings, and websites to get their points across. They know how to please customers and know the wants of professionals. Maybe all of this will lead us to a better world, as the professional claim goes. Maybe we should believe that lasers will be used more often to protect us than to harm us, that information databases will serve and not invade the public interest, and that surveillance cameras will catch criminals and not just record crimes. But even if we were to accept this (as many have), we have to also recognize that in our safer world (if in fact it is safer), we have another world that awaits us that is a more encompassing version of what C. Wright Mills was referring to in his description of the white-collar worker. Like the "lumpen bourgeoisie"—this kind of middle-class working stiff—of Mills's time, the modern professional chases after security but does so in a grander way and with a greater selection of items to choose from: distinct property lines is one thing, but how about property lines protected by a laser field? How about a school where kids are watched by surveillance cameras, searched by metal detectors, and tracked by their ID cards? What we are talking about here is a lifestyle and middle-class expectation, a manner of making one's immediate surroundings a kind of private utopia through techno-security fortification. It used to be that the suburban enclave was enough to guarantee safety, but now we need suburban or gated enclaves within the enclaves. Not just divisions, but subdivisions.

As with our creation of utopian societies in suburbs, the making of a safe school has depended on people creating what are often referred to as "safe havens" or "safety zones" in schools. It is an old concept of partitioning and barricading made new by advanced technology. It is also a kind of security premised on the belief that money can buy expertise and that expertise can get you safety. The selling of security equipment to schools depends on shared values that are filtered through business transactions where those involved agree to believe certain assumptions—where expertise resides, for example—and to enter deals because they have chosen to believe that safety is an economic good. Behind this is the assumption that the world outside—the space outside the "safe havens" or "safety zones"—is perilous and therefore in need of some "goods" to make it better. The perils of the world come in different forms. There are professional insecurities that are often economic and social in nature; there are also outright fears of invasion and attack, and worries about loved ones—images of terrorism, school shootings, and other tragedies impressed on our minds like news bits on perpetual rerun. These fears and insecurities are based on real situations; they involve physical threats as well as insecurities associated with money, status, reputation, and careers, which are used by many groups to achieve their goals—not only by governments and institutions, but also by corporations, and especially security businesses, that sell a semiparanoid society the sense that security is at our fingertips if only we will invest in it.

One's Own Private Utopia

Politicians, the news media, and even activists promoting a cause (child abuse, youth violence, etc.) can pump up people's fears, even when we have little to fear.[25] During the 1990s, as crime rates were falling, more people were convinced that society was actually more dangerous—stories about superpredators, missing children, child molesters and pornographers, gangbangers, random shooters, wilding kids, and crackheads fed us a steady stream of mayhem. In one survey, two-thirds of Americans felt that crime was increasing when it was actually decreasing, and 62 percent felt "truly desperate" about crime, which was about twice as many as in the 1980s when crime was actually increasing.[26] To allay fears, people bought into security and justified it not only on the basis of needs (we buy it because we need to protect ourselves) but also on the basis of free will and choice (we buy it because we have the choice to do so). Individuals look for safety in the same way that they look for a new style, prestige, and love—through their buying power. This is a kind of safety that is called upon and consumed by free market agents who see threats and dangers around them and who trust in mass-produced things to free them from worry.

In her study of gated communities, anthropologist Setha Low pointed out how individuals, who were almost always wealthy and white, used fortification, self-policing, and self-surveillance to control activities in their walled-off neighborhoods and sought out a security that was reminiscent of an idealized childhood.[27] She described a San Antonio gated community by calling attention to its exclusiveness and security components and how apparently the attainment of one depended on the other.[28] It was a suburban development of cul-de-sacs centered on a private golf and tennis club with swimming pools, a restaurant, and a clubhouse, and it was surrounded by a six-foot masonry wall—in its own way, it was like a walled-in utopian village. But this was also a high-tech village. The main entrance was controlled by a grid-design gate that swung open electronically and was controlled by a hand transmitter or by a guard contacted by an intercom and video camera connection. There were also neighborhood associations and neighborhood watch programs made up of residents who kept an eye on the comings and goings of the place.

The gated communities described by Setha Low, as well as by Dennis Judd, Michael Davis, and others, are not places where security is imposed; rather, they are places where it is self-imposed.[29] This is not a world of Big Brother. It is a world of opportunity—where individuals have the opportunity to buy security and to self-enclose themselves in their own private and exclusive havens. When people fret about a world overrun by security, they envision a police state, robots that track our movement, and cameras that watch everything we do. But if this has happened—and it has, to a point— what has also happened is that individuals have accepted the terms of security businesses even while fretting about a world overrun with their stuff. We have bought into the professional claim and the professional idea that Everett Hughes and other sociologists talked about, that belief in expertise and knowledge and utility to solve our problems. We have also bought into the idea of the professional as innately good, and as the moral backbone of our society, as described by Émile Durkheim. Security businesspeople invite us to question the safety of our safety zones (our schools, our suburban neighborhood streets, and our workplaces), which many have done gladly as they retreat to gated communities, ultrasecure malls (or "club" superstores), suburban enclaves and subdivisions, and supersecure schools and office buildings. The pursuit of this kind of security requires that individuals rely on the possibility of advancement through consumerism and put trust in things to solve the problems that advancement (in the form of science, industry, and technology) has helped to create. The world is dangerous because danger is more advanced and more pervasive, security professionals will tell you; the only thing to do, then, is to make security more pervasive and more technologically advanced.

To buy into security, we have to be convinced that we must solve our own problems, and that professionals in the private sector (our own "security consultants") and not in our public sector—not our fellow citizens, not our safety nets, not even our police—are the ones who can protect us. But what does this mean for us who are given these options to spend or not to spend? To some extent, we are required to take initiative and invest in our own safety and the safety of people around us. After all, if we—or our school administrators—will not do it, who will? School boards and school administrators feel a moral imperative to invest in technology; it is an expectation, often pushed by communities. For most of us, it is not only a matter of keeping a place safe but also a sign of keeping up with the times. We take matters into our own hands and use everything at our disposal to make schools "safe havens." But at the same time, we sometimes self-enclose and accept for our own good the greater surveillance of ourselves. We let ourselves be coaxed to let fear motivate us to buy and participate in a mostly middle- and upper-class agoraphobia, a retreat from public spaces and the formation of what David Sibley described as "geographies of exclusion"—enclaves that are racially, economically, geographically, and physically separate from one another through various kinds of manipulations of people, space, and items of trade.[30]

To convince us that all this is in our best interest, an image of utopia is held before us. The instruments are not intimidating—they offer us restful living and peace of mind, and they look sleek and trendy, more space-age than clunky. They show us a path to a better world and speak to us about the future: they show us how to be forward-looking and optimistic. Rather than constraining and overpowering us, they make it possible for us to leave our houses at night, to sleep peacefully when we get home, and to send our children to school without worries that they will harmed. Peace of mind has a price tag, and for those of us who can afford it, we buy it partly to make ourselves feel better, partly because we are willing to accept that equipment will do what it is purported to do. At another level, it also warms our hearts to know that the people who make and sell the equipment are good, honest, hardworking businesspeople—professionals, like you and I. They too, like all of us, do what they do in order to play their small part in advancing society and providing for its needs. We share utopian ideals, love our technology, choose items because of what they look like, try to allay fears and insecurities by buying stuff, and hope that professionals with the expertise and the inside scoop on things know what they are doing. These aspects of the security industry are significant because they, in a sense, grease the sale before people even meet or an advertisement is read or a consultation is made. All this is in place for the security industry—the utopianism, feelings of insecurity, and assumed expertise—before industry professionals even do anything, and naturally the industry does all it can to keep it in place, even if that means boosting our fears, playing to our fascination with technology, or pumping us up with utopian ideals.

Security professionals remind us of our general discontent with circumstances around us; sometimes they tell us what to fear, and present stylishly crafted silver or dark-colored plastics as ways of guarding ourselves from dangers that lurk about. All this occurs, of course, with the explicit intent to sell inventory and to improve business. Therefore, security professionals market carefully to their customers. They highlight their expert knowledge but also note the expertise of their customers, and while they are working with facilities that range from schools to prisons and with mass-produced equipment that is used for everything from warfare to elderly care, they aim to convince their customers that they will receive individual attention, that they share values of social betterment, and that security can be bought, at a price that is reasonable. They use utopian imagery to tap into our yearnings and hopes as well as our insecurities in order to sell a product. They are business savvy but also see a great mission in what they do. All they expect is that we should buy into the deal and convince ourselves that we are safer with the more equipment we have and that our underlying fears, often partly caused by technology, can be solved with technology.

CHAPTER 3

The Safest Society That Technology Can Create and Money Can Buy

This funding marks a major step forward in the creation of the School Security Technology and Resource Center. With this funding, we're saying to our kids that their safety is a top priority.

Senator Jeff Bingaman (D-NM), on the founding of the School Security Technology and Resource Center at Sandia National Laboratories[1]

As Senator Bingaman's remark makes apparent, for most people investments in technology mean investments in something good—they prove that we have the best interests of people at heart. In this case, we show our dedication to schoolchildren who will apparently benefit from the devices created at the School Security Technology and Resource Center at Sandia National Laboratories. As senator of New Mexico, where Sandia is located, Bingaman, too, will benefit in political clout, as more funding goes to the research laboratory, and perhaps people in Albuquerque will benefit from an increase in jobs. These types of benefits cannot be forgotten when we are talking about what has promoted techno-security fortification in schools and whose lives are advanced when the equipment is produced and sold. Technology is the essence of security equipment; therefore, how security technology gets funded, how it gets sold, and other issues related specifically to technology are discussed in this chapter.

Security technology is promoted by people like Senator Bingaman, who help to naturalize the belief that technology is innately beneficial and therefore a necessary form of "goods" to purchase. It also gets promoted by the kind of federal funding he is referring to, which makes the development of the technologies possible and feeds businesses with products that they in turn sell to customers. It also gets promoted by companies that advertise products by appealing to our outright love for technology and our faith in it to make life better. Behind the sales pitches, advertisements, and descriptions of equipment are worlds imagined by H.G. Wells, Francis Bacon, Thomas More, and other utopians.[2] While the previous chapter discussed utopianism through the making of enclaves, here utopianism is discussed in relation to technology. Utopianism through technology is a starting point for understanding the promotion of security equipment in schools and other public places, for this basic premise that technology will lead us to a more perfect world underlies all security sales, providing a rationale for why one buys and one sells the equipment. Before we get to the funding and marketing of technology, the chapter explores how individuals throughout the ages have endowed technology with a kind of power that in some cases verges on a religious fascination.

The Making of Utopia through Technology

For hundreds of years, there has been a tradition (especially in Western society) to associate the betterment of society with technological development, something seen in the writings of philosophers and political scientists of the nineteenth and twentieth centuries, in the writings of Charles Darwin, in the ideals of the French and American Revolutions, and in the writings of utopians and social critics, both socialist and capitalist. The Age of Discovery and the Enlightenment were spurred on by technological development and new understandings about the world achieved through the creation of glass, gunpowder, the compass, and other inventions. In 1532, the German geographer Apianus summed up the sentiments of the time when he stated in the preface of his *Quadrans Astronomicus* that without inventions "life would return to the state of the ancient man who lived without laws or civilization, similar to beasts."[3] What Constantine Hadjilambrinos called the new scientific knowledge of the sixteenth century replaced the old by emphasizing the importance of empiricism rather than theory, which was made possible with the advent of newer observational equipment, including telescopes and microscopes.[4] Other technologies, such as the compass, helped individuals to travel the world, to discover, and to see for themselves. The different uses of glass (in the creation of "scopes") had great bearing on ideas about seeing for oneself as a means of gaining truth, giving rise to notions of empiricism and positivism. Technology was an enabler, helping to make new discoveries possible and altering visions of the world. Where there was technology, there was the ability to see what was previously invisible to humans and to discover at a level that was unprecedented.

One characteristic of utopianism is the importance that is given to the capabilities of human products and utility to improve society. Part philosophers, part armchair scientists, and part social critics, many utopians throughout history held strong to the belief in technology as a means of social advancement and had a wholehearted love for rational science and empiricism. H.G. Wells, for example, a student of T.H. Huxley, was a true believer in rationalism and the scientific method, and his take on safety looked very much like a techno-security society. In his *A Modern Utopia*, everybody in the World State is classified by physical traits such as fingerprints, and records are kept about individuals that track their travel, marital status, and convictions of crimes. There is a governing class of "organized clairvoyance" that carefully supervises all citizens, assuring the general improvement of society and heading off anything that would undermine efficient, rational progress.[5]

As Nell Eurich explained in her study of science in utopias, when utopians imagined their worlds they were guided by the principles of utility and applied science.[6] Francis Bacon especially was enamored with what he called "instruments and helps," though he cautioned about overdependence on them. He lived during a time that saw the advent of printing, gunpowder, the magnet, the compass, the microscope, the telescope, and other instruments that changed the way individuals saw the world and their capabilities of imagining new paradigms about the cosmos—it is no wonder he was enamored. Instruments and helps also figured prominently in the World State of H.G. Wells and much earlier in Thomas More's *Utopia*.[7] So, while utopian writing may honor the natural world and humans' closeness to it, these are often set within or accompanied by the ability of humans to use technologies to manipulate the world for the better.

This mastery of the environment by humans through technological development is something that sociologists Joel Nelson and David Cooperman recognized as well in the technology revolution and dotcom boom in the 1990s, stating that there was and remains the assumption that "the revolution in information technology will provide greater control over society and, further, that this control affords an opportunity to advance utopian aims and ameliorate social problems."[8] The anti-utopian books of Aldous

Huxley, George Orwell, and Kurt Vonnegut ended up turning technology on its head and made it a key characteristic of the modern dystopia, but for utopians, though there was concern about overreliance, they were infatuated with the potential of instruments and helps to achieve utopian aims.[9]

Another important element to achieving utopian goals was a governing class that promoted the ideals and provided the needs for the society. Many utopians hailed what Max Weber referred to as the "maximum formal rationality" of a world governed by a benevolent class that safeguards the principles of positivism and capital production.[10] But utopians were neither wide-eyed Pollyannas nor short-sighted positivists. They were critics of society who expressed their dissatisfaction with the status quo and remarked on the circumstances in which they lived. Wells appreciated the efficiency of the Industrial Revolution, but was also a member of the socialist Fabian Society in London for a time and was an archcritic of English class divisions, which he parodied even in his science fiction novels, such as *The Time Machine* and *The Invisible Man*. In his last book, *The Mind at the End of Its Tether*, written at the end of World War II, he presented a scathing and sad description of humankind's future.

Utopians blended futuristic fantasy with wary prediction, idealism with pessimism—much like security professionals. If Wells's motivation for pessimism was the devastation of London during World War II that he witnessed, for the modern security professional the motivation is a more hidden evil, one that did not really exist in Wells's time. This is not an enemy that is always seen, or attacks from the outside, but rather one that can be in kids' clothes, living down the block, or boarding an airplane with you. Like utopians, security professionals have an unerring belief in technology and science to solve social problems; they are also part social critics, remarking through their conferences, sales pitches, and advertisements on the sorry state of current affairs in our world. They are promoters of improvement, selling utopianism to a public that is a little on edge. The public's assumption that technology solves problems, and the security industry's boosting of this idea—combined with hundreds of years of thinking that equates technological advancement with social advancement—have laid the groundwork for the modern security sale.

In an article about the security system in the Indianapolis Public School District, which was updated in 2003 by Honeywell, we get a glimpse of the important role technology plays in the newest security installments, and since such articles are also advertisements for companies, we see how the boosting of technology is used to sell equipment. The Indianapolis School District employs a "technology foreman," Richard Joest, who is obviously quite proud of the technology at his disposal. The system uses

Honeywell's Enterprise Buildings Integrator (EBI) platform, a system that links the district's ninety buildings including their control devices, surveillance cameras, a database archive of information and surveillance camera images, and an asset tracking system (that monitors the movement of security staff, buses, and equipment and valuable artwork). Explaining how the upgraded system provided by Honeywell improved their surveillance camera system, he stated:

> We always had the capability of using our network for video, but when you have 400 cameras going, there was no way that our network would support that traffic all the time. Honeywell's digital video solution solved that problem for us…Five years ago, we thought it was impossible to find a company that could tie all of our systems together, but here we are today on our way to a fully integrated system. [11]

In case we did not get the point about the importance of technology, the article is titled, "Integrated Technologies Spell Improved School Safety." Given the blind admiration that most people have for technology, most will not even question the assumption that technology "spells" improved school safety. This fascination with technology, and our generations-old belief that it automatically leads to improvement, provides the rationale for the use of the equipment, and is the hook for selling the equipment to schools and other public places. Security professionals need only mention "cutting-edge technology" and people automatically think it is a good thing.

Federal Investments in Security Technology

Naturally, there is more to the promotion of techno-security than utopian ideals. There is also the money that the U.S. government puts into technology research and development at federal and private research laboratories and at universities that support the creation of the devices. Since the mid-twentieth century, the security industry has been heavily supported by the federal government. Wiretapping and listening devices, metal detectors, hidden microcameras, and other security technologies were developed during the Cold War primarily because U.S. presidents, with military advisors and backing from Congress, considered it a matter of national security. Later, biometric technologies, including finger and palm scanning and facial recognition systems, were developed as part of the Star Wars missile defense program of the 1980s. The long relationship between the federal government and the security industry is wrapped up with the popularization of computers, as well, especially the Kenback-1, Altair, Radio Shack

TRS-80, and Apple Computer—once again, technology that was initially developed for military purposes. In the 1980s, the development of micro-chip technology propelled the computer business forward and also aided in the advancement of smaller security devices with greater capabilities for information gathering. Later, the popularization of the Internet provided the general public, including small workplaces and schools, low-cost, digi-tal surveillance.[12] The federal government's support of these technological developments is an essential component of techno-security fortification. Private businesses rely on government scientists, as well as university sci-entists (often with government grants), to create the products, and gov-ernment and university scientists rely on private companies (sometimes founded and headed by the scientists themselves) to make their products available to the military, police departments, prisons, schools, and, lastly but perhaps most significantly, the general public.

In terms of schools, the U.S. federal government provides security fund-ing through the Safe & Drug-Free Schools Act, the Safe Schools Act, COPS (Community Oriented Policing Services) grants for police departments, and the Secure Our Schools matching grant program. These funds are often channeled through the U.S. Department of Justice, Office of Juvenile Justice and Delinquency Prevention, and National Institute of Justice. Fur-ther, the No Child Left Behind law, passed by George W. Bush in 2002, has a provision requiring states to identify "persistently dangerous" schools. While this provision in the law does not deal specifically with techno-security, if a school is defined as "persistently dangerous," students would have the option to transfer to a "safe" school in the district, which may help to convince administrators to invest in techno-security, if only to appear not "persistently dangerous" and to therefore head off an exodus from the school.[13] If this is not enough to boost techno-security, the No Child Left Behind law also includes a provision that assures funding for the School Security Technology and Resource Center at Sandia National Laborato-ries, mentioned earlier by Senator Bingaman.[14]

Sandia National Laboratories, which was founded in 1941 to develop nuclear weapons as part of the U.S. Department of Energy, is run by Sandia Corporation, which is a Lockheed Martin Company; Lockheed Martin runs Sandia Corporation for the U.S. Department of Energy. This puts school security under the leadership of one of the largest pri-vate contractors to the military. In 2003, Lockheed Martin received about $24 billion from the U.S. government to develop weapons and to finance other projects, including a surveillance system overseeing ports in Phila-delphia and Camden, New Jersey; information management systems for the FBI, Department of Health and Human Services, Social Security

Administration, and Department of Homeland Security; a project to supply about 6 million people in transportation with biometric identification cards; and now, development and research work to outfit schools with the latest security technology.[15]

Pushed heavily by Senator Jeff Bingaman, the School Security Technology and Resource Center at Sandia serves as a resource center for school district administrators, law enforcement officials, and security professionals. At the Center, there are security consultants who can visit schools and advise administrators and school board members on security options and teach them about their new technology developments. The Center's advisors also consult with security professionals. Sandia National Laboratories researchers also conduct "vulnerability analyses" of school grounds, and sponsor public meetings with principals, teachers, parents, and law enforcement personnel. The laboratory also sponsors conferences attended by school administrators, security professionals, and law enforcement officials. In 2002, their conference was cosponsored by the National Institute of Justice, the COPS program, and the Center for Justice Leadership and Management at George Mason University—again, a powerful set of players promoting the sale of equipment to schools.

The 1998 founding of the School Security Technology and Research Center at Sandia established a legitimate federal center devoted exclusively to the development and distribution of school techno-security. The Center was originally made possible by the Safe Schools Security Act of 1998 that provided Sandia about $1.4 million per year to establish the school security center and to advise and train school administrators. Another chunk of money went directly to schools. The Safe Schools Security Act made available $10 million per year to help schools to purchase security equipment. One such school district, closest to Sandia—the Albuquerque public schools—implemented a system that uses hand scanners to identify parents and guardians of children. When parents or guardians register their children for school, they are assigned a personal identification number (PIN) and are asked to place their hand on a pad that uses biometric technology to record hand features. Each time someone picks up a child, he or she enters the PIN and places his or her hand on the pad. If the PIN and the hand geometry match the information in the system, the person is allowed to take the child.[16] The district implemented the program with federal money provided that they permit the Department of Justice to study the effectiveness of the program and parents' responses to it. The U.S. Department of Justice also provided funding for some of the first iris-scanning systems in schools including those in the Plumsted Township School Distict (discussed earlier) as well as schools in the Ocean County

School District. Both systems are located in New Jersey and were installed by Iridian Technologies with $293,360 grants for each project.[17]

The federal government has also supported the installation of school security technology through publications distributed by the Office of Justice Programs and National Institute of Justice of the U.S. Department of Justice. The most comprehensive of these publications, *The Appropriate and Effective Use of Security Technologies in U.S. Schools*, was written by Mary Green, an employee of Sandia National Laboratories, and released by the U.S. Office of Justice Programs and National Institute of Justice.[18] It includes information about CCTV systems, metal detectors, handheld scanners, access control, duress alarm devices, and biometric technology, including the palm scanner being used in Albuquerque and elsewhere. The publication also instructs school personnel in how to use the technologies. Relationships between schools and security professionals are forged as well by conferences sponsored by Sandia National Laboratories and other organizations, both federal (National Institute of Justice, U.S. Department of Justice, and Office of Juvenile Justice and Delinquency Prevention) and professional (American Society for Industrial Security and National Association of School Resource Officers). Relationships are also established through outreach, as when research laboratory and businesses offer schools free threat assessments, site visits, and demonstrations of their products, and through advertisements distributed by the tens of thousands of security businesses that exist.

The installation of security technologies in schools is also boosted by worldwide events, as when war triggers greater use and acceptance of security technologies. In 2002, the Department of Homeland Security, which was established after the attacks on the World Trade Center and Washington, D.C., in 2001, declared schools potential sites for terrorist attacks and provided money for schools to expand their security systems and plans. In 2003, $17 million was available to the security industry for the production of school security technologies and for training school and police personnel in how to use them; there was also $15 million available through the Safe Schools Initiative; and for police departments, $200 million was available for hiring police officers, including school police officers. Though not directly related to technology, the Emergency Response & Crisis Management program makes available money to combat terrorism and other emergency situations. Through this program, the Department of Homeland Security awarded schools in 2003 between $83,000 (Macon County School District, Alabama) and $1 million (School District of Hillsborough County, Florida).[19]

Changes in the tax code, as well, give governmental support for security technologies. In 2001, the U.S. Congress amended the Internal Revenue Code of 1986 to allow building owners to deduct qualified security devices. The act passed as the Securing America Investment Act of 2001, and inserted into the Internal Revenue Code an allowance of deduction, stating, "A taxpayer may elect to treat the cost of any qualifying security device as an expense which is not chargeable to capital account. Any cost so treated shall be allowed as a deduction for the taxable year in which such device is placed in service."[20] This made the purchase and installation of "qualified security devices" a tax write-off. According to the law, qualified security devices included nearly every device on the market, including the following:

1. An electronic access control device or system
2. A biometric identification or verification device or system
3. Closed-circuit television or other surveillance and security cameras and equipment
4. Locks for doors and windows, including tumbler, key, and numerical or other coded devices
5. Computers and software used to combat cyberterrorism
6. Electronic alarm systems to provide detection notification and off-premises transmission of an unauthorized entry, attack, or fire
7. Components, wiring, system displays, terminals, auxillary power supplies, and other equipment necessary or incidental to the operation of any item described in subparagraph (A–F)

With the Securing America Investment Act, the U.S. government added an incentive for people to buy the equipment—a new tax savings. But even before this latest incentive, all U.S. presidents, every Congress, and all military advisors and FBI and CIA directors have supported the development of techno-security (to varying degrees). This is a powerhouse group, especially when they work in tandem. And with all this power, they considered techno-security development top priority, a matter of national security, which kept government support on high speed. In the latter part of the twentieth century, this support expanded to include not only military, prison, and policing sectors, but also support for more popular uses of the devices to include, for example, schools. Federal funding, the establishment of research centers, conferences, and publications that draw school authorities into the "national security" sector partly explain what has promoted the development of the equipment and how its intended use has expanded to include schools. However, in spite of all this high-powered support and activity at the federal level, security equipment depends on the distributors to get it out to people. Ultimately, popularization of the equipment has depended on private enterprise, security companies that have taken what is essentially military technology and turned it into an item that a school administrator would want.

Getting Techno-Security Sold

Once security technology begins to move out of the laboratory and away from the hands of researchers and scientists, its federal backing diminishes and private businesses take over to a greater extent and begin their push to get the technology out to not only divisions of the military, police departments, and prisons, but increasingly to stores, schools, universities, and the general public. Initially, the newest technologies are picked up by corporations with the closest ties to government research labs and with their own laboratories supported, in part, by taxpayers (such as Lockheed Martin). These corporations contract with other companies for various kinds of services, such as sales, promotion, shipping, and installation. They also contract with other companies that provide components for the equipment, such as glass for lenses or plastics for housings. Through this subcontracting, greater numbers of companies get involved and benefit from the production of techno-security equipment. In time, other businesses with the resources to do so develop their own versions of the technology and begin sales to the everyday consumer. Sometimes these businesses deal security equipment exclusively; sometimes they are companies that have sold other accessories, but develop new departments to deal security equipment. This is true of Honeywell, GE, and Sony, for example. Not all security equipment follows this trend, but this is a typical story, one that would make sense to people in the business. Once in the domain of the private businesses, security companies use advertising divisions or subcontract with advertising agencies to begin their work on making the product available to the public. While the federal backing makes the technology development possible, the advertisements' portrayal of technology gives it the allure to appeal to the everyday consumer who is choosing from a wide selection of security technologies, many of which look the same and do the same kind of things.

To get security equipment sold specifically to schools, security professionals offer incentives and perks. For example, security businesses donate security equipment to schools and install it for free. In return for the donations and *pro bono* work, the school is sometimes used as a prototype and featured in trade magazines and advertising distributed by the company. Schools also receive equipment for free and at reduced rates because monthly payments and other forms of reoccurring revenue compensate for the initial donation and *pro bono* work. The Massachusetts-based company Vanguard has done this with surveillance equipment and access control devices that would ordinarily cost a school $40,000 to $300,000 depending on features. WorldNet Technologies in Seattle and AvalonRF of San Diego have consulted with schools to install WeaponScan 80™ for free in order to showcase their advanced metal detector, which in addition to recognizing metal also recognizes plastic used in gun making and was originally developed by the Navy during the Cold War to track Soviet submarines.[21] West Hills High School in Santee, California, accepted donated equipment from Sony and PacketVideo that included wireless handheld computers and video cameras and powerful smoke detectors. The CCTVs were installed to record students and students' license plates, and administrators in 2002 were considering adding facial recognition technology to the cameras. Hall monitors were also outfitted with wireless computers that could instantaneous access information about students.[22]

WebEyeAlert, developer of the SOS Littleton Initiative discussed earlier, includes articles from the *Boston Business Journal* and the *Derry News* of New Hampshire reporting on their Web-CCTV monitoring system installations in schools, and though I am uncertain whether or not the schools mentioned received security at reduced rates, a sale representative was clear that "accommodations are always made to meet the needs of schools."[23] The WebEyeAlert technology allows police officers to monitor students from the police department, the school, or their cars through surveillance cameras, wireless computers, and the Internet.[24] Part of what many advertisements do is present a world where police, schools, potential emergencies, and middle-class lives of security all coexist. The WebEyeAlert advertisement creates a visual connection between the police officer on the left and the photograph of the school, which are connected by the white bubble that tells us, "WebEyeAlert provides real-time video surveillance, easily and remotely assessed via the web" (Figure 3.1). The school is connected at the bottom to a photograph of an ambulance racing out of a hospital emergency room garage and a young, good-looking professional couple standing outside their neat suburban home. Using layout techniques and provocative images, we quickly get presented to us a lifestyle image of what a happy middle-class life should look like.

In general, security professionals attempt to convince prospective buyers that technology is the way of the future, that its increasing use is inevitable and good for them, and that it will help them to achieve this secure lifestyle: "Take a closer look at the LG IrisAccess 3000—it's the look of things to come," claims an advertisement by LG Electronics U.S.A., Inc.,

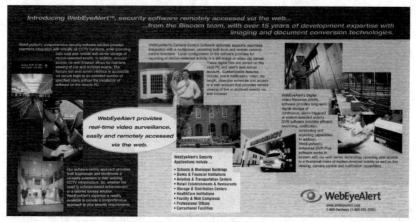

Figure 3.1 The white oval connects the school to the police officer, who is accessing school surveillance cameras through the Internet. The couple above and intersecting with the school photograph is the image of what a middle-class life should be like. Also, at bottom right, is the WebEyeAlert logo of an eye. WebEyeAlert, brochure (WebEyeAlert, 2002), inside spread.

for an iris identification system.[25] Melanie McGee, president of Evolution Software, Inc. (itself a revealing company name), explained at a 2001 security conference that "wearable security computer systems" would have technology "integrated in everyday life."[26] The integration of technology with everyday life is a popular security industry motif, a staple of security advertisements, and a common allusion made by school security dealers when they explain the "integration," "natural fit," or "harmony" between technology and humans.

Because technology cannot always live up to the promises of those who develop and sell it, the production of school security equipment—from scientist to manufacturer, distributor, vendor, and end user—relies not on proclamations about protective qualities, but on scientism and utopianism, images of power and omniscience, and claims about cost-effectiveness and simplicity of use.[27] Security professionals know that individuals purchasing equipment do not need hard data showing decreases in violence and crime in places where their products are used. Security professionals and advertisements rarely discuss how their items make people safer; and when they do, most information is anecdotal or passed on in commonsense kinds of ways (of course it makes us safer, so let's talk about features, looks, and durability). Most information is about the technology, and specifically about its looks, its efficiency, the speed of what it does, and its great capabilities for doing amazing things—not things that will directly make us safer, but things that we are asked to assume will make us safer. "Technologies to manage people, openings, and assets. A flexible design, seamless integration capabilities, and state-of-the-art technology make InterAccess an essential solution for any organization," claims a brochure from IR Interflex, in Forestville, Connecticut, for access control equipment for offices, government buildings, and schools.[28]

An advertisement from CEIA states,

> CEIA, the world leading manufacturer of Metal Detectors, presents the *Classic*. This walk through Metal Detector is engineered and designed to meet the specific needs of public facilities such as: schools, hotels, amusement parks and city halls. The *Classic* provides the required security with a high level of operating efficiency. The leading edge of technology features a high flow rate of people through the gate with minimal alarms.[29]

"The leading edge of technology" of the metal detector is hailed, not necessarily for the safety that it provides, but rather for its efficiency—its "high flow rate." In a similar way, the access control systems from IR Interflex are promoted for their "flexible designs, seamless integration capabilities, and state-of-the-art technology," but not a word is said about people actually being safer when they have their bodies scanned or their eyes touched with lasers.[30] Advertisers know that individuals need to understand the "securityness" of their products, which does not necessarily mean they must be convinced that it will actually make them safer. We need to be convinced that because an item is able to magnify something four hundred times, we are safer; because it can process a lot of information, danger is lessened; and because it rotates, tilts, or uses digital rather than analog, we can worry less.

Products must also look appealing. Science has not only given us more advanced technology but also enabled technology to look less clunky, be smaller, and therefore fit in more with the environment in which it is used or installed. Equipment that had once taken up rooms can now fit in a carrying case; items that had once stood up in a kind of ugly display of utility can now resemble entertainment equipment. The devises sold by LG Electronics, CEIA, IR Interflex, and other companies are silver and black, sleek-looking, and futuristic, and appear durable and rugged in a satisfying kind of way (Figure 3.2). This is a design style that sociologist Arnold Pacey referred to as a "combat-ready look from military equipment to symbolize no-nonsense functional rigor" in his description of home electronics gear marketed to men (with their black matte finishes, digital displays, and push-button controls).[31] Security professionals want their products to convey ruggedness and sophistication, functional rigor and fun. By promoting utility (that equipment serves its purpose) combined

Zodiac SmartCard
FINGERPRINT VERIFICATION READER

Zodiac reads a Portable Fingerprint Template stored in a contactless SmartCard or a stick-on BioPatch !

"Zodiac Prox" for Non-Biometric Doors

FEATURES

- Template stored in contactless SmartCard
- User capacity of reader is unlimited
- Built-in visual and audible indicators
- Wiegand line encryption option available
- 26 Bit Wiegand or Track 2 ABA output
- Quick and easy centralized enrollment
- Fast, accurate and easy to use
- Plug & Play installation

Figure 3.2 Fingerprint verification reader. Sleek and futuristic, gray and silver, as if presented from the heavens. In the top left corner, the smartcard is the brain of the human outline. Cansec Systems, Ltd., single-page advertisement (Cansec Systems, Ltd., 2001), front cover.

with appeal (that it will be fun to possess and use), security professionals begin their forays into the school market. They are hard-pressed to actually prove that their products make people safer, and to get us to forget this detail, we are given a set of images and appealing designs that make the purchase seem almost necessary. We trust the equipment not because we know it will make us safer, but because we trust in science and see the "science-ness" of the equipment in the way it is designed and in the way it is described.

The science-ness and technical durability of security equipment are seen in illustrations and in verbal and visual cues that promote an unabashed acceptance of technology and human life as natural partners. These images and verbal cues are what Roland Barthes referred to as a "constantly moving turnstile" of meanings that are constituted within language, visual representations, and our interpretations of things, which create what he called "myths" about items such as security equipment.[32] These myths must be at least loosely connected to reality (that technology can be efficient, for example, is true) and must convey meanings that associate the idea of a thing with truths that appear logical and natural—that, for example, efficiency inevitably means safety or that because an item can process information fast it naturally provides greater protection. That the technology myth is based in truth is an important aspect for selling products. Advertisers and dealers claim that their equipment is accurate and efficient, and this is mostly true. But this is also part of the irony of technology: correlations between, for example, accuracy and safety are presumed but not necessarily true. Who is to say that because something is fast and efficient, it makes life better?

Getting techno-security sold also depends on buy-in from the public, who accept assumptions about technology's appeal, potential, and power—and its naturalness. Security professionals aim to convince individuals that it is only natural to have technology used on them. When young people are asked to stand spread-legged at a school entrance while a guard searches them with a metal detector, or workers are asked to have their hand measurements taken before entering an office, the interaction between the guard/technology and the "suspect" depends on the compliance of the "suspect." Part of the reason we obey security checks is because we are forced to do so, but compliance is also achieved by convincing individuals that what is being asked of them is a (perhaps unfortunate) part of modern life. To resist the security check would be suspicious behavior: one would have to make a scene, and most onlookers would see sinister intent in anybody not submitting to a routine check. Resistance to techno-security has therefore been minimal, even when the technology is used on innocent adults.

When security professionals sell equipment to schools, they have their sights on protecting individuals from dangerous youths; certainly preventing youth violence is a large part of what security equipment aims to do. But security professionals continually seek to broaden the market, and they know that historically technology has had a widening effect: what starts small and with a particular focus ends up increasing in scope. Though security professionals present this as a natural progression and an inevitable aspect of technology, the widening effect is not natural or typical of technology; rather, it is typical of businesspeople who set out to broaden their market. What looks natural is really business being served. A small system will usually become a more advanced system ten years later; what starts with a few cameras keeping watch over a school parking lot will most likely evolve into a system that includes hallways. School bus surveillance systems that were originally installed to observe goofing-off youths are now equipped with cameras that also focus on bus drivers. Once a school system has become fortified against student aggression and crime, it will begin expanding its security installations to include teachers. This is due to the concerted efforts of businesspeople to "upgrade" and "integrate" systems and therefore increase the breadth of the markets they serve.

Consider a school security system in Philadelphia that employs finger-scanning machines in their schools, not for the students (who already use ID cards and are on surveillance cameras), but for the 30,000 employees of the school system, including the teachers. This is the same kind of finger-scanning system used on military bases, in some casinos, and recently by Kroger Corporation, a large grocery store chain, to facilitate the purchasing of groceries by customers.[33] By 2003, several hundred of the finger-scanning machines were installed in Philadelphia and teachers were required to have their fingers scanned and to enter an identification number when reporting to work.[34] The biometric system was manufactured by Accu-Time Systems Inc., based in Ellington, Connecticut, and was installed by TimeTrak Systems of Glenn Mills, Pennsylvania. In 2004, Governor Jeb Bush in Florida was considering using the machines in schools through-out the state; they are already used in several schools in Florida, includ-ing Pinellas County, where administrators use a system to keep track of students who ride the 750 school buses, and in a middle school in Boca Raton (Don Estridge High Technical Middle School), which uses a biomet-ric hand reader to take attendance and for libarary check-outs and meal purchases by students. Edwin Darden, senior staff attorney for the Alex-andria, Virginia–based National School Boards Association, compared the new technology to ID cards, and school officials in Philadelphia felt they were a logical upgrade from the broken-down punch-in/punch-out machines that many school districts already employed. But Darden also stated, "It really is new, and I don't think there's anyone anywhere who's thought of all the implications of it."[35]

Techno-security has become what appears to be a natural part of our lives partly through the efforts of the security industry to broaden its markets to the point where school administrators, parents, teachers, and students see techno-security fortification of schools as normal; they get our buy-in and promote our acceptance of the equipment even though we know little about the devices and what they do. Security professionals want us to trust them and to believe conflicting stories: that the technol-ogy is cutting-edge, but really no different than earlier equipment; that the equipment will change things, but not really affect us. It is technological, yet natural, they will tell you. But we know that technology changes things and does affect us, sometimes negatively, and yet we sometimes manage to forget this or we see the change as always beneficial. Imagine that a device that did not even exist fifty years ago can now be viewed as essential to our lives. This is true of not only security equipment but also personal computers, CD players, DVDs, digital cameras, and cell phones. One could say that technology takes over our lives and changes everything. But people do this. We buy the technology and make it essential to our lives. The process is facilitated by companies that have the products for sale and know how to spin them and create their images to make them appealing to our senses.

While the techno-security market has broadened from military and police sectors into school and housing sectors, the technology has become more advanced. When Edwin Darden, senior staff attorney for the Alexandria, Virginia-based National School Boards Association, compared the finger scanners used in schools to ID cards, he was hoping that the public would not think too critically about this. In many ways, the finger scanners are similar to ID cards—he may be right in this regard—but the comparison leads us to believe that ID cards are simply cards with one's identification on them. ID cards can be much more sophisticated; some are embedded with microchips with Geographic Positioning Systems (GPS) that can be used to track the card holder. ID cards can also be integrated with databases that archive information and can mark and call up information. ID card scanners are also equipped with alarms that can be triggered when somebody swipes a card and information raises a "red flag." School adminstrators can program scanners to recognize, for example, a student who has been expelled or a student who has moved out of the district.

Even surveillance cameras in schools have in only a few decades evolved from stationary video recorders to digitalized and mobile units integrated with databases and viewing capabilities (zooming, panning, infrared) that were once only processed by the military. One of the more significant advances involving surveillance cameras has, like ID'ing, involved biometric technology—in this case, facial recognition technology. Biometrics is used in the finger and palm scanners used in schools in Pennsylvania, Texas, New York, and elsewhere, and in more sophisticated ways in facial recognition technology that was being tested in Royal Palm Middle School in Phoenix, Arizona in 2004. The equipment was installed through the urging of the Maricopa County Sheriff's Office and with the help of the Phoenix-based company Hummingbird Defense Systems. Hummingbird donated $350,000 worth of security equipment, including the facial recognition system, to the Maricopa County Sheriff's Office, which the Sheriff's Office tested, liked, and wanted installed in a school as a pilot program.

Facial Recognition Technology

Though schools have begun using various kinds of biometrics (hand and iris scanners, for example), facial recognition technology has yet to make a strong inroad into the public school market. However, given the widening effect of technology and its use in at least one school in Phoenix, it is only a matter of time before school administrators and school boards start approving the use of facial recognition technology and begin pilot programs of their own. This will happen as the technology becomes less expensive and more accepted, and as school systems in Pennsylvania, New Jersey, Florida, and elsewhere make iris scanning and other forms of biometrics seem routine. It is only a short jump from scanning to facial recognition systems, and a shorter step yet from high-tech surveillance cameras to facial recognition–equipped cameras. Some school authorities, such as those in the Santee, California, contracting with Sony and PacketVideo, have openly discussed their intentions to install facial recognition technology. Security company representatives are also clear about their intentions. At a security conference, I spoke to the director of communications for a facial recognition technology company who could not "rule out the possibility that schools will become part of our consumer base." She remarked that police departments and airports were using the technology but that the "technology needed to reach the consumer level," including the level of school districts.

One could imagine administrators using the facial recognition technology to scan the faces of students as they walked in the hallway, running their features through a database that checked for individuals who were not students in the school, or of students who have been suspended or expelled. The technology could be installed in the surveillance cameras already mounted in many schools, as it was in cameras in the downtown district of Tampa, Florida. In Tampa, security professionals, with the backing of police, installed facial recognition software in each of the thirty-six cameras in the streets around the downtown entertainment district. The technology was also tested in Florida at the Super Bowl, where 75,000 fans unknowingly had their faces screened through a database of digitized mug shots.[36]

Facial recognition technology is advanced for at least two reasons. First, it is surveillance that incorporates a new form of technology involving the reading of bodily patterns (biometrics). But equally important is the fact that the technology involves not only high-tech surveillance but also the warehousing of information about individuals in order to compare surveillance recordings to databases that contain sometimes millions of digitalized images. Jane Wakefield, in a news magazine article, described how federal agents at the 2000 presidential inauguration wore tiny cameras that were designed to record the faces of individuals and compare "facial landmarks" to a database of faces of those who have been accused of terrorism.[37] The FBI has begun digitizing 40 million criminal records at its National Crime Information Center to make them conducive to facial recognition technology. The U.S. Department of Defense has given Visionics, the makers of the FaceIt facial recognition system, $2 million to adapt facial recognition technology for military uses, and the Defense Advanced Research Projects Agency (DARPA) is working with Visionics to develop an upgraded form of FaceIt that would be able to not only recognize facial patterns through disguises and facial hair but also pinpoint faces from five hundred feet away in an urban environment and, further, recognize behavioral patterns, such as frequent gatherings of people at particular spots and hesitant or jerky walking through a parking lot (which may identify a potential car thief).[38] This is the same type of product that is being used in Chicago to identify odd behaviors through their 2,500 cameras stationed throughout the city.

States and localities have also begun to develop databases of images to be used with facial recognition technology. Authorities in Illinois compiled a database of 2 million facial images and have contracted with Viisage Technology to provide expertise in their development of a facial recognition system. PhotoMug, Visionics' Integrated Law Enforcement Identification System, and Smith and Wesson's Suspect Identification System are facial recognition systems used by police departments and sheriff's offices in the United States. The New York Police Department (NYPD) has also begun plans to use facial recognition technology in their street surveillance cameras, and according to Howard Safir, a prominent ex-commissioner of the NYPD, facial recognition technology will become increasingly available to officers in their police cruisers.[39] New Jersey state troopers could use the technology in cameras that have been already installed in police cruisers.[40] Police vests have also been equipped with surveillance cameras that could employ the technology; in 2003, the Los Angeles Sheriff's Department outfitted fourteen deputies with video camera-equipped vests that transmit the goings-on of police interactions with citizens to recorder equipment in police cruisers.[41] Already, the police cruiser and vest cameras are used for information gathering, which is the first step in creating a database of "facial landmarks." At a security conference, Stephen McAllister, director of the Technical Assistance Research Unit (TARU) of the NYPD, said that they were working with the Public Housing Authority to put facial recognition technology in some of the three thousand surveillance cameras already mounted in public housing projects, turning the technologically advanced cameras on people who are nearly all nonwhite and poor.

Facial recognition is a development that came out of the Reagan administration's Star Wars program of the 1980s. The technology also piggybacks off of other devices that many have already accepted as a natural part of life. The primitive precursor to facial recognition technology is the video cameras of the 1960s installed in commercial buildings, warehouses, hospitals, all-night convenience stores, and gas stations. These early cameras were plagued by grainy images and were stationary things with nothing even close to pan-tilt-zoom capabilities. But in the 1980s, video surveillance improved with new camcorder, digital, and multiplexer technology. By 2000, many surveillance cameras had sensors (to turn on when there was movement), night-vision technology, and pan–zoom–tilt capabilities, and cameras in the near future will have the abilities to record through physical barriers and to pick up conversations from great distances.

Surveillance cameras are an obvious mainstay of the security industry. A survey of security companies in the mid-1990s found that over 75 percent sold video surveillance equipment; a leading CCTV manufacturer reported net earnings of $120 million in 1995, compared with net earnings of $16 million the previous year.[42] The increased sales of surveillance cameras were spurred on by the 1994 Violent Crime Control and Law Enforcement Act, which provided funding to city officials and police departments to purchase and install various kinds of surveillance technology, especially mounted cameras, mostly to fight urban gang and drug violence. Funds were also allocated for support and training of police in the use of geographic information system (GIS) technology to track and monitor gang activities. GIS was developed as a research mapping tool, and has been used in academic research as well as by the military, SWAT teams, and the police.

Facial recognition technology is a potent force because it can be used in conjunction with GIS, behavioral pattern and profiling software, various kinds of iris or palm scanners, and massive databases of information about individuals. Its surveillance capabilities are only the tip of the iceberg. Being watched is one thing; having your facial patterns compared to databases of facial images, having your movements analyzed by software that can alert police to atypical behaviors, and having maps of people's neighborhoods broken down into quadrants, subdivisions, and sectors that inform users about each sector's income levels, educational attainment, race, crime levels, voting patterns, and even the kinds of shopping people do—all this is different from even the most advanced solitary surveillance camera. Cameras networked into databases with personal and GIS data and working with other profiling software are a force to be reckoned with. Security professionals, among them some of the most influential people in the business, are not blind to the potential abuses, though their concerns are usually expressed in ways that do not hamper business.

Joseph Atick, CEO of Visionics Corp. and creator of FaceIt, has joined with the Security Industry Association to request that Congress create guidelines for the responsible use of security equipment by authorities, especially facial recognition technology.[43] In a 2001 address to the National Press Club in Washington, Alick proposed the following recommendations:

- Require agencies to inform the public with signs and media alerts before using facial recognition systems.
- Mandate that acquired images be immediately purged from the system if they do not match one in the database.
- Require the use of encryption and authorization protocols.
- Establish guidelines controlling the inclusion of an individual's image in a database and its dissemination to other agencies.
- Create oversight and enforcement procedures, including penalties for violators.

Joseph Atick's proposals for regulation are reasonable, but although we may "create oversight and enforcement procedures, including penalties for violators," as with all technologies that give people power over other people, we will never be able to stop misuse of the equipment, as when a top-ranking police officer in Washington, D.C. was caught using databases to blackmail patrons of a gay bar, or when Michigan police were caught using a database and surveillance cameras to stalk women.[44] Another problem with the recommendations has to do with the speed of technology development. By the time laws are passed regulating facial recognition technology, there will be a new technology raising newer issues. The federal government does not work nearly as quickly as technology develops. In general, the recommendations are common sense, yet nearly inconceivable. Keep in mind that the USA PATRIOT Act of 2001 opens up lines of communication between federal agencies such as the FBI and the Central Intelligence Agency (CIA). This is because some federal agencies and police departments were criticized for not sharing information that may have thwarted the plans of the terrorists who attacked New York City and Washington, D.C., in 2001. To request that the dissemination of information about us be controlled, as Atick's fourth recommendation does, is unrealistic and counters the USA PATRIOT Act.

Consider, as well, the first recommendation—that we have signs and media alerts forewarning people. What if there were signs reading "THIS IS A FACIAL RECOGNITION ZONE"; what do we do? Not walk there? Cover our faces? What happens when we do not have the choice to avoid facial recognition technology, as when students are compelled to go to school? And in reference to the last recommendation—to create oversight and enforcement procedures—one wonders if these procedures will be as effective as those purportedly regulating junk e-mail, spam, and porn on the Internet, all fine examples of fighting losing battles. Though it makes perfect sense to regulate the technology, how do you regulate something so well supported by the federal government, the military, police departments, school systems, the security industry, private businesses, technology gurus, and people like you and me who buy the stuff?

As mentioned earlier, by 2005 only one school in Phoenix had begun using facial recognition technology. As with all new devices, it was first proposed as a way of dealing with a dire concern, in this case preventing children from being abducted and protecting them from sex offenders. ID cards and surveillance cameras (without facial recognition technology) were also first proposed in schools as a way of dealing with things such as school shootings and child abductions. However, in many cases the concerns did not manifest themselves in reality; in other words, beginning in the late twentieth century, schools that were already safe began to install the equipment, claiming to deal with weapon violence, for example, when there had never been threats of weapon violence. In the case of facial recognition technology, its first use was in a school that had never had problems associated with child abductions or sex offenders. Mike Christensen, principal of Royal Palm Middle School, volunteered his school even though such problems did not exist among the 1,180 seventh and eighth graders. Frank Frassetto, MIS director of the Washington Elementary School District, said that the district had been selected because Hummingbird Defense Systems, and another company they worked with to secure the Phoenix deal (Darcomm Network Solutions, a company that already provided some services to the school district), "thought of us because we are a very large system and have a solid network."[45] The school district had been chosen primarily because it was willing to have the equipment installed, but also because it was a perfect testing ground: it was large and already had a system on which to build. The expansion of techno-security in schools is not going to occur because of threats of danger, but rather, the expansion will occur because school systems have become a lucrative and willing market for the security industry, and once we understand this—and grasp the significance of it—we can start to determine what this will mean for schools and for the children educated in them.

Weighing the Good and Bad of Technology

Whether a security technology is beneficial or not depends on an incredible amount of factors, so it is not possible to either hail or condemn security technology on a wholesale basis. A security camera that captures on tape a thief who has just robbed a convenience store and that leads to his arrest is a good thing. If you doubt this, put yourself in the position of the convenience store clerk next in line to be robbed. But what if the camera is used to conduct marketing for the convenience store without us knowing it? Is it a good thing still, or is it now a benign thing? What if the marketing technique leads to an information database that includes your buying habits? What if the camera is used to misidentify an individual who is then arrested, or is used in order to secretly document individuals in the store without us knowing it and for reasons that are not explained to us? What if the camera has capabilities to run your features through a database of recorded facial images? What if it can be linked up with databases that contain information about your banking, home, family, travel, health, school, and consumer activities, or that can access tax records, cable bills, rentals, and all kinds of information we give each day even at the checkout counter of the grocery store or at the post office to get a package sent? We may be lulled into thinking that our privacy is protected, and to some extent it is, but most laws and new policies have supported broad uses of security technology and the relaxing of constitutional rights to privacy.

Even when laws protect us, national crises can prompt presidents, Congress, and the courts to bend laws, to interpret them in different ways, and to sometimes amend them, as the U.S. federal government did with the USA PATRIOT Act. Mark Monmonier, a geographer, saw a similar thing happen in the 1940s when the U.S. Census Bureau colluded with the military in aiding the internment of Japanese Americans.[46] Though the Census Bureau is and was at the time governed by policies meant to protect identities and personal information, the Bureau supported the Western Defense Command's 1942 "evacuation" to internment camps of over 110,000 Japanese Americans. Though the Census Bureau would not hand over household questionnaires, they did give the military block-by-block counts of residents with Japanese ancestors. In this case, and others more current, one must consider not only the actions of the Census Bureau but also the incredible amount of pressure on the Census Bureau to turn over the forms. Even when collected for the good of society, one never knows when a time of hysteria, new laws, or any number of developments could lead to the release of information about us for questionable purposes. In many minority neighborhoods, census takers are looked upon with suspicion, and perhaps rightfully so. Even if Census Bureau policies safeguard information, who is to say that a federal directive, perhaps through the Department of Homeland Security, will not trump Census Bureau policies? Certainly, libraries have policies about safeguarding patrons' information, but this does not stop USA PATRIOT Act provisions that empower law enforcement personnel to collect library patrons' records without the patron being notified.

Similar circumstances can occur in schools, where information may be given out for questionable purposes. As with the USA PATRIOT Act and the Western Defense Command's use of Census Bureau information, private information about students may be made available because new laws and directives broaden access to the information. For example, though student information is protected, with the passing of the No Child Left Behind law in 2002, military recruiters are permitted access to students' contact information, which had previously been off limits. Prior to the law's passing, the Family Educational Rights and Privacy Act (FERPA) had kept students' contact information concealed; but the No Child Left Behind law makes it mandatory that a school release the information unless a parent states in writing that he or she wishes to keep the information concealed or a school can show an adequate reason for denying recruiters entry (a religious or philosophical opposition to war, for example).[47] Once school administrators begin releasing student information to military recruiters, what is to prevent them from releasing it to other federal personnel—keep in mind this is information that is released not for investigative reasons, and not because there is a threat, but for recruitment into the armed forces? Additionally, as more information is collected through more high-tech devices, what other kinds of information will be accessed or released? Some day, will we be debating whether or not schools should release surveillance camera images of students or daily itineraries of their movements captured through tracking devices in their ID cards?

Technology has the ability to both free us from worry and cause us to worry more; to improve and hamper life at the same time—to be used for good and bad, to make life better and worse. Some social scientists refer to this as the "paradox" of technology. This is a "technology comes with a cost" theory, or what Edward Tenner called the "revenge of unintended consequences."[48] So the question is not whether techno-security is good or bad, but rather, Will the better outweigh the bad? Will we come to regret the fortification of schools? Or, fifty years from now, will we be patting ourselves on the back, saying that it was a job well done?

One way to get a glimpse of what we can expect in the future—and what schooling may be like in years to come as techno-security fortification continues—is to look at the people selling the equipment and what they wish for us and our schools. Security professionals at all levels of the business aim to convince us that a better world is within our grasp and that they are the people to work with because they have the knowledge and technologies to lead us to this better world. They want us to believe that "better" means more technology even when we are talking about education, and that modern school administrators must use technology because bearers of technology are powerful and more advanced. Once this belief about technology is established (an understanding that has developed over centuries), sale of equipment to schools is easier, because individuals are already convinced that the equipment is developed and used for their own good, even in cases when schools are already safe or when private information about individuals—about students, ID card carriers, parents, Internet users—can be revealed with the simple change of a law. Through their sales pitches, conference presentations, advertisements, and conversations, security professionals also convey a particular vision of humankind. This vision is one where humankind integrates happily with technology, where buildings such as schools become complete—or "integrated" or "networked"—only when they make use of the latest techno-security devices. Whether we are talking about schools or people's use of techno-security equipment in their communities, in order for us to buy into the techno-security fortification our humanness needs to blend in with the equipment and the equipment ultimately needs to become a part of our being—and we in a sense need to become cyborgs, a blending of human and technology.

Security equipment is also sold by highlighting the pleasures that technology can give users; design styles highlight the aesthetic qualities of equipment, even when the equipment is a metal detector used on children in schools. Hunks of equipment are turned into nice-looking devices, a feast for the senses for people who expect nothing less from their equipment. Security professionals know that people buy equipment not only because of what it does, but also because of the gratification, feeling of empowerment, and sense of progress that it can give them—and that school administrators are no different from anybody else, that they too want these abilities.[49] Security industry professionals know something that some technology critics have difficultly admitting: that individuals like making technology part of their lives, and that we not only "use" technology but also "connect" with it—we connect psychologically and viscerally (loving the feel of our new devices). We also literally connect through wires, keyboards, lenses, and other items that become extensions of the body. Even scientists—who pride themselves on impartial, objective science and utility—are guided by powerful social images and feelings about technology.[50] As Arnold Pacey pointed out in his research, scientists are guided by their memories and their experiences of society, their wishes for humankind, and even their preferences for certain designs and forms of product style.[51] Technology can be thrilling, and our use of it is a kind of communion with fantasy and power, for technology can enhance the senses like a drug. It makes us feel modern and gives us expertise, mobility, and personal power. The techno-security fortification of schools has little to do with safety and social control—it is really about image and the attainment of these abilities. Security businesses do not convince school administrators to purchase equipment because the equipment will make their buildings safer or they will be better able to control populations, but rather, because the equipment is a symbol of being future-oriented, advanced, and part of the modern world.

CHAPTER 4

The Promises of Techno-Security Fortification

If the police addressing Columbine had had such devices, they would not have waited so long to go into the school, they could have "pointed and clicked," saw what was happening, responded appropriately by taking quick action and by having the bearings on the perpetrators.

Jon Herttua, vice president of Worldwide Carrier Sales, Packet-Video, describing new technology his company was developing[1]

In spite of the advanced capabilities of products distributed by PlanetCCTV, WebEyeAlert, and other surveillance camera companies that enable police officers to access surveillance cameras in a school from any place where they have an Internet hookup, their products are rather standard and have a more cutting-edge version in what Jon Herttua, the vice president for Worldwide Carriers Sale, PacketVideo, referred to as "point-and-click" technology. In 2002, Herttua's company started working to develop handheld monitors that would be able to record through physical barriers in order to "catch live video reports"—that could have stopped, for example, the two youths at Columbine High School. He explained that such technology could be modified to enable parents to check in on their children at day care centers not only from a desktop computer, but also from handheld monitors. Though this technology is in the works, high-tech "nanny cams" are quite popular and are sold by many companies, including ParentWatch, whose cameras are less than $100 and can be installed in houses or day care centers. PacketVideo had recently won a bid to outfit new schools (referred to as "Schools of the Future") in Las Vegas with surveillance camera software that could be upgraded (i.e., are "scalable") to incorporate more advanced surveillance capabilities such as "point-and-click." In a conversation, Herttua told me that he wanted to develop a line of what he called "public security devices." These would adopt what has been used primarily by the military, mass produce them, and make them available to all consumers at a moderate cost so that everybody could have their own public security device.

The world that is envisioned here is not one involving a state takeover of ordinary people by higher-ups. It is a shopping spree. It is consumer utopianism. How will the PacketVideo businessman and others like him get the technology available to consumers—how do you get people to accept the cameras, information gathering, ID'ing, and metal detector searches? Forcing it on them will seem too tyrannical. So let consumers buy themselves into it—let them use the devices (for their homes, their cars, their day care centers, and their schools), add some to a city intersection or downtown area, and before you know it you have started a trend where individuals purchase their way into a life where the devices are as commonplace as your clothing and as indispensable as your computer. With advertisements, companies do all they can to demonstrate the naturalness of their products and how we would benefit by using them. But to think that companies have so much power over us—that they can advertise a product and we like sheep automatically buy it—is a rather simple way of thinking about people. Certainly, advertising can be powerful. But there is something on the receiver's side of the deal that helps us to be critical even if we are ultimately receptive to the promises made by advertisers. Advertisement messages do not introduce us to new ideas; they bring out what is already in us, summoning emotions just under the surface of our consciousness. In the case of security, advertisements tap into our yearnings for safety, our fears, but also our hopes for peacefulness within the bordered areas of our lives, urging us to buy into a world where we live, travel, communicate, and even meander streets through technology, with technology, by using technology, and by having technology used on us.

As a capitalist enterprise, techno-security fortification—whether in a school or not—needs to appeal to middle- and upper-class professionals who are the primary consumers of the equipment. In order to do this, security professionals cater to particular professional wants and make certain promises to their customers: not only that the equipment will provide safety and social betterment, but also that it will grant its users professional clout, pleasure, expertise, social and economic mobility, and personal power. This chapter explores these promises and demonstrates how they are used by security professionals to take equipment invented for military and national security purposes and turn it into an everyday "tool" for the on-the-go professional. One of the first steps in doing this is convincing critical consumers that equipment, devices, machinations, and other technological attachments to the body should become a part of our daily existence, that life should be technology mediated, a part of the way we do work, take pleasure, relax, communicate, and do virtually everything else. Security professionals want us to accept this lifestyle, to buy into this worldview; they want us, for our own good, to become this blend of human and technology—this kind of cyborg. Making it seem natural that we are attached to technology—physically as well as emotionally—is an essential part of promoting techno-security equipment.

Becoming Cyborgs

Melanie McGee, president of Evolution Software, Inc., was one of the more obvious promoters of human/technology integration, and a clear cyborg at heart. At a security industry conference in New York City, she was an invited speaker with some of the biggest names in the security business, including Dr. Joseph Atick, primary inventor of facial recognition technology; Thomas Berglund from Sweden, president and CEO of Securitas Services Limited; and executives from Protection One, Inc., Iridian Technologies, Inc., and Siemens. Unlike the formal addresses by the other speakers, McGee's presentation was part performance art. She stood before the group demonstrating a wearable computer: she had a strap around her head that held a monocle that protruded forward from her forehead (the computer screen), a little pouch on her hip (the CPU), and in one hand a keyboard that she used with her thumb (which she admitted takes some time to learn how to use). She also had a hidden camera on her shoulder that recorded what was around her and could project the images onto the monocle computer screen. As she strode before the group of about 750 security professionals, she explained that the computer could be equipped with voice recognition technology, which could eliminate the need for the unwieldy thumb-operated keyboard.

In her presentation, she stated that the wearable computer helps users integrate with their environment. No longer do people have to sit at a desk to do computer work "but [they] can be walking in the environment doing it." She admitted it was a bit like *Terminator*, referring to the

Arnold Schwarzenegger series of movies. She explained that the wearable computer introduced us to an "augmented/mediated reality" that put us in an environment that is more secure: "It is a form of protective wear. It enables one to acquire personal security. It's taking security into your own hands." She also mentioned as an aside that one could record police activities and that multiple cameras could be attached to enhance viewing; again, appealing to the everyday consumer who would like their technologies to be a bit subversive and to have power usually reserved for police and military authorities. To boost the significance of the product, the CEO also explained that the U.S. military was interested in "military adoption of the technology for motion tracking systems and 3-D augmented systems." In collaboration with scientists, her company was also developing "wash-and-wear computers" and "fabric displays and embroidered circuits." She explained that newer "covert designs will be integrated into everyday life and allow people to take personal responsibility for their safety."[2]

Wearable computers. Covert designs. Integrated into everyday life. Mediated and augmented realities. This is a world where everybody can be a Terminator, a place where individuals are no longer tethered to the inadequacies and limitations of the human body. Security professionals are not appealing to our yearnings for safety; they are appealing to our yearnings for fantasy and our desires to improve the body and life experiences. In many ways, what we expect from security technology are the same things we expect from other technologies, including pharmaceuticals, computers, and cars. We not only expect medicines to make us healthier, but also expect techno-meds or lifestyle drugs to expand experiences and overcome the limitations of the human body (to make us more social and more peppy, and to improve sex). We expect our clothing (and not just wearable computers) to also expand our experiences and to at least give us the feeling of overstepping the normal capabilities of the body. Through our clothing, we can associate ourselves with different people, live out personal fantasies, and feel what it is like to be rich (or poor), important, or even a member of the opposite sex. We also expect to expand human possibilities—at least, these are some of the promises made by companies that tell us we will be able to jump higher with the right brand of sneakers, have more energy with particular pantyhose, have greater sex appeal with the space-age razor blade, and feel on top of the world with the right kind of business suit. Clothing covers our bodies not only in machine-manipulated fabrics but also in meanings expressed through fashions, which allow us to interact in the world with a veneer of mostly our choosing. The fashion can be sexy, goofy, serious, modern, artsy, or casual. To some extent, the wearable computer is just another fashion, more modern than modern, more technological than artsy; it is a blend of several fashions reshaped by technology to express the hipness and cutting-edge style of the wearer. That the technology described by Melanie McGee becomes part of our clothing is significant, for clothing is the most pervasive interconnection between humankind and technology, and the one that we least recognize. Textiles, plastics, and silicone fibers are so much a part of our bodies that we can hardly imagine ourselves without them. It is nakedness that is abnormal; our natural state of being is the body sheathed in machine-manipulated cottons or laboratory-created fibers and maybe someday "embroidered circuits."

When security professionals discussed their consultations with schools, they also highlighted how they try to make the equipment seem natural to school district officials. Who would have thought that a school building would need surveillance cameras as much as they need chalkboards or books? But this is what several vendors told me. One said, "Let's face it, things like books, chalkboards, desks, and security equipment are the basic facts of schooling." Scott Dennison, Director and CEO of CEIA, stated:

> My job is to make your security installation a normal part of the school day. We do not want our customers to feel burdened by the installations . . . really, the opposite is true, because we want people to feel proud of their equipment, to know that they are incorporating the best that money can buy. School administrators and teachers have too many other things to worry about. That is why we have equipment that is easy to use. If you look at our surveillance cameras, they appear advanced, and they are, but being advanced also means being easy to use and feeling good about using them. We know how many people have difficulties with their technologies . . . through our consultants and on-site visits to schools, we make technology as simple as school officials need, so you don't even notice it, or don't have to worry about it. We are talking about equipment that can do incredibly important surveillance work for a school, is completely scalable, but is no more difficult to use than the lock on your front door.

Ross Fidler, manager of business development for LG Electronics U.S.A., Inc., explained what he viewed as the "normal process of investment in security" for any school, which included an "epiphany" once school administrators and guards got used to the equipment: "First, school district officials have many questions, then they start getting used to the equipment, then start wondering how they were ever able to run the school system without the equipment; next thing you know, they have an epiphany and say to themselves, 'This equipment makes me feel good about my school, my job, and myself.'"

This integration of humankind with technology is one of the more dominant themes in the security industry, and one that facilitates the security equipment sale. When advertising to schools, the security industry makes obvious references to school-related realities, but even before marketing directly to schools, the industry establishes a shared language that is meant to underpin all their marketing efforts, and human/technology integration is a big part of this language. This, of course, is tied to their promotion of utopia and social betterment; but the point is that security professions need us to not only buy equipment but also make it essential to our lives. We have to do more than just use it; we have to feel unnatural when not sheathed in technology, behind the times when not using the latest stuff, and even a bit nutty when not buying what everybody else is buying. How many people feel "naked" or "not right" without their PDAs (personal digital assistants) or without their cell phones on their hips? How many people are viewed as wacky because they use simpler technologies? Security professionals want us to reevaluate what it means to be human— to feel this nakedness and abnormalcy when without technology. After all, what does nakedness mean to us? Certainly not a natural state of being: it represents being exposed, open, and unprotected. It is an exaggeration to say that security professionals want us to feel naked, but they certainly want us to feel exposed and unprotected. No matter if they are marketing to schools, prisons, or offices, there is always the assumption that humans and technology are natural partners. One gets this sales line when asking about equipment; you can see it in security magazines and in advertisements, and hear it in comments by security professionals when they refer to the natural fit between people and devices.

Consider, for example, IR Interflex advertisements.[3] In 2000 Interflex was acquired to head the security sector of Ingersoll-Rand, and by 2002 the sector was bringing in about $2 billion a year and was composed of about 450 employees operating in twenty-two branches in eleven countries. This is their description of facial recognition technology:

> The IF7000 operates on the basis of ZN Face, a biometric verification method. Using automatic face comparison, the system checks whether the ID and the ID holder match. A video camera, a software based on neuronal algorithms enable the identification of individuals. The fundamentals are unique person characteristics which are stored in the database of the system. A person gaining access must present his/her ID or enter a PIN code. Then, a facial image is captured, evaluated with regard to characteristics, and

compared with the stored template. Changes in a person's appearance do not affect the system.[4]

The highly technological language is made to seem everyday, as if everybody should have a daily biometric verification done. Shouldn't we all know what an IF7000s is, or ZN Face? In this world, people go about their lives expecting that they will be managed through the mathematical sequencing of their body traits. People can even change their appearances, and the technologies will not be hampered. In many advertisements, individuals seem to wade through technology effortlessly and without regard for the information stored about them and the lasers used on them. They expect to be broken down into neuronal algorithms and to have their face geometry compared to a database of profiles. In sales pitches, I have heard metal detectors described as "an extra set of hands" and surveillance cameras as "eyes on the world." At security industry conferences, assistants to vendors have equipment demonstrated on them as if it were the most natural thing to do; they stand spread-eagled, with someone running a metal detector over them, without a second thought about it. This is a state of affairs where all of us will be so completely integrated with technology that we will no longer even notice it; putting on your embroidered circuits will be as natural as putting on your socks. We will no longer really care about our dependency on technology because we will not notice our dependency or care to understand where the body ends and the technology begins. All of this calls to mind what Donna Haraway referred to as the "cybernetic organism," the modern human who is actually a hybrid of machine and organism.[5]

In order for us to become so completely dependent on technology, we have to see it as a natural and commonsense part of our lives. This is quite a feat, given that technology represents almost everything that is not natural: it is manmade, invented, and produced; it has no life and does not arise out of our natural world (except when the natural world is manipulated by humans); it is the product of scientific achievement, not a normal by-product of our cosmos; and it is knowable and its origin is clear, not shrouded in mystery. And yet, technology has become in the minds of many a part of nature; it has taken on an almost spiritual significance and has been given the grandeur once reserved for the natural world. It can be beautiful and inspiring, and can have a life of its own; we attribute to technology human qualities and see it as an integral part of the normal evolution of the human race. Evolution, Inc., PlanetCCTV, WebEyeAlert, and other companies all make reference to human qualities, the cosmos, and human development even in the names of their companies. It is no coincidence that these companies are named with references to parts of the human body and/or in relation to our natural world: company names aim to project an image, and while there are plenty of techno-images in company names, there are also many names that want to give us the sensation of being in touch with the world by being in touch, and being touched by, technology.

Establishing the Naturalness of Security Technology

When I asked security vendors to describe what they intended to achieve in a school building, most explained—in one way or another—that they wanted a complete integration of school duties so that everything from attendance to security would be controlled and monitored through a central network. Everything that goes on in school will have some element of security attached to it. Taking attendance, for example, will involve the use of ID cards and scanners, teaching will be done under surveillance cameras with equipment that has been tagged with tracking devices, and teachers will have communication equipment that makes summoning a guard easier. Parents will pick up students using palm scanners, children will ride buses that are tracked with geographic positioning systems, coming into school will entail a metal detector search, and even buying a lunch will be recorded and the information will sit in a database (what Vigilos calls its "Central Data Vaults") and perhaps be downloaded one day for some investigation by police or federal agents. The routines of teachers, students, administrators, bus drivers, and parents will involve techno-security devices—the most innocent of us will be attached to machines, codes, systems, and templates. Technology will have a face, and people, on the other hand, will be "cardholders," measurements to be taken, a sequencing of traits to be compared to a database of other body traits. It is not that we will lose our humanness, though perhaps to some extent we do. But more to the point, humanness will be redefined—what it means to be human will be slightly altered to take into account the pervasive role of technology in our lives. This is an essential part of techno-security fortification—that it has us accept a particular lifestyle where technology mediates almost everything we do and serves multiple personal and professional needs. For new generations of people, this will involve a shift in thinking about what it means to be natural; for example, traditional symbols that we associated with nature (trees, hills, gardens, and so forth) will be redefined according to technology (cars, cell phones, the Internet, and so forth). Advertisers have already led the way in establishing this way of thinking. Notice, for example, in advertisements how easily cars seem to blend in with mountain roads or, as we shall see, security equipment blends in with its natural surroundings. Why should a log cabin in the woods with a post fence seem natural and not a house in a gated community with a security system?

In IR Interflex advertisements, images of a human/technology integrated world can be seen not only in their descriptions of products but also in their brochure photographs, which give us a visual representation of what the security industry wants to convey to us about the naturalness of technology. One of the company's primary symbols is a butterfly, which always seems naturally at ease in highly technological and professional worlds (Figure 4.1). This partially silhouetted butterfly appears in many of their advertisements, often, as in the advertisement shown in Figure 4.1, in the most out-of-place contexts. In other advertisements, humans are contentedly attached through their hands to technologies (Figure 4.2). In this case, a prominent picture of a hand is seen being transformed as it merges with technology; it also seems to be broken down into quadrants, as if being scanned and read by a biometric device. That the entire image is framed by a circular light adds a sense that the hand is under surveillance, in the sight of a lens, perhaps, or even at the center of a bull's-eye.

Security businesses contracting with advertising companies or using their own advertising divisions convey messages about humans and technology by using layout techniques that juxtapose parts of the human body

Figure 4.1 A montage depicting a highly professional and technological world mixed with leisure— and a butterfly in flight. IR Interflex, "Interflex Product Overview," brochure (IR Interflex, 2003), front cover.

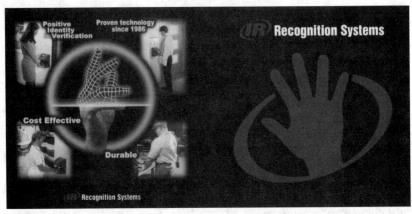

Figure 4.2 Claiming to have "Proven technology since 1986," the images show humans melding with technology through hand scans. At center, the hand seems to rise into the technological age. IR Recognition Systems, advertisement (IR Recognition Systems, 2001), front cover.

Figure 4.3 The face of the cyborg—half human, half machine. Many photographs juxtapose surveillance cameras with human eyes. LG IrisAccess 3000, "Iris Recognition System," single-page advertisement (LG IrisAccess 3000, 2002).

with technologies that almost resemble the body, as when advertisements show a human eye intersecting with a surveillance camera, which is a very popular image. Headquartered in Seoul, Korea, the LG Technology Division of LG Electronics U.S.A., Inc., produces the IrisAccess 3000, an iris-scanning device for surveillance cameras. In their advertisement, the silver-and-black surveillance camera looks eerily like an eye, albeit one of a robotic quality, a kind of *Terminator* eye (Figure 4.3). There are many advertisements, by different companies, that use this kind of eye/surveillance camera image. To some extent, the image represents the face of the cyborg, this new type of human we should gladly become. Part of why we should be glad for what the company offers us—telling us, about the IrisAccess 3000, "It's the look of things to come"—is because we can experience the omniscience of surveying all that technology can capture. The electronic eye of the surveillance camera is, of course, omniscient, always "scalable" and "smart," and gives us what promises to be unlimited possibilities. Another example, the Axis Communication advertisement, demonstrates the omniscient eye, which appears almost like a god, ever watchful and slightly unnerving, telling us, "See anything. Anywhere. Anytime" (Figure 4.4). This concept of omniscience is seen, as well, in the provocative company name PlanetCCTV, a company that also describes their devices as "smart."

Figure 4.4 The eye of power and omniscience, as if viewing from the heavens. Like towers, film strips (presumably from surveillance cameras) feed into the eye. Axis Communications, advertisement, in *American School and University* 76 (February 2003): SS9.

In addition to discussing "smart" technologies, security professionals will refer to buildings that use their technologies as "intelligent," as in the following excerpt from an article about building security:

> The term "intelligent building" is at least a quarter-century old. It generally refers to the computerized, networked integration and control of a building's internal environmental systems—lighting, temperature, fire/safety, air quality, hydraulics—and electronic security systems. The latest generation of intelligent buildings extend this control further by providing acess to and integration with key business functions such as manufacturing and process automation, financial and personnel management, and supply-chain management.[6]

The intelligent building is one where all aspects of the "internal environmental systems" are integrated, from air quality to electronic security systems—much like the school building, with everything from attendance to surveillance cameras integrated. When individuals give technology and buildings that use technology human qualities, such as being "smart" and "intelligent," they help facilitate the integration of humans and equipment. Who, after all, does not want to be "smart" or use "smart" things ("smart" technology, "smart" boards, "smart" bombs)? The technologies are smart because they make us smart. They are also smart because they are advanced, which after all shows our "smartness" to create and use them.

WebEyeAlert, a key participant in the Columbine Initiative discussed earlier, also relies on these eye, omniscience, and smart concepts to sell their equipment. In 2000, the company was successful in winning a contract over thirteen other bids with the Londonderry school system in New Hampshire. According to School Buyers Online, an Internet marketplace and clearinghouse for school professionals, the regularity of bomb threats at a school in Londonderry cost the district $30,000 in overtime police fees and created tension especially as the threats increased to the point where seven threats were made in a ten-day period.[7] Using language uncannily similar to advertising language, the director of facilities for the Londonderry school district remarked that "WebEyeAlert's open architecture enabled an easy integration with our CCTV system. The WebEyeAlert team of experts had us up and running quickly and the software has been running flawlessly since its installation." The system included forty-eight surveillance cameras that could simultaneously give the viewer both live-streaming video and archived clips from any Internet-accessible computer via a Web-based account on the company's website.

When the director of facilities for the Londonderry school district referred to the "open architecture" and "integration" of the surveillance system, he spoke like someone who had been in the security business, which is possible since school district administrators often prefer to hire security personnel (and sometimes teachers) with backgrounds in private security (as well as policing and the military). The WebEyeAlert surveillance system is similar to other systems that enable multiple individuals to log onto a company website and view images through surveillance cameras. These systems are almost always described as "integrated." A sales representataive for Vigilos, Inc. referred to this kind of integration as "network addressable capabilities that synchronizes [sic] with host cameras and store transactional data"—more high-tech language that conveys expertise and scientism, as well as the idea of one powerful megasystem. Software dealers in particular (as opposed to those in hardware) were keen on this idea of integration, for they saw their software as the link between humans and technology hardware.

In their sales proposal, Vigilos explained what they could offer schools in a section called "How Can Avanta Solve the Issues of Schools Today?"

> By providing a cost effective way to integrate information Avanta [the software produced and supported by Vigilos] offers schools a means to incorporate pertinent information to be used to determine potential threats and notify the proper governing authority. Avanta is browser-enabled, allowing schools to assign as many users as needed without loading software for each user to access the security system information. Each user can use their existing web browser to log on, review and manage the security system. With schools depending so much on external support from parents, local police and other community participants this allows for easy implementation and access for anyone.[8]

Using Avanta software, school administrators and guards can program into their systems specific rules such as "if a metal detector is triggered capture that information with an associated video clip and store as an event." This archives the information for later viewing in case evidence is required for an investigation. Avanta software will also send automatic notifications of an intrusion through an alarm system or an automatic e-mail to the local police. It can also be programmed to send telephone or pager messages. Like other software, police (with user IDs and passwords) have full access to the system, which could be used from the school, the police precinct, or from patrol cars.

What makes us buy into the deal? Certainly, technology has obvious benefits. Who, after all, would do away with the thousands of machines, gadgets, and tools we use to make life easier and safer? But there are other aspects of technology that urge us to buy into what salespeople have to offer. Security professionals are very clear that the equipment is meant to give us a feeling of omniscience; we can feel empowered by their devices and above the world when we use them. We can feel that we are taming nature, taking control of time, or conquering space. Security professionals will tell you that surveillance cameras can "stop time," "capture an event," and "let us see all things." We will extend human possibilities—see, hear, sense, and feel more clearly and beyond what is humanly possible. And for the critical consumers who, though fascinated, may be wary of the techno-world we are creating, they are informed that they should rest assured because techno-security is a normal part of life, as natural as the chalkboard in the school, a butterfly in flight, or the clothing on your back. These are promises made by meaning makers—advertisers working for security companies—who take mass-produced hunks of plastic and metal and give them an aura of omniscience and power.[9]

Techno-security fortification of schools is one part of the development of a technology-mediated and capitalist world—where even things like safety are brought to us by businesses. The "safety" part of techno-security equipment is the label that puts the technology in a particular class of products: essentially, it lets us know that the product is a thing to make us safe, rather than, for example, a thing to make us travel faster or communicate over long distances. And yet, the sale of techno-security is boosted when it is sold not just as a safety thing but also for its entertainment, communication, and even leisure qualities. Security equipment is sold to school officials by convincing them that they will be able to "process students faster" or "keep better records" or "free up your time for more quality and efficiency." And why shouldn't security vendors make these promises to school officials—or to city planners, homeowners, or anybody? Even outside of schools, when selling to the general public vendors know that people expect a lot from their technologies, so there is security equipment that fits into many classes of products. It is sold to us to make life more comfortable, it gets hooked up to our entertainment systems, and it is sold for the pleasure that it can give us. This is a process of mass production—an ingenious working of meanings and images and hardware construction, which has helped to create an item so versatile. It is quite a feat that in such a short time security professionals have been able to take such daunting equipment and turn it into something so trendy and so integrated with so many aspects of our world. This is another success story for businesspeople to share in boardrooms, at shareholders' meetings, and at conference gatherings. And yet, the success was inevitable and was accomplished with the willingness of consumers who over the years have found technology fun to use. It brings out something in us that is childlike and adventurous. We play with our technology, sometimes dangerously, because technology can be thrilling. Even technologies used to catch criminals should be fun to use.

The Pleasures of Security Technology

Offering individualized services, and stating that their metal detectors "Meet the Demands of Airports, Law Enforcement, Schools, Courthouses, Correctional Institutions, Loss Prevention, Event Security, and Governmental Public and Private Facilities," Garrett Metal Detectors is one of the largest and most successful producers of handheld and walk-through metal detectors. As their ads will tell you, they were proud sponsors of the 2002 Olympics in Salt Lake City and produce the metal detectors of choice for most schools. Their SuperScanner is one of many handheld metal detectors marketed to schools.

Advertisements for the SuperScanner offer visual representations of a happy society even as individuals submit to scanning. In photographs that accompany SuperScanner advertisements, most individuals are shown to be clean-cut and smiling, with their arms spread in satisfied resignation while being scanned by an individual with a metal detector prominently displaying the Garrett company name. In one brochure, the Garrett Super-Wand (a variant of the SuperScanner with a slightly more sleek design) is shown scanning the feet of an individual, who, though we cannot see his or her face, is represented as a youth by the sneakers and fringe cuffs of the jeans. Not only are we to assume that the youth happily (or at least contentedly) submits to the scan, but for the user as well, including those working in schools, the advertisement claims that "the new Garrett Super-Wand makes everyone an effective security scanner" and is "very easy and fun to use."

Should metal detectors be fun to use? In the cyborg world, yes, because pleasure is paramount. We want to feel fantastic and above it all when we use technology—even metal detectors. When Garrett advertisements claim that their metal detectors are fun, they are drawing on our yearnings for pleasure and even fantasy. They are also referring to technology's toylike quality. In his studies of technology, George Basalla pointed out that invention is a playful endeavor and that people want their technologies to be playful things, even if it is a technology used to scan people's bodies for weapons.[10] One can imagine gripping the solid, black body of the SuperWand, of holding what a sales representative called its "well-balanced placement and feel," and sliding it up and down the contours of a person's body in a way that can never be devoid of sexual implications. Sociologists have described the driving of a car in a similar way, the invigoration of speed, motion, and control that is so pleasing.[11] If the Internet were just an information-gathering tool and not an instrument of pleasure, it would not have the appeal that it has for children and adults. We expect pleasure from our cars and computers; why not from a metal detector?

A sales representative for Kalatel, a subsidiary of Interlogix Company, which specializes in surveillance cameras, had this to say about their CyberDome Day-Nite Cameras:

> These are a joy to use. The capabilities are nearly limitless. You get clearer pictures, 360-degree views, 24-hour coverage, day-night, color capabilities. You will be happy with this system because, foremost, it is easy to use. If you're not happy, then I have failed. I never fail to please, that is really important to us [nods to an assistant, who agrees with her].

No cyborg society is complete without happy people who easily integrate with technology, who submerge themselves in its magic qualities, submit to those who use it on them, and are rewarded themselves with the joy of technology that is both fun to use and fun to have used on them. At security industry conferences, sales representatives are more than willing to show off their wares, but additionally they want people to use them and to know what it feels like to hold a metal detector and to scan somebody. I have had opportunities to do this and have felt odd sensations while holding the equipment, feeling mischievous, as if I was doing something wrong and yet everybody said it was right.

Using a metal detector at a booth at a security conference, a vendor for the equipment kept telling me to slow down as I moved the metal detector over a manikin: "You have to take it easy. It's like a sport. You have to get the feel of it." He showed me how to stand, how to hold the metal detector firmly but comfortably, and how to wave it over the plastic body, telling me, "If you are not feeling good about your use of it, you're not going to like it and you're not going to do it right. It's like a good golf swing."

One vendor, who sold software for security integration, said this about his systems:

> The best thing about the software is that it is easy and fun to use. You can like being the boss of your own terrain . . . it's completely user-friendly, easily navigated. No significant development [of our

product] is without attention to making it easier and more plea-
surable for the user. Why should we be hampered by technologies? That's the main impetus for technologies today, that they can
actually make our more advanced technology easier to use. More
advanced doesn't mean that we have to be more advanced to use
it. Instead, really, more advanced means that it is actually simpler
and more gratifying to use so that people's comfort levels with
software and hardware rise.

One sales representative for Infinova, a company specializing in surveillance, fiber optics, and access control, had this to say about his equipment:

> You take our surveillance systems and try them, and we will let
> you try them, we will visit your site and set up a model of how it
> would run, and you do this, and you will never want to be with-
> out the system. Primarily, because you are going to see the great
> power it gives you. And primarily because you are going to like
> using it. If you don't like using it I will eat this modem [holds up
> a modem]. This is very important to us because we know that if
> you don't like the equipment—I don't care how effective it is—if
> you don't like it, you will not keep with the security program. It's
> like dieting. You may know it's good for you, but if it is awful to
> do you won't do it, and this is how we end up with this [pats his
> rotund belly].

Vendors sometimes have manikins so they can demonstrate their
wares, but it is likely that people working as assistants will act as models if
a potential customer wants to see a demonstration of the equipment—or
try the equipment themselves. The people who model for equipment demonstrations are often women, are always professional-looking, and do not
seem uncomfortable with standing spread-eagled for a demonstration. In
advertisements that focus on schools, as well, individuals who are being
scanned, have ID cards, or are recorded by CCTVs are often depicted as
clean-cut and upwardly mobile youths who seem to enjoy the experience
of being a part of the techno-security world.

Security professionals know that their customers want to feel good with
the things that they buy and use. They market to educated professionals
who have certain expectations, are schooled members of either the working elite or professional classes, and want their technologies to meet many
human and business needs. Professionals are the vanguards of the cyborg
world, the trailblazers, those eager for the newest devices—the ones to buy
them first—partly because their professions depend on them, partly because
of the pleasure they get from them. In schools especially, the devices are

becoming an expectation: even in the safest school, we expect to have security equipment about. Part of this is the "you never know" phenomenon, where even our safest places seem to us potentially dangerous—as shootings in Columbine and other middle and high schools remind us. But also, in time we can seem almost obsolete, less developed, and even negligent when we do not use or apply the newest technologies, especially when others around us are. Professional people expect their everyday "tools" to help them gain status, improve productivity, and advance in society—and we have the same expectations when it comes to security equipment. Security professionals know that people want many things from their systems. They want to feel good using them, they want to feel powerful, and they want to be able to advance in the professional world. When school officials invest in techno-security, they want to invest in a system that will make schooling more efficient and their own work easier. Techno-security cuts down on manpower, replaces bookkeeping with databases, and makes a place look modern, with equipment that seems to gleam with new-age possibilities. Even the idea that techno-security involves equipment can mislead those who have yet to grasp how techno-security has become an integral part of all aspects of schools—the best representation of techno-security may not be the individual surveillance camera in the hallway, but the diagram of its operation in relation to other aspects of the school, including other techno-security devices (alarms, automatic locking doors, etc.) but also the heating system, lights, and other basic utilities.

The Abilities of the Can-Do Professional

PacketVideo, Evolution Software, Inc., Infinova, and other companies give upwardly mobile people what is often called a "complete package" of equipment and accessories for pleasure and business. Techno-security equipment is an enabler and is uniquely adaptable to various environments (prison, school, and office) and needs. If you need it to help you be safer, it can do that. If you need it to update you on weather conditions or to click into a website, it can do that as well. Like cell phones that do more than just let people talk to each other, security equipment is becoming part of larger systems involving entertainment and professional and life management. At an international security conference in 2004, I attended a training session on using surveillance cameras. The surveillance system software was part of a kind of house management system that controlled lights, the heating system, pool equipment, and potentially all modes of utilities in the house. With the same software that controls your surveillance cameras, you can also control when your thermostat should be turned down or when the stereo should kick on. These kinds of integrated systems are becoming the norm in the industry.

With their advertisements declaring, "You Name It, SimplexGrinnell Can Secure It," the security company, which advertises to schools, describes an interconnected system embedded with all kinds of "abilities":

> Isolated, dedicated security networks and databases have been standard practice for years and in some cases are still mandated. But the industry is also driven by a new set of rules fueled by today's enterprise-level security challenges—challenges that require unprecedented communications and interoperability. The security network of the future must link controllers, databases, file servers and other vital network resources in a seamless, integrated security environment delivering high configurability, scalability, and survivability.[12]

Though the description is mostly about the security industry, it is really about you, the professional, and what you will need—controllers, databases, file servers, and other vital network resources—to be a part of a future governed by a whole "new set of rules." Like PacketVideo, SimplexGrinnell sells software that helps users update what they have in place to create a more elaborate but clearly logical security system that is integrated, scalable, and a model of what is sometimes called "information architecture." The company provides a host of "abilities" to the buyer: "interoperability," "configurability," "scalability," and, rather ominously, "survivability." At one level, what the advertisers are referring to here is quite simple: it is a macroenhancement of equipment and lifestyle, where one has a complete security system (where fire alarms trigger cameras, or cameras are operated from multiple stations) within one network. But at another level, this is a conceptual enhancement. The description also signals a new era of security, where systems have "unprecedented communication" to deal with "enterprise-level" challenges. They "link," "network," and are "seamless." When buying this equipment, people not only update obsolete systems but also are propelled into the future with one leg up. The equipment, and the language that goes with it, become a kind of professional capital—language that one needs to know, as well as instruments that one needs to have, to make it in the professional world.

Security technology is partly about mobility, keeping ahead of the game. The technologies are a marker of the can-do professional—the person on the move. When an institution such as a school is outfitted with the equipment, it becomes a part of this professional, future-oriented world. Just the name of PacketVideo's "Schools of the Future" captures this idea, as do the schools with the latest of everything (from urinals to security equipment) portrayed in architecture portfolios and catalogues distributed by the security industry. It is common to hear that newly opened schools represent "school districts on the move" or that changes in schools, including installations of security equipment, represent schools "moving forward." Conveying mobility is important, because we associate it with good things—advancement and improvement. So when security professionals talk about mobility, they are trying to appeal to professionals who know this language and need evidence that they are in fact "on the move."

Starting with mobility, the security sales pitch follows a particular logic: you get mobility that can lead to success that can lead to power, respect, and, ultimately, one's own private utopia, where all needs (pleasure, safety, business) are at one's fingertips. The mobility is actual, in the sense that people are no longer bound to their desks and that devices are more portable (for the on-the-go professional) and also mobile in the economic sense, in that the devices allow professionals to rise in the business hierarchy, giving them a competitive edge in a world where other people are also buying technologies and using them to their advantage. The best security technology also increases profits, whether we are talking about the remaking of a mall or downtown center, or about efficiency and "flow" that increase productivity for a company. For schools, security equipment enables officials to save on insurance premiums and to "process" students faster. It helps schools better compete in a free market school system, where districts must attract students who have a broader range of choices through voucher programs, open-enrollment policies, and some magnet and charter school options.

In order to promise so much to the professional—not only safety, but all of these advantages—security equipment must surpass its utility and offer more than just safety. No longer can a surveillance camera be just a camera; it must be networked into a system that includes fire alarms, databases, record-keeping programs, and utilities. Additionally, the camera must record with great capabilities, and also be able to call up information and archive and mark sections of data.

One of the realities of the security business is that it is less and less a security business and more and more a technology business. Security is just one capability (along with entertainment, scheduling, communication, etc.) of newer life management systems. As a PacketVideo advertisement states, the security mode of their devices is one part of your complete "quality multimedia experience":[13]

> PacketVideo, the recognized leader in wireless multimedia, provides MPEG-4 compliant software that enables the delivery,

management and viewing of one- and two-way video, audio and multimedia applications over current wireless networks to mobile devices such as telephones and personal digital assistants. Packet-Video's pioneering end-to-end solution delivers the highest quality multimedia experience possible in every mobile environment, globally. The company markets its software to wireless operators, wireless device and silicon manufacturers, and content providers to ultimately enable mobile consumers to access a variety of applications, including news and financial stories, sports highlights, music videos, weather and traffic reports, and home or work security cameras, from any location. Mobile consumers can gain access to multimedia content today by visiting PVAirguide™, the world's first wireless streaming media showcase.

Wires, which were once signs of advanced technology, are passé; they bind and tether and hark back to an old world when people unitasked. On the other hand, wirelessness represents mobility, which again is an important part of being the can-do professional. The mobile professional is given unbounded power and freedom by software that is "compliant," enabling multiple forms of viewing for purposes of safety, profit, entertainment (for the pleasure seeker), and information gathering about sports, weather, (naturally for the "mobile consumers") traffic, and, for the consumer, financial stories. Like the performance art of the wearable computer by the Evolution Software president, this is a "multimedia experience possible in every mobile environment, globally."

Again, we are in cyborg land, where successful people are the ones with the greatest technology and therefore the greatest abilities. Whether we are talking about education, security, war, or information gathering, technology is power. The company description of Evolution Software echoes sentiments related to mobility and works hard to tap into that professional market, where one knows the value of power, information gathering, mobility, and profit wrapped up into one package:

> From developing & designing Internet applications & sites to Database design & administration, Melanie [President of Evolution Software] and her team provide a complete range of IT services focusing on utilizing existing resources, and preparing new information systems for the future. Through Melanie's capabilities Sandra Jones & Company [a security industry consulting firm] clients are assisted with database design, information architecture, database development and implementation, data retrieval (multiple techniques), data sharing and integration and data analysis

and reporting. If information is power, Melanie's skills translate data to usable knowledge. Evolution Software provides productivity software to sales forces that deals with complex proposals to help accelerate and streamline their sales process in order to improve profitability and business without tethering people to their desktops.

For those seeking professional power, Evolution Software offers customers access to information for "data sharing," "information architecture," and "data retrieval." Again, this is a system for individuals who cannot afford to be "tethered to their desktops" and who know that information is power. The mobile classes of cyborgs (or "mobile consumers" described by PacketVideo) are clearly among the privileged classes, which unlike the crotchety wealthy of yore are constantly on the move, interacting in physical and digital spaces, traveling at great speeds, and working in a world where money is new, transferred digitally, and made and lost quickly. This is the future that professionals know awaits them, and to prepare themselves for it, they buy technologies that enhance their abilities to be successful. Possession of new life-management security equipment is like having your own personal techno-assistants—or PDAs—letting you communicate instantly with others in the world, record what is around you, access news programs and the Internet, operate surveillance and detection devices, and even get you going on some online gambling. Whether you are a school administrator, homeowner, or just a regular person looking to get ahead, security professionals let you in on a secret: you want to be safe, enjoying yourself, successful, and ahead of the game—here are the products to buy.

Promises of a Profitable Future

Because security advertisements lack data showing that their systems actually make people safer, and there are few references to safety in what security professionals say about their equipment, it is clear that being safe is only a minor part of the package. Having mobility, power, and control over your environment is what security is about. These are aspects of technology that appeal to nearly everybody, especially those professional working people striving to get ahead who are able to afford the equipment. But there is another level of consumer that stands slightly above that of the everyday professional, that has another intention, another something to be gained from security. Security equipment has a long history of being used by the highest levels of management to increase production and to watch over workers.[14] Surveillance and information gathering have always been at the heart of capitalist production, and security professionals know that the big contracts are often made with high-level buyers who have certain business expectations, in that all new acquisitions should lead to the ultimate goal of profit and efficiency. Marketing to CEOs, presidents of companies, business owners—and increasingly, school officials—security professionals are clear that their equipment will meet the bottom line. Almost all articles in security magazines that feature installations in new facilities discuss the economic benefits of the equipment, as do sales reps and vendors.

A vendor for Videolarm was very clear about the advantages of his equipment, ticking them off with his fingers.

> You have the immediate benefits of reduced crime and vandalism. Schools spend tens of thousands of dollars a year due to vandalism and crime. And especially for schools, you don't have as much litigation, because you have better documentation. That's right off—immediate savings. Many insurance companies give deductions when you have new security installed, and this is especially true of surveillance cameras. So you have that savings. You have better efficiency and flow of your resources. Human resources and otherwise. You also avoid activities that cost you money, whether we are talking about stealing or just laziness. These are the monetary savings right off the top.

An advertisement for Northern Computers, Inc., drums up fears, but they are not the typical fears due to external dangers—they are the fears that upper management must feel when confronted with their own disgruntled employees:

> Now how about that disgruntled employee you had to fire last week? That hardware technician you swear by, did you know he can open any lock? What if information security is a lot more menacing than you originally thought? You may have information security licked, but is your facility at risk? Is there a solution to reduce the risks involved with theft, vandalism . . . even espionage? If there is a solution, are you using [it]? Combat the mounting risks your facility faces with solutions from Northern Computers.[15]

The surveillance systems being installed in schools and other public places are connected to a history where security itself—even before the mass use of equipment—was used to benefit capitalists. We see in the above quotation that it still is. When teachers, such as those in Philadelphia, start having hand scans done and bus drivers are on surveillance cameras along with the kids, or classrooms are installed with cameras, we see the potential for schools to follow in this long history. Security—in one form or another—has always been used by businesses and governments to increase profits, to make people work harder, to minimize illegal and unsavory activities, and, in some cases, to bust unions and to infiltrate activist groups on both the left and the right. This was seen in the earliest days of private security in the nineteenth century, when Allan Pinkerton (generally credited with founding the first private security business) provided security for the new railroad industry, for the U.S. Post Office, and for Abraham Lincoln.[16] In the world of security, he was an almost legendary figure who was hired to also track the Reno Gang, Butch Cassidy, and Jesse and Frank James.[17] But businesses had other uses for Pinkerton, and some of his agents were recognized union busters and infiltrators of groups such as the Molly McGuires. In July 1892, Carnegie Steel Company hired three hundred armed Pinkerton agents to expel striking Amalgamated Association of Iron and Steel Workers from the Homestead Works in Pittsburgh. After the shooting stopped, several men on both sides were dead and many were injured. After the incident, the U.S. Congress began to draw up legislation to regulate private security, something still going on today but with the opposite intention—these days, Congress has moved to deregulate security.

The use of security by upper management has a long history, but it has entered a new era of surveillance, especially with the private use (and not just military use) of global positioning satellite (GPS) systems. Today, even workers on the open road—ones you would least expect to be under surveillance—are tracked with GPS by trucking firms. GPS systems use transmitters that beam coordinates to twenty-four satellites owned by the U.S. Pentagon. Trucking firms contract GPS services through security companies such as OmniTracs (a division of Qualcomm) and HighwayMaster Communications in Dallas. Describing the benefits of the devices, *Fleet Equipment* magazine got right to the point: "Computer software programs and global positioning satellite (GPS) systems have given fleets a way to route, reroute, and track vehicles, loads and drivers to make the most of their rolling assets."[18] Remember, as well, the school bus surveillance equipment discussed in Chapter 3 that kept watch over the kids but also had a camera trained on the bus driver. The truck maker, Kenworth, is starting to build trucks with pre-installed "telematics tracking systems," which will be able to track trucks as well as download information about the driver, the route, the speed of the vehicle, and other information. One line of freight trucks includes the T800, which is a biometric finger-scanning system for verifying the driver of the rig—this is not only to prevent theft but also to prevent drivers from switching trucks or getting a buddy to take the load.[19]

If you are part of upper management and you are told that a security system will help make your employees safer and protect assets, you are pleased. But there is another incentive when you are told that you can also increase revenues by making workers more efficient and honest. Consider, for example, how IR Interflex puts it in their advertisements. The following excerpt is repeated in slightly edited forms in several of their brochures:[20]

> Interflex offers customer-focused, innovative integration of tech-nologies, providing comprehensive system solutions that revolu-tionize the management of people, openings, and assets. A single database dynamically manages the flow of people and assets. By doing so, Interflex contributes to its customers' attainment of business goals by helping to increase revenues, decrease opera-tional costs, and increase the productivity of employees and other assets. While most system providers concentrate on one piece of an offering, Interflex's vision of combining the management of people, openings, and assets, has created an environment where modules of software applications reside around a common data-base infrastructure. The benefit to organizations is the opportu-nity to invest in technology that can grow and be used in multiple facets of business operation.

Interflex specializes in access control, time and attendance, personal scheduling, production data recording, mobile communication, identifi-cation devices, and biometrics (again, a completely integrated system of security, life management, and communication), and its vision is purely about business: "A single database dynamically manages the flow of people and assets" in order to "increase revenues, decrease operational costs, and increase the productivity of employees."

To be blunt, security technology is part of a larger economic structure: the rat race of life. It is tied into profit making and used to keep workers on track. It is also part of the everyday life of on-the-go professionals who are often on the receiving end of security (the ones being watched, hav-ing information taken, and being scanned) at the same time that they too make use of their own security equipment to get ahead and to sometimes subvert surveillance from above or use it on people below them. When not using actual security devices, individuals use the same technologies for life management, entertainment, and professional advancement. Used one way, GPS is surveillance; used another way, it makes cell phones operate. The use of security equipment—according to the people who should know best, the vendors—is primarily about business advancement. Security vendors, who are always looking for the big sale, know that upper-management people are their best bet for a profitable contract, and they give their top-notch customers exactly what top-notch people want: better ways of increasing assets and cutting costs. So why should schools be any different?—vendors will ask. Especially with reforms that give students greater enrollment choices and where school officials are dealing with tight budgets—why shouldn't a school official, like a good businessperson, make decisions even about security that have the dual benefit of increasing revenues? Since profit is at stake, inevitably the use of techno-security will manage more lives and more aspects of our lives; it is one thing to say that techno-security will involve surveillance cameras to oversee hallways, but when those cameras become mobile, are placed in classrooms, and are part of building management systems, we may find that our most important tasks in life—the education of children, for example—will depend on items with names like Rugged Eye, LED Bullet, and Warrior Elite.

Getting Self-Assured and Well-Secured

Professionals use technology, including security technology, to keep up with the Joneses—to prove to people around them that they are up with the changes and are professionals on the move. Videolarm advertises their Warrior Elite vandal-resistant cameras in *Security Magazine* with an ad that features a dog with its head buried in sand. There is a question in bold next to this picture that asks, "Is Your Head in the Sand?" And, below this, "The Threat is Real. Videolarm has the Solution."[21] Nobody wants to be a dog with its head in the sand. The advertisement also tells you that their surveillance cameras can withstand a .22 caliber bullet. Things that can withstand bullets (and whacks with baseball bats—as a WizKid Opto-Tech surveillance camera advertisement claims) are the necessary components that we need in order to keep ahead, and apparently to educate youths. Advertisements such as this one are effective even in the public school market because school professionals use technology to keep up with other schools and to show their forward-thinking sides, too—that they are ahead of the game, up on the latest advances, well-fortified, and therefore a "school of the future," as PacketVideo puts it. Similar to the points that Larry Cuban has made, technology is often hailed as a panacea for what ails schools—low academic achievement, buy computers; concerns about safety, buy security devices.[22] As with the "wiring" of schools since the 1980s, security fortification is one part of a larger reform effort that touts a free market approach to school improvement, and as with computers often does not achieve its desired result but becomes established anyway.

Techno-security devices become established in schools for many reasons: federal support for development and research of the equipment; businesses promoting the wares; school reform that has opened the school market to (security) technology businesses; legitimate concerns about safety that we attempt to deal with through the buying of technology; the fascination that people have with technology; a school's desire to appear up-to-date with the latest technology—these are just a few of the reasons. Additionally, techno-security fortification has become a kind of competition of professional wills. The highest levels of management use the technologies to profit and will do so as long as lower-level professionals and workers allow them. The government pushes it into the most private parts of our lives and deeper into the public realm partly for social control purposes and partly to promote private enterprise (free market school reform, for example). Professionals use it as part of their set of tools to get ahead; and for each item they buy, the more they need to buy, for, as we all know, even the newest, most cutting-edge items are soon obsolete. As soon as businesses get people like you and me to buy their stuff—and when places like schools become part of the market—the items are already popular and do not have the same grand stature as when they were the exclusive items of the elite or the military. So the ante is always raised: the next set of equipment must be even faster, more efficient, and more stylish, and must provide more pleasures and power and stature than the last.

All this, of course, suits security businesses just fine, and they do all they can in press releases, advertisements, sales statements, and other pronouncements to keep people moving in this direction of buying techno-security for competing, profiteering, and image-building. When someone calls foul—perhaps the ACLU complaining about yet another iris-scanning machine in a school—the security industry retaliates with stinging accusations. Anyone who still has the gall to complain about surveillance or information databases is a crazy hippy, a potential terrorist, or a flake. In these public controversies involving techno-security, the arguments are usually focused on the invasiveness versus social control aspect of the equipment—whether it is violating our rights or is an effective means of maintaining control in a building. Though important issues to raise, the idea that techno-security is another step in the business takeover of schools is cast aside. We have put our trust in businesses to run even our schools, and we deal with safety with a "full-scale assault" of technology, as one vendor put it. So businesses push security, state and federal governments push security, and just when you think the educated classes will start pushing back, they hop on board and find that they too can benefit from the technology; that it feels good to use a metal detector; that they like their gated community; and that they feel better with their superse-cure school. They even find new entertainment at their fingertips.

Businesspeople could not dream of a better situation. If they had simply told people they would be safer with the equipment they would never have had such success. As any security professional will tell you, people want more than safety: they want self-assurance, instant information, power, respect, and even the ability to move beyond mere humanness—to see and hear better, operate more efficiently, and live life at higher speeds. This is the real power of techno-security equipment and a key part of mak-ing the sale—convincing people that they will be lame ducks (physically, socially, and in their professional lives) without the devices. When this logic is played out in schools it is effective, especially in light of school shootings and the September 2001 attacks in the United States. No school official wants to appear to be a lame duck, and usually with the backing of school boards, administrators, and parents, they follow in the footsteps of other schools that use technology to the hilt for all purposes—for edu-cation, for school management, and of course, for safety. In many ways, security professionals have half their work done for them because people already like this kind of cyborg world; they like their toys and their man-ufactured pleasures and prestige. These aspects of technology cannot be forgotten when we are considering the factors that have promoted school fortification; techno-security is another technology provided to schools to improve some element of schooling, in this case the safety of students. We accept the fortification just as we have accepted other technology buildups in school—including the use of computers and earlier generations of tele-visions, slide projectors, and overheads, all of which were hailed as forms of school improvement, but often did not live up to their promises.[23] School fortification is another element in this long history of sometimes blind belief in technology and private enterprise to improve human endeavors.

However, techno-security is also different from other technology pro-motions; boosting the fortification is a fear factor that was not as dramatic in earlier promotions of technology. Though promoting computers in the 1980s was accompanied by a "crisis" in education, the crisis involved aca-demic standards, not life-threatening attacks. Propelling the sale of secu-rity equipment is fear, a very powerful force, as security professionals have learned. To some extent, fear is manufactured in that security profession-als draw on fear—make explicit reference to school shootings and terror-ism—to sell their wares and to drive the market in a direction of continual expansion. Several books have shown how fear is used to shape discourses and social policies, but few have analyzed how fear is used to establish a business niche and then exploit it. As the next chapter shows, security corporations advertise danger, they try to fill us with fear, and sales representatives and vendors use people's insecurities to promote their products. In doing so, they also promote the privatization of security. They try to convince us that only the private sector—that bastion of capitalism—can protect us. They use stories and images of horror to show us how important they are—to boost themselves and to elevate their role in making us feel safer. Without them, we are told, we are as good as dead.

CHAPTER 5

Horror Stories That Sell

I project that sales to schools will probably double in the next year. Three or four years ago, we would hear parents saying, "We don't want metal detectors. It looks like a prison." Now they are demanding that schools provide a safe environment.

Jim Dodrei, vice president of marketing for Garrett Metal Detectors[1]

Security professionals talk about their wares with great urgency. The vice president of marketing for Garrett Metal Detectors explained that people are "*demanding* that schools provide a safe environment." And if it means that their kids will be safer, parents are willing to ignore or forget that they used to think that schools would look like prisons with the equipment. Security professionals sometimes give the impression that people are rushing into their offices and banging at their doors demanding equipment from them. One told me, "The general public has just woken up, are facing the facts, that they need protection and need it now." Another told me, "I wouldn't say that people are hysterical, but they are definitely desperate." I do not know if people are really hysterical or desperate, but they are most likely demanding, which accounts for the skyrocketing sales that Jim Dodrei and others in marketing talked about. But if they are not hysterical or desperate, then security professionals have failed, for they try in earnest to spread the presumption that people are and should be hysterical. This can be seen in what security professionals say, in their statements to journalists, and in interviews I had with them. It can also be seen in articles in trade magazines.

Access Control & Security Systems is a popular trade magazine for security professionals, including those in the school market. On the inside front cover of each issue, there is a "Datelines" section that carries blurbs reporting on major security-related news. In one issue in late 2002, there were four blurbs. The first three were rather typical. One reported that a Transportation Security Administration security screener who fell asleep on the job caused Miami International Airport to evacuate five concourses and delay forty-one flights. Another noted that the Westchester District Court (in New York) approved the use of flashlight scopes that can detect forged licenses, opening up their use in 2,300 bars, delis, and other establishments in the state. Another discussed the firing of five hundred security screeners at San Francisco International Airport, the result of legislation requiring screeners to be citizens of the United States.

Each of these blurbs deals in some way with a rather significant security event of the time. However, the fourth blurb was quite different, for it mentions nothing about security (except to mention a security guard who was attacked) or much of anything relevant to the primary readers of the magazine, who are security professionals. However, it is about violence and most specifically about out-of-control kids, which, though it does not give practical kinds of information and news, has its own kind of appeal for security professionals:

> Philadelphia—A 17-year old Philadelphia boy escaped from a juvenile detention complex, the third such escape there in as many weeks. The boy smashed through a window and escaped. Two weeks ago, seven boys at an adjacent unit punched a pregnant staff member, then attacked a security guard with a flagpole during an attempted breakout. They were quickly apprehended in the front of the building. A week before that, four youths broke a window and escaped from the Pennsylvania Clinical School, a privately-run center for juvenile sex abusers. They were found hours later hiding in a trailer park.[2]

If *Access Control & Security Systems* were the magazine of choice for people buying the equipment, this blurb would make more sense. I could see the editors' point if they were passing on information to school administrators who may be dealing with such issues, or, on the other hand, using the blurb to stir up worries in order to boost sales of the magazine or security equipment in general. But this trade magazine is specifically for security professionals, not end users. Why, then, a blurb that mentions virtually nothing about security? One could guess that security-related news at the time was scarce; therefore, the school-related blurb was filler. But at the end of 2002 (when the issue was published), this was not the case. In addition to new federal security regulations for airports, the U.S. Department of Homeland Security was being formed, H.R. 2970 (the Securing America Investment Act of 2001) was close to being signed into law, and a number of lawsuits, buyouts, and consolidations were occurring in the business, involving some of the most prominent security corporations in the world, including ADT (settling a lawsuit regarding the violation of telemarketing laws), Honeywell (buying Ultrak, Inc., for its CCTV business), and Philips (selling a security division to the German conglomerate Bosch). The security business was in perpetual motion and in a boom period. As Jack Mallon, an industry analyst and the publisher of *Mallon's Security Investing*, pointed out, "It's a little early to be consummating the deals, but there is a lot of money that is suddenly pouring into the [security] industry."[3] In short, there was much news that would have been more pertinent to security professionals than a short list of school-related horror stories.

However, horror stories are a line of rationale, a shocking reminder of why the security profession exists, and security professionals need occasional doses of them. While the sales representatives, consultants, and vendors will read the blurb about the Philadelphia attacks and express the same kind of shock that most caring people would express, they also read it for the sense of satisfaction that it elicits. Like the reading teacher examining high illiteracy rates or the mechanic learning about a new line of cars with a persistent mechanical problem, the getting of bad news is a bittersweet experience. The horror stories convey to the security professional their indispensableness. Like other professionals, they are motivated by money, obligations, and prestige, and their actions are shaped by their training, the culture of their work world, and the belief systems that circulate in the profession.[4] But in addition, professionals take stock in any indication that they are important. Along with their own personal goals, they are preoccupied with efforts to legitimize and advance the profession in a more general way, to give it recognition; this ultimately benefits them, for as the industry advances, so do they. Therefore, the horror stories are an important element of the techno-security buildup, for they legitimize the security profession at the same time that they elicit fear and worry from the general public, adding to the likelihood that sales will increase.

Because there is so much to gain from spreading fear, security business-people do all they can in advertisements, sales talks, consultations, and training sessions to create a situation where people feel that it is only logical to worry. Fear is a vehicle for selling, but in order to sustain sales, fear has to be widespread; businesses cannot flourish on one or two incidents. Therefore, incidents need to be repeated, and the slightest sign of potential danger needs to be broadcast in order to convince mostly rational people that there is a crisis passing through the nation, even in our schools and suburban and rural enclaves. To do this, they often present vignettes that describe indiscriminate danger all around us, like the one about the attacks in Philadelphia. Like dramatists, they drum up feelings of vulnerability; they make us see invasions from outside, and tell us a story that many of us believe because of the way the story is told. This chapter looks at the way the security industry tells its story—a story that ends, naturally, with them racing to the rescue.

Outside Invasions

On the evening before Halloween 1938, Orson Welles, playing the character Professor Richard Pierson of the Princeton Observatory, broadcast what many people in the United States thought was an invasion of Earth by Martians. The broadcast was actually an adaptation of *The War of the Worlds* by H. G. Wells dramatically done by Orson Welles and a series of guest actors. Some news reports stated that over a million people panicked in spite of four radio announcements telling listeners that the broadcast was a play. The next day, the *New York Times* reported on their front page: "Radio Listeners in Panic, Taking War Drama as Fact," in an article that described people running out in the streets with towels around their mouths (to protect themselves from poisonous Martian gas) and flooding police departments with phone calls.[5] Sociologists who studied the panic concluded that people became hysterical basically because they were gullible and ignorant, and due to other kinds of faults they possessed. But another author, Hadley Cantril, who studied the broadcast and interviewed people who had listened to it, concluded in his book *The Invasion from Mars* that the panic had more to do with the technique of the program and the conditions of the day than with the people themselves.

In many of Cantril's interviews, people referred specifically to the professors and other experts depicted on the program.[6] There was, of course, the professor played by Orson Welles, but in addition there were scientists and others identified as newscasters in the field, Red Cross officials, commanders, and others with highfalutin titles, who gave their view of the situation with much serious-sounding expertise. There were also first-person accounts by "people in the street" and people who had been looking out their windows when the invasion had begun. The "experts" in the play also expressed their own alarm. Just when parts were becoming unbelievable, they expressed their own disbelief, as if to say, "Yes, even I, who have seen and studied it all, am finding this hard to believe." On top of this, there were the already-raw nerves of citizens as World War II loomed and Fascist bogeymen seemed hell-bent on taking over the world. The people who Cantril interviewed referred to events in Europe, and many felt that the Martian invasion was the workings of the Japanese or of Fascists. Hitler and Mussolini were on the rise, and only two weeks after the broadcast, Nazis destroyed Jewish synagogues, homes, and shops in what is now called the Kristallnacht. In the minds of many, world invasion was not so far-fetched.

Barry Glassner, a sociologist, saw similar things going on in more recent panics that he studied. Though different from an invasion from Mars, the "invasions" of child pornographers, superpredators, wilding teens, and gangbangers that preoccupied our news in the 1980s and 1990s shared elements with previous panics, including the one caused by Welles. Like the broadcast, each of the panics that Glassner discussed was mostly short-lived and each had its own set of experts, its "people in the street" and "concerned citizens" stories, and a social context and some element of truth that made even outlandish claims seem believable. As he stated, "Statements of alarm by newscasters and glorification of wannabe experts are two telltale tricks of the fear mongers' trade."[7] He also added the use of poignant anecdotes, the use of isolated incidents as trends, and the depictions of certain people as innately dangerous.

When we get to school shootings in the last half of the 1990s and terrorism at the beginning of the twenty-first century, we have yet again all the makings for a panic. In the United States, there are actual cases of each; there are school shootings at Columbine High School and elsewhere and the terrorist attacks in 2001 that will always act as reminders that the unbelievable can happen. There are so-called experts, newscasters expressing their alarm, first-person accounts, isolated incidents that stand in as trends (such as the one reported in *Access Control & Security Systems*), and depictions of people as out of control and hell-bent on destruction. There is also another group broadcasting the invasion: the security industry.

Many sociologists and political scientists have discussed how the media, politicians, advocacy groups, and others promote fears in our society, in a sense broadcasting to us that we should fear, telling us what to fear and, by extension, what we should do about it. But increasingly, the security industry has been joining in with politicians and media outlets to promote their angle on the "invasion." Their boosting of fear is actually rather new.

This is partly because until recently, the security industry has been a quiet partner to the military. But then Columbine, 9-11, and the Oklahoma City federal building bombing all played their part in bringing the security industry into the public fold, making all types of security measures seem like a natural outgrowth of circumstances that went way beyond our control. But the fact is that security businesses have responded in business fashion. If they are to profit, they need to fan the fire, so they broadcast steady doses of horror stories to customers through their advertisements and sales pitches, and they broadcast the horror through conferences and trade shows to colleagues, who in turn advertise to us and to our bosses and city planners and school administrators. The horror stories are the lifeblood of the industry, giving the professionals what they need to feel valued, and stoking the crisis, the panic, and the paranoia to keep people buying.

What a Dangerous World It Is

Horror stories (involving school violence, terrorism, or street crime) are circulated in security literature and are sometimes preludes to keynote addresses and presentations at security industry conferences. The images used by security companies in their advertisements can be dramatic, menacing, and portentous. Silent Witness, a company specializing in surveillance cameras, offers a series of "rugged, high-impact, and vandal-resistant" cameras, including mini- and pinhole cameras for covert surveillance and specially designed Wedgeview, 4-Way Quad, and Bullet cameras. The Silent Witness "2002 Camera Line-Up" brochure gives information about these cameras and many others.[8] On the cover of the brochure is a photograph of a typical vignette of danger. The picture offers the viewer the perspective of a surveillance camera (a very common layout technique), which a youth angrily sneers at from a distance (Figure 5.1). The youth's face, body position, and clothing represent the out-of-control kid. We thank our lucky stars that we are viewing this guy from a distance, and are separated from him by the guards. Silent Witness also carries a line of Digital Chaperone surveillance cameras that can be installed in automobiles to keep tabs on people using the car. In 2003, the Pocono Mountain School District in Swiftwater, Pennsylvania, authorized the purchase of 105 Digital Chaperone monitoring systems for use in the district's school bus fleet.[9]

The well-known security company ADT, which had been very successful in the home security market, also sounds the alarm in an advertisement in *Access Control & Security Systems* under the header "Are You Still Relying on Traditional Security?"

Figure 5.1 The horror story in action. The viewer sees the dangerous youth as if through a surveillance camera, at a safe distance. The youth glares back at you, the viewer, and the surveillance camera that foiled him. Silent Witness, "Camera Line-Up," advertisement brochure (Silent Witness, 2002), front cover.

> The world has changed. As security professionals, we now have to be prepared for anything, including the unspecific and the unthinkable. It's an enormous responsibility, but one that doesn't have to be yours alone. We understand how your job is more important now than ever before, and we want to help. Let us get to know your business and your concerns. Then we'll draw from the broadest range of products and experience available, including the latest in digital video and access control.[10]

The tone of the advertisement expresses a clear decisiveness to help through expertise, but also expresses a kind of disbelief, as if even security professionals find it hard to believe that such "unspecific" and "unthinkable" horrors can happen. The excerpt also calls to mind the fact that security equipment is used to keep ahead and to appear modern. The undercurrent of these strategies to sell equipment to schools is fear—the fear that tells us "we now have to be prepared for anything" and makes us feel dread to hear the portentous words: "The world has changed."

A Tempbadge advertisement for visitor passes shows a chalkboard with the words "Who's walking your halls?" scrawled on it. It is a menacing image, vaguely reminding us of scenes in horror movies. At security industry conferences, too, it is standard fare to allude to the dangerousness of modern life. One security professional referred to these allusions as "war stories." At a cocktail party after a day of conference presentations, a group of four men and a woman stood in a circle and bantered about current events (a case involving a woman raped in Central Park in New York City, a case involving a New Jersey boy who was caught putting a pipe bomb in the ceiling of his school, and a company's involvement in antiterrorism activities). One presenter excused himself to refill his drink, saying, "I'll join you again for more war stories in a second." At a conference in Philadelphia, one security professional joined a group, asking, "Telling war stories?" Security professionals were a great source for information about local instances of violence, often knowing about instances that were not reported in the newspaper. One security dealer explained that many professionals check websites for the latest instances of violence in the country, which they then pass on at conferences and to customers and add to press releases.

One company president, who was invited to speak about his company's new security integration system, introduced his talk by looking over the heads of his audience, striking an almost evangelical pose, and explaining,

> We in the business know that dangers lurk in our vicinities. Danger, absolute evil, can be in the next school, in the next airline incident, in the next office building where a man may be lurking with a weapon. The facts are as plain as can be. The world is not getting any safer. Just the opposite.

There is the portent of horror, of evil, of lurking beings, of weapons. Rank-and-file security professionals listen to this kind of talk with a mix of typical work boredom, moderate interest, as well as knowing nods of the head. They see themselves as people on the front lines of this dangerous world. They know that their mission is to deal with these threats in our vicinities. So they relate these stories to others, including buyers who must be convinced of not only the national crises sweeping the nation but also the belief that security equipment can protect them from crises.

Integral Technologies, Inc. and IR Security and Safety also use these images of horror in their advertising for what IR Security calls its "Engineered Solutions for High Abuse Environments," which include schools and colleges, stadiums, government buildings, and hospitals (Figure 5.2).

Figure 5.2 Advertised to "Schools and Colleges" with two blurry images of tragedy. The juxtaposition of photographs of the hospital gurney being pushed toward the school hallway photograph calls to mind school shootings. IR Security & Safety, "Engineered Solutions for High-Abuse Environments," brochure (IR Security & Safety, 2001), front cover.

The same blurry photograph of students charging away from what is presumed to be an attacker in a school is shown on the cover of both the IR Security and Safety and the Integral Technologies FirstLine Digital Surveillance advertisements (Figure 5.2 and Figure 5.3). The Integral Technologies advertisement also includes, at the top, four menacing photographs of a school hallway and a blurb responding to the assertion "He Hit Me First":

> No, he didn't. Reveal a liar, catch a thief, settle a dispute with the most advanced digital surveillance technology from Integral Technologies. Our digital CCTV recorders capture the truth with sophisticated technology that operates easily, so you can have an eye on everything that happens in your facility or campus no matter where you are.[11]

Inside the IR Security and Safety brochure, there is also a photograph of what appears to be a youth (recognizable by the sneaker and jeans) trying to kick in a door. He is foiled, though, by the Von Duprin Breakaway

Figure 5.3 The photograph of panicked students is the same as in the IR Security & Safety advertisement (Figure 5.2). At top, four disconcerting surveillance camera images taken from inside a school. Integral Technologies, Inc., advertisement, in *American School and University* 74 (July 2002): 28.

Lever Trim. The mechanism causes the lock to "break away" when more than thirty-five pounds of pressure is put on it, making potential thieves think that the handle is broken and the door is still locked, and that therefore entry is impossible or not worth the trouble. Obviously, the image is a reminder of danger, though certainly not as menacing as the sneering kid in the Silent Witness brochure or the children charging away down a school hallway as if they were being shot at. Though the Von Duprin lock advertisement is subtle, such imagery is important to security professionals because it makes us accept a certain level of fear by presenting atypical happenings as commonplace—even the jeans and sneakers that the kid is wearing are as typical as can be, right down to the Nike logo. So an "everyday kid" kicking in a door becomes part of our mental baggage as we go about making decisions about schools, where we should live, and, of course, what we should buy from the company sharing these images with us.

Though images of overt danger are common, sometimes the dangerousness of the world is implied, a basic assumption written into brochure advertisements in a more matter-of-fact than dramatic way. For example, a letter distributed during a 2002 security trade show in Philadelphia to those who visited the booth of CEIA, a prominent metal detector company, reminded them of potential horror with simple references to "recent world events" and "threats to our nation:"

> CEIA is regarded as the "World's Leader in Metal Detection Technology" and we believe that after you have had a chance to review the enclosed material you will quickly see why we have earned this reputation. Due to recent world events there has been a major focus into the area of metal detection. CEIA continues to be selected as the top choice for Local, State, and Federal Agencies based on the most recent threats to our nation. CEIA continues to develop new metal detection products with our aim to provide the highest level of detection, reliability and discrimination of personal objects that far exceeds all competitive models in the field of metal detection today.[12]

Security professionals see urgency in what they do; they want to protect us from "recent world events" and "threats to our nation" by providing the "highest level of detection." However, they are also regular working people. When they talked about their jobs, they expressed the same kind of matter-of-factness that other professionals are likely to express: "It's a good job," "It's a way of making a living," or, even less enthusiastically, "A job is a job" were common sentiments. They were what one vendor called off-handedly "working stiffs," with petty complaints, plodding along in their jobs, pretty happy, and doing their best to get ahead, like many of us. But they also had another something to add: they had in common with their fellow business associates and customers a world-weariness that comes with fighting the good fight uphill and against all odds. Like those in social work and education, and in some branches of medicine and law, in spite of the daily grind that comes with any occupation security professionals saw their work as part of a grand undertaking. Naturally, this connects to what was discussed earlier in reference to their mission for social betterment. But the aspect of fear adds another dimension to their mission: it gives the grand mission its grandeur.

When presenting their mission, the backdrop is almost always the world in turmoil. The mission would be lost without it. In the world of security, various elements of helping, of tough times, and of business come together, providing the rationale for the security sale. One security professional, echoing the comments of others, remarked,

> My job is about helping people. That's what I do. And these are tough times for that. Protection is a natural need, and people are

fearful, really fearful. What I do is a drop in the bucket for making this world a better place to be for the future, but that's because
things have gotten so out of control. It's a decent job, a tough job
really, one that makes me think I am doing something good and
making money and being part of a group working for the same
goal, though we all have different products and capabilities.

Another sales representative remarked, "Without us, there wouldn't be
safety or maybe even people, at least not people living lives I would consider good."

These comments reflect the utopian ideals of the security profession,
but they also show how utopian ideals are cast within the context of a dangerous world, one where, if we were to survive, it would not be with lives
that a normal person would consider good. Like all manufacturers of utopianism, the security industry will not let us forget that there is plenty out
there to worry about. They stir up the panic for profit, but they also do it
in order to bolster their own positions, to give meaning to their jobs, and
to make the sale that might possibly get them their bonus or recognition
in the company. Security dealers are spin artists, dramatists, people who
present stories to us and count on our own insecurities to buy into the
deal. These constant and sometimes subtle messages about fear come to us
through rhetorical devices, images, declarations, and layout techniques. To
explore this point further, the next section focuses on one type of equipment—metal detectors—and concentrates on two of the most prominent
companies in the business, Garrett Metal Detectors and Metorex. Again,
the world that is presented to us is full of invasions from the outside, sneering kids, and even gun-toting middle schoolers. It is a scary, scary world,
told by people who have the expert knowledge, the scientific-sounding
devices, and even the social milieu and the actual incidents of unprecedented violence to back up what they are pitching.

Metal Detectors

Garrett Metal Detectors is perhaps the most successful metal detector
company in the world. As the comment by the vice president of marketing for Garrett that opens this chapter highlights, sales to schools have
increased dramatically since the late 1990s. By 2003, Garrett sales to
schools surpassed sales to prisons and airports, and accounted for about
20–25 percent of the company's business. The company provides direct
services to schools, and news releases distributed by Garrett include information about the many schools that use its detectors. One of the company's first large school contracts was with the District of Columbia, where

Garrett Magnascanner 1000 walk-through metal detectors were installed in 1990–1991 and their Super Scanners were used in the schools by District of Columbia Metropolitan Police and guards employed by MVM, a private security guard company.

In an advertisement reporting on these school security developments, an introductory paragraph by Garrett describes a dystopian world where weapons, violence, and fear are as common in schools as books, essays, and exams:

> It seems impossible nowadays to read a newspaper or watch television without learning of another weapons-related tragedy in schools across the nation. Weapons, violence and fear have become as much a part of the school curriculum as books, essays and exams. Recent events have further underscored the need for schools to implement strict measures to prevent violence.[13]

Garrett has a special department that provides services to schools, called the Garrett Metal Detectors School Safety Department. For those interested in learning more about what Garrett can offer to schools, this division of the company distributes a video called *Safe Schools*.[14] The video is thirty-seven minutes long and provides information about school safety and violence. The tape comes with a warning affixed to the cassette: "This tape contains sensitive matter and should be viewed only by school educators and law enforcement agencies." The video provides tips for how to spot a student carrying a gun (one shoulder will slouch and one pants leg will seem longer than the other, caused by the weight of the gun; students hold their hands to their hips to prevent the gun from wiggling; and the barrel of a rifle may protrude from a pants leg). The video also features a segment on the Eddie Eagle Gun Safety Program (a school-based program financed by the National Rifle Association), even though the segment has nothing to do with metal detectors (a bit of advertising for Eddie Eagle). It also demonstrates the different ways to use handheld and walk-through metal detectors.

The narrator, Chief of the Biffs County Campus Police Department, is stiff-lipped and never-blinking, and wears intercom headgear during the filming of his headshots though he is not using it. He adds a sense of urgency, seriousness, and stalwart objectivity to explanations of metal detector searches. In his presentation, he shows us various kinds of concealed weapons (a crucifix necklace that doubles as a knife and a razor blade heart pin) that can all too easily slip through a standard search. These demonstrations are dramatically done, with crescendos and diminuendos of music in the background and other elements of high drama.

In one scene, in stop-action slow motion that gives the film a grainy reality-TV look, school police are seen arriving at a nicely trimmed suburban house. They approach the home and take their positions outside the front door (one standing slightly to the side of the door, hand held close to his gun, while the other knocks). A voice-over explains that when a threat of violence involving guns or explosives is made by a student, a house search involving school officials, school police, and police departments is highly advisable. Inside the house, a woman is seen answering the door. The school police enter, looking so much larger than the woman and almost too big for the house, and go directly to the youth's bedroom, proceed to search the room with great professional élan, and ultimately find an automatic rifle under the mattress.

In another scene, a student (who in real life is the son of the narrator) is shown in a frontal position wearing jeans and a shirt. The narrator explains the threat of concealed weapons, while the boy begins pulling guns from his clothing. First, he pulls out eight pistols from the waistband and pockets of his pants. He lays these weapons on a table in front of him. After the pistols, he reaches around to his back and pulls out a small automatic rifle with one hand and an ammunition clip with the other. He quickly assembles the automatic rifle and places it on the table. He then pulls out a shotgun from his pants leg, then, when it seems that he is done pulling firearms from his clothing, he pulls out two more pistols from his back pockets. The arsenal lies on the table in front of him—from one kid, a dozen firearms.[15]

In the next scene, in blue-tinted slow motion, young people in school are shown walking through a metal detector while two large police officers in military-style uniforms look on. The voice-over explains, "Crime prevention techniques should be used to address the threat level at each school. Most [metal detector] screening techniques are more effective with high frequency low volume [i.e., conducted constantly and randomly], which provides a greater deterrent value with less disruption to the academic process." The video also demonstrates the uses of police dogs, how to arrest a student, and how to interrogate a student. It has a section on "how to conduct random classroom and student searches when legally justified," which is discussed while the video shows school police running metal detectors over students standing in a colorfully decorated middle school hallway, not looking all too happy, but not unhappy either.

Metorex is another metal detector company that has attempted to tap the public sector, especially the school market. This may seem like a step backward for a company that also provides metal detection services to the U.S. Nuclear Regulatory Commission, the U.S. Department of the Treasury, the Pentagon, the U.S. Mint, and NASA, as well as AT&T, Six Flags Theme Parks, and the Florida Department of Corrections.[16] But though lacking the prestige of the prominent government buildings and even theme parks, schools are lucrative, and any company would be happy to have a share of the school market.

A sales manager for Metorex told me that METOR metal detectors were "deployed in over 40,000 areas worldwide and are generally seen as the benchmark for state-of-the-art detection." In a letter I received after an informal interview with him, he highlighted the user-friendly quality of their products and how they are responding to the "aftermath of school and workplace violence"—again dredging up fears:

> It was a pleasure to speak with you and discuss security needs. Please find enclosed our METOR 150 brochure, our customer reference list, and pricing. In the aftermath of school and workplace violence, we charged our engineers with the task of developing a walk-through metal detector that incorporated the renowned METOR technology into a startlingly inexpensive, user-friendly model. We asked them to make the METOR affordable for schools, courts, and others for whom security expenditures had now become a necessary line item in an already stretched budget.
>
> We are proud of their achievement and are pleased to announce the METOR 150 HIGH DISCRIMINATION WALK THROUGH METAL DETECTOR. It is, without a question, a significant accomplishment that blends sophisticated performance and easy operation. Consider the METOR 150. It is unlikely that you will find a less expensive unit. You will not find another walkthrough metal detector that is provided with better Customer Service. Its design and performance are available to you at a cost that makes it an extraordinary value.[17]

Metorex has sleek-looking walk-though and handheld metal detectors, and their cost is among the lowest in the business, which partly accounts for their success in the school market. The Metor 28 handheld detector costs $145, and the basic cost for the Metor 150 walk-through is $1,750, without accessories.[18] Imagine: for less money than one may think, metal detector ownership is just a phone call away. On top of this, they are good-looking pieces of equipment—even the walk-through detectors have style. Additionally, like other electronics, their prices are likely to fall as they become more popular; metal detectors in the 1980s that were less effective than current models cost several hundred dollars each, while today's metal detectors can be purchased for less than $200. The walk-through metal detector can also be ordered with a thirty-two-inch-wide top crosspiece (for wheelchair access) to meet American Disabilities Act requirements and to be sure that those in wheelchairs do not slip through a checkpoint.

In a typical Metorex advertisement, a photograph shows a young woman, who may or may not be in a school, standing contentedly while being examined with the unique-shaped Metor 28, with its circular head and various options, including charger, belt clip, carrying case, and earphones (so that only the user hears the detection alarm). In another advertisement for the same company, two students are shown passing through the polished silver Metor 150 "high discrimination" walk-through metal detector, mentioned earlier in the letter from the Metorex sales manager. The students demonstrate what the Garrett narrator called the "high frequency low volume" technique of metal detection, whereby metal detectors are set up throughout the school, and at random times students walking in the halls are required to pass through them. This avoids the buildup of students at a school entrance and the great amount of manpower and technology that is needed to examine sometimes a few thousand students each morning. There is also something more pleasing to the senses when we see only several students passing through a metal detector, rather than the crowds that form when all students are entering schools through security checkpoints.

In the statement that began this chapter, the vice president for marketing of Garrett talked about the expanding school market. But he also made a comment about the complaint made by some parents in the past who have felt that schools ended up looking like prisons when metal detectors were used. This is a common complaint among critics who have compared new techno-security to a prisonlike mentality that disproportionately affects poor people of color. There is much literature that points out the creeping similarities between schools and prisons—in equipment, architecture, and even disciplinary policies.[19] Whereas the factory may have been the model for the emerging school system of the nineteenth century, some believe that a prison model has overtaken schools more recently, especially with the advent of techno-security in schools but also due to security tactics, such as those championed by mayors (such as Michael Bloomberg of New York City) who have flooded schools with police officers and allowed officers, at times, to usurp the authority of school administrators.[20]

The prison (or war zone) comparison is the ultimate horror story. It tells us everything we need to know about the total breakdown of our schools and society. But the comparison takes on an entirely new dimension when expressed by security salespeople, because their intent is not to analyze a situation, but rather to sell us a situation, a bad situation, which they do by telling us that, yes, schools are like prisons, but the students and circumstances in the school are what make it like a prison—not the equipment. "Sometimes when I'm working with school administrators, I get mixed up," one salesperson explained to me. "I'll start talking about the inmates or cells and forget I'm talking with a school official, not a prison official. Then I have to start talking about classrooms and students." If we were to pit the critics against the businesspeople, the critics would no doubt have the upper hand when it comes to the way security has turned parts of schooling into a prisonlike experience. But the security professionals have something like a trick up their sleeve. Just when you are starting to feel that the pervasiveness of the equipment is making schools look like prisons, the products change form; they get smaller and sleeker-looking, and start using colors—muted grays and silvers—that we have come to expect from technology that fits with everyday decorum.

Schools and Prisons

WizKid OptoTech is a division of Extreme CCTV, Inc., and contracts with engineers in England, Canada, and the United States who develop the unique designs of their surveillance cameras. The company holds patents on CNG (conical no-grip), LED Bullet, and Rugged-Eye designs, which refer to the manufacturing of their cone- and bullet-shaped cameras. They market their natural and infrared cameras and illuminators to both schools and prisons, and their product descriptions are meant to be vague enough so that whether one is a prison warden or school principal, one gets the feeling that the advertisement is talking to you, personally:

> After night falls, many conventional CCTV cameras cease to capture their unlit target. The WZ30L provides a smart, cost-effective solution to this problem. Without flooding the area with unnecessary visible light, the WZ30L lights up the scene exclusively for an infrared-sensitive surveillance camera that can be set up further from the scene. Furthermore, the WZ30L is the toughest infrared illuminator the security industry has seen. Indeed, the unit is so tough, WizKid OptoTech put it to the ultimate test, driving a 6700-pound Ford F150 truck over it. The WZ30L survived in full working order. Needless to say, sledgehammer and baseball bat blows are not a problem. This motivates our industry-leading 5-year replacement warranty on the housing. The WZ30L has a 30-LED array mounted behind a spherical polycarbonate dome. The heavy cast aluminum base is available in a surface mount or flush (WZ32L). The LEDs come in 940nm or 850 nm wavelengths for covert and semi-covert surveillance respectively.[21]

Whether we are in a school or prison, the WizKid OptoTech equipment is tough enough to handle a Ford truck driving over it; it can withstand baseball bat blows and even blows from a sledgehammer. Pictures in the brochure show the camera being run over by a truck and a man standing next to the truck holding a baseball bat (referring to the assertion that "baseball bat blows are not a problem"). Two years before attending the training session with Extreme CCTV, I was at another conference and spoke with an Extreme CCTV sales manager who dealt with the WizKid OptoTech equipment. He was the first to introduce me to the sentiment that "schools could be like prisons"—meaning that students could be as bad as prison inmates. Security literature is also clear about the connection between schools and prisons. In the book *CCTV for Security Professionals*, for example, the author is blunt about the matter: "As sad as it sounds, many [security] designers for educational facilities use the same design approach as someone designing a system for a prison."[22] Why? Because the situation is basically the same in both places; therefore, the same system can be used. Also, from a business point of view, it makes complete sense to develop a camera that is versatile enough to be used in different places; with good advertising, you can sell the same camera to a prison warden, government official, and school administrator—all of them thinking they are getting something specifically made for their facility and their particular needs.

When I questioned the Extreme CCTV sales manager about whether or not it was possible that "schools could be like prisons" because of the security equipment, he relented, "That's possible." But he emphasized that schools should be careful not to let that happen; if it did, however, it was an unfortunate consequence of "a dangerous world that we live in." The Extreme CCTV sales manager explained that in addition to being tough, "the conical no-grip design not only makes the housing nearly impenetrable, but also prevents people from tying a rope to it." Perhaps noting a look of confusion on my face, he explained, "To prevent people from hanging themselves. It's suicide prevention. Also escape prevention so people can't tie a rope to it and put the rope out the window." When I asked him if he was referring to schools or prisons, he told me, "Both."

The illustrations in the WizKid OptoTech brochures demonstrate their toughness and the conical shape of their designs, and their descriptions of equipment make reference to prisons that could "take a back seat to some schools" when it comes to destructive environments:

> The meanest, toughest prisons in the world can take a back seat to some schools when it comes to destructive, vandal-prone environments. WizKid domes like the WZ30 can take this abuse to reliably deliver surveillance for today's remote DVR technologies.

WizKid's new WZ22 is just as tough and has features that make it ideal for the ceiling and hallways of the world's meanest environments. Using remote DVR features, WizKid digital video can be seen as it happens from *outside* of a school property. Should fire or terror attacks occur authorities could access video events before entering the premises. Valuable video information could save precious time as well as lives.[23]

For many security dealers, it is assumed that schools are part of what the ad refers to as "the meanest environments." The photographs in the brochure show the conical (escape- and suicide-proof) no-grip design and a montage of menacing CCTV footage taken from inside a Canadian school. The montage looks eerily like an arrest of a student or of an attack, though they are not clear. Though it is not stated in this advertisement, in another brochure that includes the same montage, a caption states, "The WZ32 in practice. Installed in a Canadian high school, the WZ32 inhibits theft, vandalism and violence."[24] There is a lot of heavy imagery and no holding back when it comes to portraying schools as prisons and even war zones.

There is more to the school/prison comparison than what individuals say about security technology; school security equipment is often simply modified prison security equipment. This is true of SCORMAP, for example, a mapping software program that uses geographic information satellites (GIS) and Computer Assisted Drawing (CAD) to provide information about the physical layout of schools and the whereabouts of individuals in the building. The program uses new technology that allows operators to display multilevel schools in a three-dimensional layout; each classroom on a floor becomes a separate identifiable unit that can be displayed on a computer. SCORMAP was implemented in 2003 in schools in Calhoun County, Alabama, and is modeled on a program called CORMAP, which was developed for correctional facilities in 1999 by the National Institute of Justice's National Law Enforcement and Corrections Technology Center (NLECTC)—Southeast, and the U.S. Department of Energy's Savannah River Technology Center (SRTC). CORMAP is short for "correctional facility map" so SCORMAP, presumably, is short for "school correctional facility map"—though it is also fortuitous that the first two letters of the program are the same first two letters in "school." The NLECTC has one project manager for both corrections and school safety, Rob Donlin, who was introduced to Lisa Russell, information technology director for Calhoun County Schools, by Calhoun County Sheriff Larry Amerson. Russell remarked about the arrangement: "Sheriff Amerson knew about CORMAP because Rob Donlin helped him map the local jail. He knew we were forward thinking, and he put us together." For the school district, a mapping tool used in jails was suitable for the schools; additionally, we see again how the techno-security equipment is hailed as a sign of being "forward thinking." Rob Donlin remarked that CORMAP required only a few modifications to make the correctional facility technology compatible with schools, but that the technology was essentially the same. Some passwords needed to be changed, but also, while CORMAP used inmates' assigned beds as their "location addresses," the SCORMAP program replaces the inmate beds with students' desks (in the case of elementary school children) and lockers (in the case of high school students), which become the students' "anchor points," rather than "location addresses."[25]

We see similarities between schools and prisons in that school and prison security technologies are virtually the same in both facilities, but if schools start to resemble prisons, they will be rather plain, institutional-looking prisons—not overburdened with heavy-duty technology, but rather, institutions where high tech mapping systems like SCORMAP make security seem less invasive and other security technologies blend in with the surroundings and décor. When it comes to surveillance cameras and other devices that are noticeable, new design styles have made security technology seem less daunting. Additionally, technology advancement (especially microtechnology and nanotechnology) has enabled equipment to be built smaller. The fortified entrances of schools depicted in pictures from manuals and newspapers from the 1990s already looked dated. The older equipment is big and hard-edged and looks off-putting. You get the feeling that you are entering a militarized compound, and it seems that the equipment design is meant to convey this intentionally. But the knowing eye sees a bygone era when simple utility of design was acceptable to buyers. The look of most fortified school entrances is much different now, with items that are smaller, better designed, and in many cases aesthetically pleasing. For example, in a booklet put out by Garrett Metal Detectors called *Effective Security Screening*, there is a photograph of a female student getting searched by a school guard with a Magnascanner. The handheld metal detector is no bigger than a calculator and could probably fit completely in the man's hand, except that the man must display the Garrett name for advertising purposes. Behind her is a walkthrough metal detector that blends in with its surroundings.

Surveillance cameras are also manufactured to be appealing to the eye. Compare the small, lustrous surveillance cameras of today to those depicted in photographs from the 1990s. In one photograph distributed by the National Institute of Justice in their manual *The Appropriate and Effective Use of Security Technologies in Schools*, a surveillance camera tower of the 1990s is shown in a school parking lot (Figure 5.4). Again, while

Figure 5.4 A photograph from the 1990s depicting surveillance cameras as a blatant show of force outside a school. The surveillance cameras are bullet resistant, and the cables are hidden by a protective shield. From Mary Green, *The Appropriate and Effective Use of Security Technologies in U.S. Schools* (Washington, D.C.: U.S. Department of Justice, Office of Justice Programs and National Institute of Justice with Sandia National Laboratories, 1999), 37.

this may look daunting to some, it is almost laughable to the knowledge-able security dealer and customer. New pan–tilt–zoom cameras have made such camera arrangements obsolete. A single, small, covert camera would be nearly invisible and could probably do much more than the stack of cameras shown in the photograph.

As fear of school violence spreads, sometimes justifiably, it promotes not only the use of techno-security fortification but also, ultimately, the promotion of a prisonlike mentality in schools. But this is true only to a point, because the problem is not that schools will look like prisons, per se, but rather that they will look like nice places. Once schools start install-ing shiny, mini, soft-contoured equipment, for many in the "It looks like a prison" crowd of critics, there will be nothing to complain about. If we are to question the overuse of security equipment in places such as schools, we cannot base our complaints on what the place will look like. Security busi-nesses will always alter products based on demand and even sensitivities that arise in society. Most likely, places outfitted with the latest equipment will look just fine—no worse than your dentist's office or supermarket or post office. This, to me, is the real issue, because what we see are schools not looking like prisons, but schools actually looking better, because the techno-security is looking better. The equipment looks like home appliances or entertainment gear, and even the colors of the equipment—silver and gray—seem to denote seriousness, sophistication, and style.

Security equipment is coming into our schools and other public places—and it looks *good*. Few people even notice the fortification. This is true of schools, communities, and downtown districts of cities. As Edward Blakely and Mary Gail Snyder pointed out in their study of gated communities, "fortress America" is a place of well-tended lawns, aesthetically pleasing barriers (wrought-iron fences and brick and stucco walls), and security equipment that has become almost fashionable. No doubt, there is something still daunting about security checks (in airports, at school entrances, and at stadiums), but the issue is that while they become more abundant, they are becoming less daunting. Some people may bemoan the prisonlike look of some schools, but what about the school that does not fit your mental picture of a prison? There is a form of security that is "in your face," that wants you to know that things are serious. But there is another form of security that has a pretty face, a security of smooth design and nice contours—and this is the big-seller security.

The images of chaos and violence, the isolated incidents that stand in as trends, the descriptions of out-of-control youths and portents of evil, and the comparisons to prisons that we have seen thus far add to the fear factor. They are part of the techniques used to construct a gallery of fear, to convey a drama that convinces us that the unthinkable can happen. Each horror story that is a part of this drama plays its role in bolstering the security industry and the importance of security professionals. It also plays a part in keeping the public nervous and, ultimately, in a consumer frenzy. Now that techno-security fortification has become a capitalist enterprise (and not just a matter between governments, police, and military forces), the fear factor stimulates consumerism. What is held out to us in the form of equipment not only solves the problem of violence and crime, but also is appealing. So we have something that allays fears, but also gives us so much more, and that is the key to capitalism—the production of items that meet a few needs but fulfill many desires.

Letting Laws Decide

Security designers and dealers are aware of the controversies surrounding their merchandise. They know that they are sometimes considered fear-mongers; they know that they are sometimes accused of making places look like prisons. They also know all the "Big Brother" claims and have heard every "Brave New World" cliché like everybody else. They are not blind, and in the case of schools, they are especially sensitive to the fact that schools house mostly young people and therefore raise delicate issues for parents and communities. The comments of Jeff Lupinacci, senior tele-com/security designer for Brinjac Engineering in Harrisburg, Pennsylvania, were typical:

> The cost of the [security] systems and procedures can cause much discussion at school board meetings. Providing a completely safe facility with no risk of crime or violence would not make a school very conducive to learning. How much is enough for your school district? This is a tough question, and each community must sort though the many political and philosophical beliefs and perceptions that people hold.

> School officials should find a capable firm to assess the vulnerability of each specific facility. A threat assessment normally would include: crime statistics, history, the local culture and environment, and changes in demographics. School executives, facility managers and teachers play an important role in identifying possible risks, and should be involved in a threat assessment.[26]

This designer for an engineering company asked the question "How much is enough for your school district?" How about for your downtown area, or for the streets of your neighborhood? To some extent, federal and state courts will be determining these questions for years to come as cases are presented to them dealing with more high-tech searches, new means of eavesdropping and surveying, and better ways of collecting, accessing, and categorizing information about people. All of this pulls at the edges of the U.S. Constitution, raising issues that were never dreamed of by the writers of our original laws and civil liberties. These controversial points were sometimes taken up in conference presentations and in discussions that I had with security professionals. Professional books as well have dealt with this issue. Consider what one surveillance camera manual had to say about school installations:

> If a camera system is going to be added to an educational facility, great care should be taken in advance to make sure this move is perceived as a benefit by faculty, students, school board members, and parents. It is recommended that the purpose of the system be openly discussed so that it is not perceived as martial law and/or an invasion of privacy. The purpose of the system should be not so

much to monitor the activities of the students as to help protect the students and faculty. If the system is not accepted from the beginning by all parties as a benefit and a necessity, use of video surveillance could backfire and cause more disruption than benefit.[27]

However, in most cases, when issues of privacy and civil liberties were brought up at conferences they were introduced in a kind of token fashion. This is expected, considering the purpose of the conferences I attended. The conferences were not meant to call into question the industry by drawing attention to delicate issues—they were meant to boost the industry. But at one conference, Les Gold, an attorney, presented with a panel of so-called experts on security and raised important questions about privacy. Another presenter on the panel, Stephen McAllister, was a New York Police Department (NYPD) captain and the director of the NYPD Technical Assistance Response Unit (TARU). TARU provides cellular tracking and wiretapping services to the NYPD, and "like the military we use facial recognition technology," the captain explained.[28] With great gusto, he talked about the various techno-security initiatives that TARU was involved in, including biometrics and microcamera police vests hooked up to databases with facial recognition capabilities.

The attorney spoke immediately after the police captain and offered a more tempered take on security, one that was meant to balance out the captain's more bravado talk. The inclusion of the attorney at the conference was also a sign that courts were taking on cases involving techno-security and that people in the industry had to be aware of new legal developments. The attorney was with a Los Angeles firm, Mitchell, Silberberg & Knupp, that advertised itself as the "Attorneys to the Security Industry." While he made his money representing security companies, at this conference he was also meant to cast a more critical light on the industry and to raise nagging questions about civil rights, but without offending the audience, who were after all people in the business and therefore potential clients.[29] Like the police captain, he raised issues that were not raised by those in the business. He added a bit of polish to the conference, while the captain added a bit of grit, so that with their blend of polish and grit, and their sometimes clashing viewpoints, they made a good team for a panel discussion. The attorney did not refer directly to what the police captain had said, but he discussed privacy issues that would certainly be at stake in the new policing tactics described by the captain.

The attorney was clear that many laws involving surveillance equipment depended on a person's "reasonable expectation of the right of privacy." He made the point that the word "reasonable" could be interpreted in a variety of ways, and that this has been the major dilemma for courts—how to interpret the right of privacy against the duty of the state to provide for citizens' well-being. The attorney did not go into specifics about laws and tempered what he said to suit people in the audience. But the next chapter fills in the gaps left by the attorney. To some extent, the courts are setting the standard for what is permissible and what is not; they will be answering the questions "How much is enough for your school district?" "How much privacy can we expect in our lives?" and "When does the safety of the whole outweigh the civil rights of the individual?"

The courts have been answering these questions since the first phone-tapping cases in the early twentieth century. But courts have had to deal with cases that test the bounds of the Constitution in new ways, forcing judges to revisit older cases with newer questions. Decades ago, courts had already established the constitutionality of CCTVs, based on the idea that the cameras recorded what was already noticeable to the naked eye—but what about newer cameras that can do more than what the naked eye is capable of doing?

Along with everything else promoting security technology discussed thus far—the federal research and development support, the corporate initiatives and perks (tax write-offs, *pro bono* equipment), the different fears that spur us on to buy the equipment, the array of professionals boosting the industry, and so on—the courts too will be paving the way for the future of techno-security. The next chapter reviews significant court cases and federal policies that have set the standard for what people using security can and cannot do. The cases, to some extent, indicate what we can expect to see in years to come regarding security and our civil rights.

CHAPTER 6

Security, the Law, and Federal Policy

The right of the people to be secure in their persons, houses, papers, and effects, against unreasonable searches and seizures, shall not be violated, and no Warrants shall issue, but upon probable cause, supported by Oath or affirmation, and particularly describing the place to be searched, and the person or things to be seized.

Fourth Amendment, Bill of Rights to the U.S. Constitution

The vice president of marketing and products of Westec InterActive, a surveillance camera company, was very clear about the importance of privacy laws when she stated that "Westec InterActive continually researches state laws to ensure we maintain compliance with all regulations. Additionally, we provide each customer with ample signage to notify patrons and employees that the location is subject to video monitoring and recording." Security professionals must not only remain aware of laws but also try to influence laws, often to their advantage. As the president of Marlin Central Monitoring, Barry Brannon stated, "We have been involved with the subcommittee [of the Security Industry Association] that's working on setting industry standards for video verification. Having a set of industry standards will set the right expectations for dealers, who in turn set expectations for subscribers."[1]

Part of the reason why individuals in the industry try to influence laws and set voluntary standards is to avoid federal oversight of the industry. As an article in *Security Sales and Integration* pointed out, "Industry organizations . . . [work] on establishing guidelines before legislators do it for the entire industry."[2] But security organizations and businesses need not worry about legislators, for even when they have intervened, they have often given much leeway to security professionals. Court rulings that have set guidelines for using techno-security have played an important role in promoting the use of the equipment and ushering forward the security industry, with restraints, but nevertheless with judicial and policy approval. But none of this is really new. Security incidents involving schools began going to court in the 1980s, but even by then, there was already a large body of law associated with search and seizure and rights to privacy. When incidents involving schools went to court, the circumstances were viewed in light of these earlier court cases having to do with wiretaps on telephones, listening devices, and other spy equipment.

Most court cases involving techno-security involved interpretations of the Fourth Amendment of the U.S. Constitution, focusing specifically on how much privacy individuals can expect when balanced against the state's duty to safeguard individuals from wrongdoers. Two of the earliest U.S. Supreme Court cases on this issue, the first in 1924 (*Hester v. United States*) and the second in 1928 (*Olmstead v. United States*), established significant precedents. *Hester v. United States* concluded that privacy was not protected in "open fields" or public places, and that items in plain view of law enforcement officials, who had probable cause to believe that the items were contraband, could be confiscated or "seized" without a warrant.[3] In *Olmstead v. United States*, the Supreme Court reviewed convictions based on evidence gained through the use of wiretaps on telephone wires. Chief Justice William Howard Taft, writing the opinion, reasoned that there was no physical trespass since the wiretap went on outside wires, and that the interception of a conversation did not constitute a seizure, since "seizure" referred to physical items.[4]

For the next several decades, what constituted a violation of the Fourth Amendment continued to be challenged, and subtle differences in circumstances could alter opinions. In the 1942 case of *Goldman v. United States*, the U.S. Supreme Court found that there was not a Fourth Amendment violation when a detectaphone—a device that magnifies sound waves so that conversations can be heard through physical barriers—was placed against the wall that separated authorities from a party next door in order to eavesdrop on the party, since there was no invasion of space.[5] However, in a later case (in *Silverman v. United States*), when officers drove a "spike mike" through a wall into the neighboring wall, where it came in contact with a heating duct, the intrusion was seen by the U.S. Supreme Court in 1961 as a violation, especially when the contact with the heating duct caused the defendant's conversation to be broadcasted.[6] This case was significant because it set a limit on what authorities can do with newer technologies and also began a bit of a trend in the 1960s to limit the powers of authorities when conducting surveillance and searches.

The *Berger* and *Katz* Cases of the 1960s

The strongest challenges to the *Hester* and *Olmstead* cases came in the 1960s. This was a time when more educated and influential people grew critical of authorities and some of their policing and so-called national security tactics. The United States had passed through what turned out to be an embarrassing and abusive congressional hunt for Communists in the 1950s, and was entering an era of greater cynicism caused in part by this past abuse of power by the Committee on Un-American Activities, but also because of the Vietnam War and overzealous surveillance headed by J. Edgar Hoover of the FBI. The Federal Bureau of Investigation and Central Intelligence Agency were using newer technologies to spy on civil rights groups, organized crime syndicates, and antiwar protesters, and some felt that especially J. Edgar Hoover overstepped his power with some of the information-gathering and surveillance tactics he authorized against people like Martin Luther King Jr., educator and activist Miles Horton, various celebrities, individuals in the activist Student Nonviolent Coordinating Committee (SNCC), and antiwar groups. Additionally, authorities in national security positions and in police departments were using more sophisticated equipment to address what seemed like a wave of urban uprisings and increased street crime. Many people responded with greater concern over violations of constitutional rights, and in some significant cases the courts, including the U.S. Supreme Court, agreed with individuals challenging overzealous authorities.

In one significant case, *Berger v. New York* (1967), the U.S. Supreme Court overturned a state statute that permitted police officers to enter a private premise to install a listening device and telephone wiretap after obtaining a warrant. Though the statute required "reasonable grounds" to believe that evidence of a crime would be obtained from the wiretap and required that authorities name the individual or individuals whose conversations were sought, the Supreme Court ruled that the statute entrusted too much power to authorities. Supreme Court Justice Tom Clark argued that though the statute required authorities to name the individual under surveillance, it permitted all conversations to be heard and recorded, including those of people who may unknowingly pass through the room or use the telephone, and did not sufficiently limit the length of time that the listening device could be used. He argued that "the statute's blanket grant of permission to eavesdrop is without adequate judicial supervision or protective procedures."[7]

Also in 1967, in the case *Katz v. United States*, the U.S. Supreme Court questioned the rationale of the *Olmstead* and *Hester* cases. In the *Katz* case, the Supreme Court ruled that the Fourth Amendment protects people, not places.[8] The case indicated that individuals under certain circumstances had the right to privacy even in public places (or "open fields"). The case involved police officers who set up a wiretap on a phone booth and activated it whenever Charles Katz went into the booth, where allegedly he was conducting illegal business. The wiretap was on the outside of the phone booth and was only activated when Katz was in the booth. Police did not seek a warrant to use the wiretap, and a lower court held that this was constitutional because there was no physical trespass. But the U.S. Supreme Court disagreed, arguing that the Fourth Amendment protects people, not places, stating that "what a person knowingly exposes to the public, even in his own home or office, is not subject of 4th Amendment protection," but that "what [that person] seeks to preserve as private, even in an area accessible to the public may be constitutionally protected."[9]

However, the Court concurred that if a warrant had been granted, then the surveillance of Katz would have been permissible. So, though the *Katz* case challenged the open fields doctrine of the *Hester* case, it also established that police had relatively broad powers to use electronic surveillance with a warrant. This posed a challenge to the *Berger* case, which seemed to indicate that conversations were protected. In the *Katz* case, the Court ruled that one's "subjective expectation of privacy" had to be viewed in light of society's willingness to accept as reasonable or legitimate that expectation. So, not all conversations were protected if, considering circumstances, the privacy of the individual is not reasonable. The *Berger* and *Katz* cases wrestled with this question: considering authorities' obligations to protect people, to what extent can we expect privacy and on what grounds can authorities breach our privacy? Perhaps to try to tie up the loose ends left by the U.S. Supreme Court and to answer this question, the federal government passed significant policies having to do with surveillance and crime in the 1960s.

Court Cases and Policy involving Video Surveillance

By the end of the 1960s, the U.S. Supreme Court had ruled on some of the most significant cases dealing with the uses of security equipment. To help clarify some of the rulings between the 1924 *Hester* case and the 1967 *Berger* and *Katz* cases, the U.S. Congress passed the Omnibus Crime Control and Safe Streets Act (P.L. 90-351) of 1968, which outlined procedures for state and federal law enforcement personnel when using electronic surveillance devices for crime prevention and investigations.[10] The law gave broad powers to authorities, but also set clear boundaries. Part of the impetus for the law began in the early 1960s with congressional proposals to create guidelines for techno-security use but to also give ample room for authorities when using wiretapping in national security contexts and to investigate organized crime. Among other provisions, it required telecommunications services to provide information about individuals under investigation and to "provide the technical assistance necessary to accomplish the interception [of conversations]" if requested by law enforcement personnel. The law also established the National Institute of Justice (NIJ) as an agency of the U.S. Department of Justice.[11]

The Omnibus Crime Control and Safe Streets Act did not address video surveillance. In 1968, video had yet to become a major tactic in security operations (wiretapping and listening devices were more popular). But the 1984 case *United States v. Torres*, which challenged a circumstance involving video surveillance, established that the Omnibus Crime Control and Safe Streets Act did apply to surveillance cameras.[12] The ruling, along with the *Katz* case, was key in establishing the legal use by authorities of surveillance equipment in public places. Essentially, the case conferred to video surveillance the same kinds of powers and guidelines set by earlier Supreme Court cases having to do with listening devices and wiretaps.

There were several other cases that established the constitutionality of video surveillance. In the 1983 Supreme Court case *United States v. Knotts*, the Court ruled that individuals did not have the right of privacy on public streets and byways where they could be videotaped.[13] A decade later, in *United States v. Sherman*, the Court of Appeals for the Ninth Circuit ruled in 1993 that individuals videotaped in public view do not have a reasonable right to privacy.[14] Two years earlier, in the case *United States v. Taketa*, the same court stated that the videotaping of suspects does not violate the Fourth Amendment, since the police may record what humans normally can view with the naked eye.[15] Additionally, police are not prohibited from augmenting their sensory facilities through the use of science and technology.[16] This made it possible to zoom in on a suspect.

Even in contexts where criminal activity is not being investigated, courts have upheld the right of individuals to install video cameras for everyday monitoring. Some of the most significant cases have involved workplace surveillance. In *Vega-Rodriguez v. Puerto Rico Tel. Co.* (1997), the Court of Appeals for the First Circuit ruled that employers had the right to install video cameras in workplaces in order to watch over employees.[17] The court ruled that individuals "toiling" in a work area did not have a reasonable right to privacy and that "supervisors may monitor at will that which is in plain view within an open work area." This applied the *Katz* ruling to the use of surveillance cameras, which stated, "What a person knowingly exposes to the public, even in his own home or office, is not subject of Fourth Amendment protection." Though *Katz* ruled "what [that person] seeks to preserve as private, even in an area accessible to the public may be constitutionally protected," courts in this case and most others have ruled that it is not reasonable for employees and other citizens to "preserve as private" actions at work that can be viewed by the naked eye.[18]

In another case, *Thompson v. Johnson Community College District* in 1997, a federal circuit court found that college employees did not have a reasonable right to privacy in a locker room area, where surveillance cameras had been installed. The employees argued that the surveillance cameras violated Title I of the Electronic Communications Privacy Act (ECPA) of 1986 and the Fourth Amendment, but the court ruled that the ECPA did not apply to surveillance cameras and that the Fourth Amendment was not violated because of the unreasonableness of expecting privacy in a locker room at a workplace.[19] The act referred to in this case amended Title III of the Omnibus Crime Control and Safe Streets Act of 1968. The 1986 amendment extended the guidelines that the 1968 law outlined for traditional audio communication to more advanced forms of electronic communications, especially the Internet, but not necessarily video surveillance, since the focus of the amendment was on audio and Internet "communication." It did not put greater restrictions on those seeking to use electronic surveillance, including cameras; rather, it updated the earlier law to include new technologies of communication. At a time when court cases and federal policy could have been dealing with surveillance cameras, which were becoming increasingly popular in public places, the focus in the 1980s and later by the Clinton administration was on the newly forming colossus we ended up calling the Internet.

In the United States, the 1990s was a banner decade for those espousing greater surveillance and harsher judicial sentencing in the United States. In the congressional elections in 1994, Republicans became a majority, and under the leadership of Speaker of the House Newt Gingrich they (along with many Democrats) began their work on promoting through policy more drastic policing methods and stricter judicial processes. Their mandate, dubbed the Contract with America, was in large measure a bold crackdown on crime. No stranger to "get-tough" policies, President Bill Clinton signed two significant laws related to surveillance.[20] The Communications Assistance for Law Enforcement Act of 1994 (CALEA; P.L. 103-414) required telecommunications providers to facilitate court-ordered wiretaps on Internet activity, even when it is necessary for the provider to update or change equipment to accomplish the task.[21] The other law, the Digital Communications and Privacy Act of 1994, strengthened the ability of law enforcement to conduct court-authorized electronic surveillance. After these laws broadened police powers to conduct electronic surveillance, Congress shifted gears a bit and placed some limitations on authorities, especially in cases involving cell phones and e-mail. In 2000, the Electronic Communications Privacy Act of 1986 was amended to strengthen privacy protections against unreasonable searches and seizures and information-gathering techniques. Among other changes, it requires authorities to meet the probable cause standard of the Fourth Amendment when gaining permission to wiretap a cellular phone. It also requires a warrant for government seizure of read and unread e-mail messages stored with an Internet service provider.

In general, federal policies and court cases in the 1980s and 1990s established the legality of video (and now digital) surveillance cameras in public places, due in part to the belief that they are unobtrusive, but also because surveillance to some extent slipped in under the radar screen, overshadowed by the daunting task of controlling the newly developing Internet. But though there was greater federal and judicial attention given to communication technology, significant court cases and policies dealing with surveillance ruled that privacy outside your home is severely restricted. While individualized video surveillance for investigative purposes has to meet some judicial standards, in cases of random surveillance individuals cannot expect privacy where they can be viewed with the naked eye—including workplaces, schools, and locker rooms. The open field doctrine was applied in these cases, and without much fanfare people throughout the United States and other countries have become quite accustomed to random surveillance in public places, including schools. The next significant court case is likely to involve facial recognition technology, because once the surveillance camera is networked to a database of facial characteristics and information banks, new issues arise involving not only surveillance in public places but also the capabilities of that surveillance to be used to access information about people and to create an ever-expanding database on perhaps everybody.[22]

Whereas the legal issue for surveillance cameras has been the right to privacy, for other forms of security equipment, such as metal detectors, the legal issue has more to do with search and seizure, which is the topic of the next section.

Searching Students

The legal uses of metal detectors are based on a considerable body of law having to do with searches and seizures. This section reviews these precedent-setting cases where the fundamental legal issue has been the standard by which a school official can search a student.

The major U.S. Supreme Court case involving a school search was *New Jersey v. T.L.O.* in 1985. T.L.O. (who is not named because she was a fourteen-year-old minor at the time) was accused of smoking a cigarette in the school bathroom. She was taken to the assistant vice principal's office and questioned. She had been caught smoking with a friend, and the friend admitted the wrongdoing. T.L.O., however, denied it. The assistant vice principal then took T.L.O. into his private office and demanded to see her purse, which T.L.O. handed over. When the administrator opened the purse, he found a pack of cigarettes. He took the cigarettes out of the purse and held them up to T.L.O., accusing her of lying. While taking out the cigarettes, he also noticed a pack of rolling paper, which he assumed from his experiences as a high school administrator T.L.O. used for smoking marijuana. At this point, he decided to search the purse further and found a small amount of marijuana, a pipe, several empty plastic packets, and a substantial sum of money in single-dollar bills. He also found a list of students written on index cards with tallies that seemed to be a system for keeping track of who owed her money, and two letters implicating her in marijuana selling.

The assistant vice principal notified the mother of T.L.O. and turned the case over to the police. At police headquarters, T.L.O. admitted during questioning that she had been selling marijuana at school. Based on the confession and the evidence found in her purse, the state brought delinquency charges against the girl in juvenile court. Lawyers for T.L.O. moved to suppress the evidence found in the purse, claiming that the search was unlawful and that her confession was tainted by the unlawful search. The New Jersey Supreme Court ruled in favor of T.L.O., stating that the search for the cigarettes was unreasonable. However, the U.S. Supreme Court reversed this opinion. The Court concurred that searches of students needed to conform to constitutional restrictions, but Justice Byron White, who wrote the argument, also stated that "the school setting requires some easing of the restrictions to which searches by public authorities are ordinarily subject."[23]

With *T.L.O.*, the Court established a precedent that impacts almost all cases involving school searches, including those where a metal detector is used: that school officials need not conform to the "probable cause" standard that governs the reasonableness of searches. Rather, school officials need "reasonable grounds for suspicion"—which is interpreted in law to be a less stringent form of "probable cause"—to believe that a search will turn up contraband. In his decision, Justice White wrote,

> Ordinarily, a search—even one that may permissibly be carried out without a warrant—must be based upon "probable cause" to believe that a violation of the law has occurred. However, "probable cause" is not an irreducible requirement of a valid search. The fundamental command of the 4th Amendment is that searches and seizures be reasonable, and although both the concept of probable cause and the requirement of a warrant bear on the reasonableness of a search . . . in certain limited circumstances neither is required. Where a careful balancing of governmental and private interests suggests that the public interest is best served by a 4th Amendment standard of reasonableness that stops short of probable cause, we have not hesitated to adopt such a standard.

The Court ruled that the reasonableness of a search must be "justified at its inception" and be "reasonably related in scope to the circumstances of the incident." Given these measures, the Court ruled that the assistant vice principal's search of T.L.O.'s purse was reasonable. While overturning the lower court's ruling, it did agree with the lower court that students were protected by the Fourth Amendment; the prosecutors had tried to argue that the Fourth Amendment did not apply in cases involving youths in school. So while upholding youths' Fourth Amendment protections, the Court ruled that a different version of the Fourth Amendment applied in schools because of the custodial and tutelary role of the school and the state's responsibility to maintain order. This was a Fourth Amendment that stopped short of the probable cause standard.

Since *New Jersey v. T.L.O.*, school administrators have had broad powers to search students based on the reasonable grounds standard, and in some cases the powers of school authorities have been broadened further to exempt them from even this standard. In the 2001 California Supreme Court case *In re Randy G.*, school officials, including security officers, were granted the power to search students even without reasonable suspicion.[24]

The case involved a security officer who approached two students in the hallway when they should have been in class. The security officer told the students to go to class, which they did. But one (Randy G.) acted nervous, which caused the security officer to become suspicious. So, with another member of the security staff, the security officer went to Randy G.'s classroom and asked him to step out in the hallway. The two security guards questioned him about his behavior, and then asked if they could search him. Randy G. agreed, and the security officer found a small knife in Randy G.'s pocket. Randy G. was then placed on probation. An attorney for Randy G. filed a lawsuit, arguing that he was unlawfully detained, but the California Court of Appeals rejected the argument, as did the California Supreme Court. The courts ruled that school authorities, including security officers, had the right to "stop a minor student in order to ask questions and conduct an investigation, even in the absence of reasonable suspicion." The two California courts, therefore, give school security officers broad powers to search students even without reasonable suspicion.[25]

But not all school searches can pass constitutional standards. In a 2003 case involving a strip search (*Thomas v. Roberts*), the U.S. Court of Appeals for the Eleventh Circuit in Georgia ruled that the strip search of elementary school children was a violation of their rights.[26] However, the court shielded the school district from liability, arguing that it was not clear to school personnel that strip-searching en masse was unconstitutional. The case involved a teacher who discovered that $26 was stolen from a student during a Drug Abuse Resistance Education (DARE) class. The teacher notified the DARE instructor, who was also a police officer. In court, it came out that the police officer had had many complaints filed against him by students and parents. The police officer decided to separate the girls from the boys, and the teacher and police officer took small groups of the children into the bathrooms in order to search them. The boys and girls were told to lower their pants, and girls were told to lift their dresses and skirts. Because the search was conducted en masse, it was determined unconstitutional. However, the court rejected that the school should be held liable for hiring a police officer with many complaints against him, for not training school authorities in search and seizure procedures, and for carrying out the illegal search. Essentially, though unconstitutional, the school could not be sued by parents or civil rights groups.

Searches with Metal Detectors

Though there were instances when schools employed individualized metal detector searches in the 1960s and 1970s, the random en masse use of them began in the 1980s, and soon after in the 1990s court cases occurred that tested the constitutionality of random metal detector searches. An early experimenter with random metal detector searches in schools, Detroit began their use in 1984 when seventeen large scale metal detector searches involving sixteen schools occurred. In an article that appeared in the *University of Michigan Journal of Law Reform* in 1986, Myrna Baskin and Laura Thomas noted how these searches were conducted in a haphazard way and often without much forethought.[27] They described an early large-scale search in a school in 1985 involving fifteen school security officers and seventeen uniformed Detroit police officers. The officers arrived at a high school at 6:30 a.m. with twenty-two handheld metal detectors and two upright metal detectors, which they set up at the entrance of the school. When the three thousand students who attended the school began arriving at 7:45, each was required to pass through the two upright metal detectors, and most students were required to empty their bags and pockets and were inspected with the handheld metal detectors. The hallways were crowded, and classes had to be delayed because of the huge logjam of students waiting to get in. The search turned up eight knives, one box cutter, one handgun, three marijuana cigarettes, and some pills. Eleven students were detained, arrested, and then transferred to the Special Crime Section base of the Detroit Police Department.

In spite of their continued use and the contraband that was discovered, school administrators and police officials were sometimes the most vocal critics of large-scale random metal detector searches. In Boston, metal detectors were used between 1974 and 1976 during the city's efforts to desegregate the schools, but they were soon abandoned because school and police administrators felt that their use was time-consuming and costly. New York City schools started en masse use of metal detectors in 1983, but they were also soon abandoned because the process of using them was costly and cumbersome (leading to long lines of students and delays of classes, as in Detroit). In New York City there had also been student and parent resistance to metal detectors, sometimes leading to clashes between youths and authorities. New York School Board President James Regan remarked, "We found when we used them [metal detectors], it caused more problems than it solved."[28] The chief of security of the Los Angeles Unified School District, the chief of the Baltimore City School Police Force, and the head of the Chicago Bureau of School Safety also questioned the use of metal detectors.

However, the criticisms did not last for long. The concerns raised in the 1980s were allayed in the 1990s as metal detectors became cheaper and more efficient, as school security officers capable of doing the searches became more plentiful, and as new ways of using metal detectors were developed (low-volume high-frequency methods, for example) that solved the problems that led New York, Boston, and other cities to abandon them. Also, in light of the mass murders that were occurring in schools, school administrators became convinced that the impracticalities of metal detectors were worth it, as did many parents.

Metal detector cases generally occurred at the state level beginning in the early 1990s. In one of the first cases involving a school (*People v. Dukes*), a New York criminal court in 1992 ruled that metal detector searches, even when done randomly, were within the bounds of the U.S. Constitution.[29] In the case, a female high school student coming into school set off an upright metal detector and was then searched with a handheld metal detector by a school police officer, who found a switchblade knife in her pocket. The court ruled that metal detector searches, even done randomly, were a kind of "special need" administrative search that was justified. The same year, Dan Lungren, Attorney General of California, released a statement declaring that the use of metal detectors in random searches in schools complied with the state's constitution.

Two years later, the use of metal detectors was put to the test again, this time in Florida and Chicago. In the 1996 Florida case *State v. J.A.*, a private security firm was hired by the school board to scan students with metal detectors as they entered the school. A team of security guards from the private firm arrived to a high school and was scanning students when one of them noticed a jacket being passed to the end of the line. A guard scanned the jacket and discovered a gun in the pocket. As in the *Dukes* case, the Florida court ruled that the search was an administrative search, and though random and lacking individualized suspicion, the use of the metal detectors in the search was considered justified in light of the school district's responsibility to maintain a safe environment.[30] In the Chicago case *People v. Pruitt* (1996), a random metal detector search of a student turned up a gun, and, again, the court ruled that the search was constitutional.[31] In general, in court cases throughout the 1990s (*In the Interest of S.S.* [1996], *The People of the State of California v. Latasha W.* [1998], and *In re F.B.* [1999]), the courts ruled that random metal detector searches were minimally intrusive, affected a limited privacy interest, and were warranted due to the school's responsibility to maintain a safe environment.

Courts have also ruled that it is constitutional to use metal detectors on specific groups of students, including those arriving to after-school sports events, those arriving late to school, or those in hallways between classes. In the 1998 case *The People of the State of California v. Latasha W.*, a California Court of Appeals ruled against a student in a case that involved the targeted use of metal detectors on students arriving late to school. In the incident, a high school girl was caught carrying a knife after being searched with a metal detector. The school had a written policy about the use of random metal detector searches, and on this particular day the principal asked security guards to search students if they came to school late or entered the attendance office without a hall pass. Latasha arrived late, was searched with a metal detector, and was found with a knife with a blade longer than two and a half inches (the cutoff for making it a criminal offense). The justices drew on previous court decisions in their judgment, again calling attention to the diminished rights of students in light of the special needs of schools:

> The school cases just cited are part of a larger body of law holding that "special needs" administrative searches, conducted without individualized suspicion, do not violate the 4th Amendment where the government need is great, the intrusion on the individual is limited, and a more rigorous standard of suspicion is unworkable. The searches involved here met the standard for constitutionality.[32]

As more police officers (not just security guards from private security firms) began working in schools, the courts have had to rule on the delicate issue of whether school police must abide by school law or police law. Are they police officers stationed in schools, required to follow laws governing policing, or are they "school resource officers" who need only abide by school laws, including constitutional rights that stop short of the Fourth Amendment? In the 1987 case *Cason v. Cook*, a police officer assigned to a school assisted with the search of two students for a missing change purse. A school administrator searched one student and found the missing purse, and then the police officer searched the other student. The Court of Appeals for the Eighth Circuit upheld the search, stating that the police officer's involvement was minimal and that the search was not initiated by the police.[33]

According to law, school administrators can conduct metal detector searches with only reasonable suspicion that the search will turn up contraband, and in some cases do not need even reasonable suspicion where a "rigorous standard of suspicion is unworkable." Ordinarily, police officers need probable cause, which is a higher standard, to conduct a search. But, as the *Cason v. Cook* ruling indicates, police officers working in schools have broader powers than police officers working the street, due primarily to the tutelary and custodial role of schools and what is seen as the non-invasiveness of metal detectors. Also, searches in schools are considered special needs administrative searches, not physical searches, even when conducted by a police officer. According to law, when school administrators request the search, and when administrators and not police take on a decision-making role in the process of a search, the search itself can be viewed as a search conducted by the school administrator even though it is carried out by police.

The Exclusionary Rule

Though it does not bear directly on the promotion of techno-security, the exclusionary rule governs what can and cannot be done with evidence gathered through surveillance or a search. In essence, the exclusionary rule states that evidence discovered in an illegal search cannot be admitted to court as evidence, but rather must be excluded from all proceedings. The U.S. Supreme Court characterized the exclusionary rule as "a judicially created remedy designed to safeguard 4th Amendment rights generally through its deterrent effect rather than a personal constitutional right of the party aggrieved." [34] The rule is meant to safeguard the constitutional rights of individuals by deterring illegal searches, and it is also meant to uphold the integrity of the courts.

However, courts have ruled differently when proceedings involve schools. Generally, if evidence is going to be used to prosecute youths in criminal and juvenile courts, the exclusionary rule applies—all evidence presented in court must be gathered legally. But if the extent of the proceedings will involve only school discipline and not criminal prosecution, then the exclusionary rule does not always apply. In other words, students can be expelled from school based on evidence found in an illegal search. However, in one case, *Jones v. Latexo Independent School District* (1980), the court ruled in favor of a student who was searched illegally and was going to be punished by the school. The boy's car was searched, and inside it school administrators found drug paraphernalia. But the boy could not be expelled, ruled the court:

> Having obtained evidence against the plaintiffs by means of an unconstitutional search, the defendants could not use that evidence as a justification for imposing punishment. Although criminal proceedings were never instituted against the students, the Fourth Amendment protects citizens against unreasonable invasions of privacy by government officials in the civil area as well. [35]

Other courts have stated that the exclusionary rule does not apply to school discipline proceedings because it is inapplicable in high schools where the safety of so many youths is at stake. Generally, though, most schools have sidestepped issues dealing with the exclusionary rule because they have learned how to conduct legal searches, avoiding the displeasure of being accused of violating the civil rights of youths with illegal searches. Additionally, laws are broad enough to permit a wide range of searches, so few except the brashest are challenged and found to be unconstitutional.

FERPA, USA PATRIOT Act, and No Child Left Behind

Information gathering is also becoming more high-tech and is therefore becoming a part of the techno-security fortification of schools. This is especially true of systems that include biometrics, information databases, and scan cards with implanted transmitters and data chips. As this technology becomes more prominent in schools, court cases will no doubt hinge on policies and rulings from the 1970s that have established the legal procedures for collecting and accessing information about students. The Family Educational Rights and Privacy Act (FERPA), passed in 1974, is the original legislation dealing with student records. FERPA allows students and their parents or guardians to review their own records. It also prohibits schools from sharing student records with outsiders, specifically stating that federal funds will be withdrawn from a school "which has a policy or practice of permitting the release of educational records . . . of students without the written consent of their parents to any individual, agency, or organization."[36] FERPA also requires schools to annually inform parents about FERPA and to provide hearings if a parent deems something inaccurate in a student's record.

One of the most significant amendments to FERPA was made through the USA PATRIOT Act of 2001 ane the No Child Left Behind Act, signed into law in 2002.[37] FERPA was amended in two ways: one relates to investigations concerning terrorism, and the other concerns military recruitment. In the case of terrorism, the USA PATRIOT Act added a provision regarding terrorism-related investigations, stating that schools should hand over student records if law enforcement officials believe there is information in the records that could aid an investigation into domestic or international terrorism. The USA PATRIOT Act lowers the standard for obtaining a subpoena of students' records and grants schools immunity for complying in good faith to subpoenas. This means that school districts are released of responsibility in the event that a lawsuit is filed charging that a school had unlawfully released a file. The original FERPA also stated that under certain circumstances, information can be released—to comply with a subpoena, for example—but only "upon condition that parents and the students are notified of all such orders or subpoenas in advance of the compliance therewith by the educational institution."[38] However, the USA PATRIOT Act prohibits schools from informing parents, guardians, or the student that a FERPA request has been made in conjunction with an investigation regarding terrorism.[39]

Additionally, the No Child Left Behind (NCLB) Act allows military recruiters to have access to students' contact information. Ordinarily, under FERPA, in order for student records to be released to third parties, permission from the parents or guardians must be obtained in writing. Under the NCLB Act, recruiters for the military can access students' addresses and phone numbers, unless a parent states in writing that the information should not be released.[40] Previously, parents and students needed to write if they wanted the records released; now, they need to write to keep the records sealed. This is because the NCLB Act amended FERPA directory information protocols. In general, schools are allowed to designate some information as public information, such as sports information or information about a student's award or membership on the dean's list. This is called "directory information," and it may be released to journalists, for example, without written consent of parents or guardians. According to the NCLB Act, a student's name and contact information are now directory information for military recruiters.[41] Additionally, under the original FERPA, a school administrator could contest the release of information even when an appropriate FERPA request was granted. However, under the NCLB Act, school administrators no longer have this option and therefore must release the information. Exceptions can be made when a private school shows a documented history showing a religious objection to military recruitment or if the governing body of a school votes in favor of barring military recruiters. As with the original FERPA legislation, schools that do not comply risk losing funding through the Elementary and Secondary Education Act of 1965.

Though the law does not deal specifically with techno-security, FERPA will face challenges as more information is collected about youths in schools, which will be an inevitable outcome of newer security technologies. Consider student scan cards, which can document when students enter school; access information about them, including library fines and disciplinary actions against them; detect where they get off school buses; and track their movements as they walk down a street. Consider as well databases of surveillance images that can now be stored more easily and without taking up much office space—that are, in fact, becoming entirely mobile. Consider too mobile computers that can be used to enter information immediately as police or administrators make their rounds ("At 2:30 p.m., I found Juan in the west hallway without his books and looking suspicious"). Imagine databases for each youth in the United States who attends school that keeps not only the massive amount of information that is already kept (academic records, health records, disciplinary reports, results from psychological tests, etc.) but also bodily readings (databases of students' images and characteristics) and information on students' movements. Will CDs of images taken from surveillance cameras be added to student records? How about map images garnered from computer chip–implanted ID cards that document the whereabouts of people at particular times? Who will have access to all this information? Generally, all information can be saved, so the only real guidelines dealing with information gathering have to do with information releasing. Under most circumstances, students' records cannot be released, except when there is written consent by a parent or guardian, there is a proper subpoena of records by appropriate authorities, or there is a bona fide emergency situation. But these safeguards have been chipped away by newer legislation, especially the USA PATRIOT Act and the No Child Left Behind Act, but also by new technologies that make the gathering of information and retrieval of information so easy and nonintrusive.

Beginning in the 1920s with the *Hester* and *Olmstead* cases, continuing through the 1960s with *Katz* and *Berger*, then focusing on schools with the *T.L.O.* case, and continuing into the early twenty-first century with the *Lindsay Earls* case, the courts have generally ruled in favor of authorities to search, watch over, and collect information about individuals, including youths in schools—with and without techno-security. Various policies and laws, including the USA PATRIOT Act, the No Child Left Behind Act, and the Omnibus Crime Control and Safe Streets Act, have also supported broad powers for authorities and have therefore helped to promote the fortification. These policies and laws have not only broadened the powers of authorities but also diminished the rights of youths. As Justice Scalia stated in the *New Jersey v. T.L.O.* case, "unemancipated minors lack some of the most fundamental rights of self-determination—including even the right of liberty in its narrow sense, i.e., the right to come and go at will."

While security professionals may not know the court cases discussed in this chapter, they certainly know that the law puts very few obstacles in their way when it comes to selling us the fortress. Though there are still gray areas, school administrators also know that they have few legal restrictions when it comes to a decision about purchasing security equipment. As long as they do not act in an overly brash way, they can use whatever equipment they like, including equipment intended for the military. Imagine: as a school administrator, you can be reading in the newspaper about some new, incredible piece of spy equipment being used by the military, and you can expect that in time, a version of that equipment will make its way to your desk in the form of an advertisement from a security company or recommendation from a facility manager or board of education. This is especially true as the equipment becomes less expensive and as grants from federal agencies become available. Additionally, the law will be on your side—your authority is broad, and the rights of students are diminished. Though school administrators may not know the legal jargon, they know, essentially, that their school is a new "open field."

CHAPTER 7

Transactions on the Open Market

In the councils of government, we must guard against the acquisition of unwarranted influence, whether sought or unsought, by the military industrial complex. The potential for the disastrous rise of misplaced power exists and will persist. We must never let the weight of this combination endanger our liberties or democratic processes. We should take nothing for granted. Only an alert and knowledgeable citizenry can compel the proper meshing of the huge industrial and military machinery of defense with our peaceful methods and goals, so that security and liberty may prosper together. Akin to, and largely responsible for the sweeping changes in our industrial-military posture, has been the technological revolution during recent decades. In this revolution, research has become central; it also becomes more formalized, complex, and costly. A steadily increasing share is conducted for, by, or at the direction of, the Federal government. Today, the solitary inventor, tinkering in his shop, has been overshadowed by task forces of scientists in laboratories and testing fields.

President Dwight D. Eisenhower, 1961 speech given three days before leaving office[1]

While the previous chapters focused on the federal, corporate, and judicial promotion of techno-security equipment, this chapter takes a slightly different tack, and talks more specifically about the broader implications of techno-security fortification, especially as it relates to the kind of military and economic forces Eisenhower talked about decades ago in his famous "military industrial complex" speech. We already know that school fortification in the United States and many other countries did not begin as a result of school shootings (though incidents of school violence and subsequent worries, along with threats of terrorism, have escalated the fortification). Nor did it begin with a government foisting security on schools in order to observe and control populations. School shootings and government foisting play a role, but the problem of looking at it from these two perspectives is that, in the first case, we end up viewing security as a natural by-product of school shootings and terrorism; and, in the second case, we come to understand techno-security as an imposition of power divorced from the agency of individuals who act on their wants and fears.

What if we were to start with the understanding that security is really about big business, and then view techno-security fortification within the larger economic system of which it is a part? Let us say that it is ordinary business being done—simple as that. Not an "imposition" or "logical response," but a *transaction*—that old mainstay of the business world.

Techno-security fortification is the result of several kinds of transactions. Naturally, there is a transaction between buyers and sellers who strike a bargain and expect to benefit from the exchange of goods for money, each in their own ways. But this is just the start of it. There are also transactions of equipment, of knowledge and tactics, and of ideologies. For example, there are transactions of equipment and knowledge involving different professional groups, as when police and school personnel come together and work together in a school, each with their own culture, equipment, and ways of doing things. These transactions also include tactic and strategy sharing, as when police bring their high-tech gear into schools and train teachers, school resource officers, and administrators in lockdown and "hallway sweep" tactics. This particular transaction creates a techno-security link that extends from schools to police departments, and because police departments also transact with the military, to some extent what we see in schools is a military/police/school process rolled up in one. After discussing this particular process, the chapter turns to transactions that have occurred on a global scale that have influenced the security industry and ultimately, the fortification of schoools and society. As big business, the security industry is very much connected to worldwide economic changes and developments. Overall, the chapter shows how school security connects with militarism and then economic internationalism, and has us look at school security as it relates to power elites—those who have been the prime beneficiaries of our new techno-security society.

Schools, Police, and the Military

Security dealers are quite up-front with the fact that they intend to change the look, shape, and very culture of what constitutes security in schools. The cover of a booklet about school security distributed by Garrett Metal Detectors (described as a "Basic Planning Handbook by the Garrett Academy of Metal Detection") shows the direction we can expect security to go in. In the photograph, the yellowed page of the past is peeled away and a new, crisp, professional era in school security is beginning (Figure 7.1). The children on the left, a student safety patrol in 1945 (which includes Charles Garrett's, front row, far left), are reminiscent of a bygone era when a bunch of boys with safety patrol hats and ribbons was all that was needed to keep a school safe. Today, the nature of security is much more professional

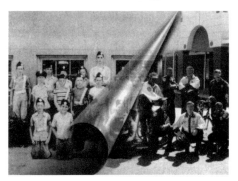

Figure 7.1 The old world of safety involving boy patrols giving way to the new world of safety involving security professionals. Charles Garrett, founder of Garrett Metal Detectors, is kneeling in the front row, far left. From the Garrett Academy of Metal Detection, *Using Metal Detectors: A Basic Planning Handbook* (Garrett Academy of Metal Detection, 2001), front cover.

looking, and we see that the boy scout-looking youngsters have grown up and now look more like police. Today, in their pressed uniforms and with all their equipment, they convey vigilance and no-nonsense duty.

Perhaps we should accept what the experts at the Garrett Academy of Metal Detection tell us and welcome this new era in security. Maybe we should be pleased that school security has become a serious issue, being addressed by trained police officers who make use of the most advanced forms of crime-fighting equipment available. When we do, we accept a kind of school–police transaction that inevitably includes the sharing of weapons and equipment and the infusion of cultural norms. We also create a new profession that includes private security guards, school resource officers, and municipal police stationed in schools—this is the "school security profession" in the making. Their presence introduces a new kind of professional to the school, so that security teams, like counselors, social workers, and psychologists before them, become part of the school, and in time people expect that schools will have professional security personal just as they expect them to have counselors.

As with other professionals, police bring to the school a particular culture. There has been much writing about the culture of policing that has focused on what one criminologist, Steven Herbert, called its "normative orders"—aspects of police work involving bureaucratic control, adventure, law, safety, morality, and competence—that shape the worldviews and actions of officers.[2] These aspects of police culture pass into the school as schools hire police, though of course the culture is not a complete whole and is altered in the school.[3] But in addition to culture—and the point significant here in our discussion of techno-security—is the equipment that becomes a part of school security tactics, for professionals also bring their tools of the trade, and in the case of school police their tools are beginning to resemble the most sophisticated equipment used to fight street crime.

Howard Safir, who was commissioner of the New York Police Department from 1996 to 2000 and was hailed by former Mayor Rudolph Giuliani as the "greatest police commissioner in New York City's history," was a stalwart promoter of techno-security. His sentiments were typical of many police chiefs who have made policing into a techno-war against crime:

> Police departments must stay on the cutting edge of technology to maintain the upper hand, using twenty-first-century techniques like digital and wireless technologies, Enchanced 911, on-line complaints, global-positioning systems, and CompStat, a computerized mapping system that tracks incidents of civilian complaints, administrative data, and crimes, and crunches those numbers into statistical information.[4]

The easy transfer of police weaponry from city streets to schools is seen in the obvious, such as guns, shoulder microphones, and restraining equipment, but also in the less obvious digital and wireless technologies that Safir mentioned. As we have already seen, these include mapping systems that use global positioning technology in ID tracking devices, database linkups between schools and police departments, and Internet capabilities that give police access to school surveillance cameras. But it was not always the case that school police would be outfitted as if prepared for urban warfare. The first school resource officers often did not carry weapons, and most were thought of as helpers and advisors, not security teams.[5] But here we are back again to that image of one bygone era of security passing and another beginning. We cannot let ourselves be captives to nostalgia, we are told by those who promote techno-security. We must ultimately recognize a basic fact put forth by both police and security professionals: the new school security team must be better equipped because perpetrators are better equipped, a point Howard Safir is very clear about:

> All of these technologies and others will soon be part of law enforcement's arsenal in the fight against crime—the technology exists; it is just a matter of funding. Computer-aided dispatch (CAD), greater e-mail and Internet accessibility for officers, integrating numerous databases into a central database, and the use of laptop computers, digital cameras, and wireless handheld devices by officers are on the horizon for the NYCP [New York City police] and other law-enforcement agencies and police departments. Soon officers will be able to type in your social security number or your telephone number into a handheld device and be able to retrieve information from the national Crime Information Center (CIC), get downloads from DNA, forensic, financial and criminal databases, check crime alerts, and compare your face to images of wanted criminals.[6]

School administrators have already begun to use handheld devices to access information about students. They also have databases, which they have begun to merge and update in order to make them compatible with surveillance cameras, automated attendance devices, ID cards with tracking devices, and other equipment. In fact, much of what the commissioner says here about the future of street police relates to schools. Inevitably, law enforcement will make these kinds of technologies part of everyday policing—whether policing the street or schools—and in many cases, they already have.

If the call to arms by police commissioners and other authorities is not enough to set the techno-fortification in motion in schools, then federal support for school–police partnerships and transfers of police technologies to schools certainly help. In the United States, the federal government has supported the sharing of knowledge and equipment between schools and police departments, especially with a 1998 amendment to the Omnibus Crime Control and Safe Streets Act of 1968, which helped to establish and fund school-based partnerships between police and school personnel. Another amendment to the same law, the 2003 Secure Our School Act (which includes the Matching Grant Program for school security), funds the transfer of police equipment to schools and also gives additional support to school–police partnerships.

According to the law, grants may be used for the following purposes: [7]

a. Placement and use of metal detectors, locks, lighting, and other deterrent measures
b. Security assessments
c. Security training of personnel and students
d. Coordination with local law enforcement
e. Any other measure that the director determines may provide a significant improvement in security

The last provision—"Any other measure that the director determines may provide a significant improvement in security"—virtually gives school board members and top-level administrators funding for any form of security measure or equipment they may want. In 2003, the reauthorization of the Secure Our Schools Matching Grant Program made available funding to schools provided they pay 50 percent of total costs. The program is run through the Community Oriented Policing Services (COPS) program, and in 2002, when the COPS program expanded its services to include the school security initiative, the program distributed $5 million to sixty-eight schools in twenty-seven states.

By federal standards, $5 million is not a lot of money, but though a rather small program it is one of many to provide funding to schools to boost security and to create alliances with police departments. It is also a way of spurring on the security market, for it requires school districts to invest in security technology, which inevitably becomes a long-term investment (as with most technology investments). Furthermore, the investment is not just in technology but also in new kinds of people who end up working in schools, foremost police officers, but also tech support and surveillance camera operators. There will also be new training, funding for training, and the slow development of a new way of conducting security—a new professional culture imbued with technology and security teams. To some extent, transactions between the federal government, police, and schools get all this rolling.

Transactions between schools and security businesses account for much of the techno-security buildup in schools. But also, so do transactions between school personnel and police that are made possible by federal grants and even by the ideas of ex–police commissioners such as Howard Safir and others in law enforcement and the military who use their positions to promote techno-security. Additionally, security organizations such as the Security Industry Association (SIA) and the Security Industry Alarm Coalition (SIAC) have contributed to training for police officers. For example, the SIAC worked with the Law Enforcement Executive Development Association, a division of the Federal Bureau of Investigation, to conduct twelve workshops in 2004 with five hundred law enforcement agencies.[8] These workshops and training symposia introduce police departments to newer equipment and tactics, which they then use in their policing efforts on the street and in schools. But the transfer of techno-security equipment from police departments to schools does not tell us the entire story. The link between schools and police is one segment of a longer line of exchanges, for techno-security fortification in schools ends up being partly influenced by what influences the police. Where is Howard Safir getting all this technology he is talking about? While police techno-security was making its ways into schools, police equipment was also changing; it too was being influenced, mostly by the military. In addition to the equipment Safir talked about, new (especially urban) police gear and uniforms borrow heavily from military stock, including helmets, "body bunkers," combat boots, padding and vests, and shoulder microphones. In time, as police adopt the devices and equipment of the military, they will introduce these items to school officials. At first, these items seem cutting-edge, but they soon become typical tools of the trade.

As with federal funding of school–police partnerships, sometimes relationships between the police and military are institutionalized and legitimized by federally sponsored programs that bring police and the military together. In the 1980s, the Defense Advanced Research Projects Agency (DARPA), which had been focused almost exclusively on military matters, began focusing on criminal justice applications for the equipment that they developed, especially as more police began to claim that they were not so much "out-gunned" but rather "out-teched."[9] The U.S. Department of Defense and the National Institute of Justice, which partly support Sandia National Laboratories, also conduct technology transfer and training symposia for both police departments and military personnel. As Samuel Nunn pointed out, it is often through these joint training sessions and meetings that many nonlethal weaponry developed for the military is passed on to police departments, including pepper spray, "sticky shocker" (a wireless projectile that sticks to a target and emits an incapacitating electric shock), and "web shot" (a ten-foot Kevlar net that can be sprung upon a person from as far away as thirty feet).[10]

Some day, will we be shooting sticky shocker or web shots at students in hallways? If you are skeptical, consider that rational and intelligent people fifty years ago did not imagine that we would be using iris scans and ID tracking devices in schools. Consider, as well, the visions of the future described by security professionals. One vendor for a digital imaging company had a way of summing up the sentiments of the business, and what we could expect to see in the future:

> We want to give principals and other authorities in school districts and other people interested in our equipment the best of the best. This is as sophisticated as any equipment used by the military [facial recognition technology]. And this is what schools need. Why shouldn't we give the best to our schools—aren't our kids worth it?

It would be overstating the point to say that these kinds of comparisons to the military were extremely common. Most security professionals just wanted to explain their equipment in more utilitarian terms and forgo the bravado talk. But certainly, even when talking about school security one would hear references to the military. It was also typical that this sales pitch was framed around giving children the "best of the best" and that the vendor pulled at the heartstrings and guilt mechanisms, asking, "Aren't our kids worth it?"

Another security vendor had an image of schools where a version of sticky shocker would be used; but rather than having a sticky substance stop a kid, this vendor discussed a device that could be shot at youths to stun them and, perhaps someday, a device that can be implanted in kids:

> These guns [stun guns] are hitting the public market, and people are buying them up like crazy. Let's face it, they are less lethal than guns that police officers use, and sometimes more effective if what you want to do is not kill somebody, but rather incapacitate someone, which would be the case, most likely, in schools. We also have devices that can be used to keep people under restraint, that can be set to an alarm if somebody steps out of bounds. We would like to see kids having with them at all times devices to determine their

whereabouts—little devices that can be implanted if desired—and with this technology, we may be able to develop technology that to some extent can program children not to go particular places or can emit a warning sensation.

Is it possible that we will implant children with devices to track their whereabouts and "emit a warning sensation" if they step out of bounds? Such items are already being developed, and are sometimes used by pet owners to keep track of runaway companions. The devices are also being developed for humans. The provocatively named device called Digital Angel by Applied Digital Solutions is described in the company's patent as an "apparatus for tracking and recovering humans [with] an implantable transceiver [designed] to remain implanted and functional for years without maintenance." Jerry Dobson, a geographical information systems expert at Oak Ridge National Laboratory, told a scenario that could be the future of such implants: he described a little girl walking home from school. She stops in a field and something attracts her attention—perhaps a flower or small animal—and she runs over to it, "but suddenly her bicep twitches. Before she can stop, her arm stings—then aches. She turns back and her pain ceases at the sidewalk. Simultaneously a commercial service provider reports to her parents."[11] In comparison to the Digital Angel, the sticky shocker and web shot are actually primitive. We may one day be pining for simpler times when we only had to toss some sticky shocker at a kid.

The history of security technology shows us that nearly all security technology gets used in more than its intended context. What starts as military development—or an item to be used on pets—eventually becomes a product for public consumption and use. The products also become a natural part of our institutions, such as schools. Police are sometimes the middlemen between schools and the military, making military equipment available to schools through their own adoption of it. In a similar way, companies are sometimes the middlemen between governments and schools, making the federal support of techno-security use a reality through their direct dealings with school officials. The difference between these two statements is very slight, though; in essence, governments, the military, and businesses work together to bring techno-security to schools.

We have seen in recent years a blurring among these different groups, where sometimes the difference between a police officer, school resource officer, guardsman, military enlistee, and private security officer is little more than the organizations paying their salaries. They not only look similar, use similar tactics, and receive training from similar government and professional groups, but one profession is also often training for another. It is typical that police officers had been in the military, or that retired police officers work for security firms, or that students are directed toward the military through their high school's JROTC program and one day will have a job in a security firm or police department, perhaps working in a school.[12] Howard Safir, after retiring as commissioner of the New York Police Department, became a partner for the security consulting firm SafirRosetti; also, Jack Maple, who was the developer of the CompStat program mentioned by Safir, became a private security consultant and helped to sell CompStat to other police departments in Philadelphia and other cities. Military men and women, as well, find jobs in the security industry. It is not a coincidence that a U.S. military website in 2004 featured a very professional-looking African American man whose biography can be read in their "Life Story" section: from high school, he joined the Army, and then became founder and CEO of a private security firm. Another life story highlights a young white boy who claims that he wants to become a police officer after his military service.[13]

The Military Industrial Complex

When President Eisenhower warned people in his 1961 farewell speech that the United States faced the challenge of dealing with a military industrial complex, he stated in no uncertain terms that individuals better protect their liberties, that they should be critical of federal funding for scientific research in defense, and that the military industrial complex would be a menace as grave as any threat from the outside. In spite of his emotional plea, though, the military industrial complex has become so ingrained in U.S. society that people no longer notice the higher level of militarization in everyday life and the immense defense budget (dwarfing that of every other country in the world), or care to know about the companies calling the shots when it comes to the types of equipment that are used in times of war, by police, and in domestic fortification.

The military industrial complex is composed of not only the military but also politicians and especially businesspeople; it is also a means for the federal government to bankroll companies through government contracts. Consider, for example, the $127 billion project called Future Combat Systems, which is a joint effort between politicians, businesspeople, and the military to create robot soldiers. In spite of the implications of having robots fighting wars for humans, the project is merely another development in techno-security fortification, and should not surprise us. Politicians paved the way for the development of the Future Combat Systems project with a 20 percent increase in the Defense Department's budget, which is then in large part passed on to corporations and research laboratories, such as Robotic Technology in Potomac, Maryland; the Computer Science and Artificial Intelligence Laboratory at MIT; the iRobotCorporation; or the Joint Forces Command research center in Suffolk, Virginia—all of which are involved in the development of the robot soldiers.[14]

There is a lot to be said about robots fighting wars for us, but also significant is the corporate–political–military link that becomes evident when we look at what is behind their development. This is part of the problem of discussing the federal role in techno-security fortification and defense, because the federal government has truly become what C. Wright Mills saw as a "power elite," a group of politicians, military personnel, and corporate people running the country.[15] This mishmash of power brokers is a less tangible group to reckon with than what we perceive to be a president and Congress running the country. The military industrial complex is seen at this high level of command, where people (including Eisenhower) get their political starts in the military and where national leaders are as much businesspeople as politicians. But even in smaller contexts, in face-to-face conversations with security professionals for example, we see that business, politics, and the military are in alignment. In my interviews and conversations with them, security professionals were clear that what they were doing was nothing short of fighting a war; as mentioned earlier, though they tended to discuss their equipment in more utilitarian terms, they also made allusions to "doing battle" and "combating" violence and crime. Often I heard these points in passing—such as when overhearing a conversation—but they were also points that security professionals wanted to make in interviews and discussions I had with them. The following are just a few examples of typical war language that they used. The first is by a female sales representative for a digital software company who I had spoken to on the telephone; the second two are by male vendors who I had met at different security trade shows:

> The danger in our schools is more imminent, and coming from many directions. I am not just talking about the Columbine kinds of shootings, but also terrorism. That can be homegrown terrorism too. We have militias—and we already know they will kill children. Look what happened in Oklahoma. . . . It isn't beyond our conceptions that those militias could start joining forces with terrorists like the ones that crashed the planes into the World Trade Center.

> The danger is much more hidden. It isn't like the old days. That was easy. You knew who you were fighting. It's like in Iraq now [where] our servicemen do not even know who are the enemies

and who are our allies. It's all guesswork—and intelligence gathering, and trusting your instincts. You used to know who were the bullies in schools, the ones going to cause the problems. Now, you just don't know. Somebody like you can just snap.

Combating school violence is like fighting a secret war. We live side by side with enemies, but the war is hidden. . . and you want the response to be hidden. This is a war that nobody—or few people—know is really going on. Just some police, maybe some administrators, and of course the students involved in the war. Otherwise, everybody else is going about their business.

There have been other cases in the history of the United States when war language was used to bolster both liberal and conservative social policies and movements. In the case of school security, the war language is important, especially when the enemy is seen in terms of a terrorist, hidden and in close proximity to us. Techno-security fortification in the United States has actually been mild in comparison to countries that have fortified due to terrorism. The military industrial complex that Eisenhower referred to developed during the Cold War and then later as police departments began to adopt military equipment to combat urban violence, gangs, and drug networks. In other countries, such as England, Israel, and Northern Ireland, the fortification process was slightly different; these countries fortified primarily under the threat of terrorism, and sometimes their fortifications were more expansive than in the United States; you are likely to see in places like London, Belfast, and Israel techno-security tactics involving high-rise walls, "rings of steel," multiple checkpoints, and more overt forms of military policing.[16] Until recently the United States had not experienced the types of terrorist attacks known to these countries. But the Oklahoma City federal building bombing, the shootings at Columbine High School, and especially the terrorist attacks in 2001 have put the United States on par with these other countries that have fortified as a result of terrorism.

If we ask ourselves whether or not to welcome the new era of school security depicted in the image on the cover of the Garrett Metal Detectors booklet, we should keep in mind the military and business context of the transformation. Fueling the techno-security buildup (in schools and elsewhere) are people from the military world, from politics, and from the business sector, who with their power, influence, and money aim to make deals that will promote their agendas; and though they can have different agendas and disagree on many topics, in the area of techno-security they are in agreement, they have the law behind them, and they eagerly promote the wares in their different ways. Regardless of how distant or noninfluential they may seem to the everyday person, they benefit from the fortification and provide the basic ingredients to keep it going—the funding for research and development, the national security rationale for the fortification, and the corporate marketing and distribution of the equipment. This is what is meant by a military industrial complex. It is the forming of a military business, with complete political (and legal) approval, that uses every ounce of its energy to perpetuate itself and to profit those who are in the business, even if that means that they promote the use of military tactics and equipment in all corners of our society, including our schools.

Security, Industrialization, and Postindustrialization

Though there are clear transactions among the military, police, and schools that contribute to techno-security fortification, those transactions would not take place if it was not for the fact that security is foremost a business venture. Businesses are involved at all levels of the equipment's creation to installation. The security industry is one of many international business enterprises that have arisen in recent years due in part to the technology-information revolution. This section briefly discusses two developments that have also contributed to techno-security fortification: industrialization and postindustrialization. The latter deals with more recent economic changes that shifted manufacturing to countries where industry was booming while the United States experienced a movement into a service sector economy. The other has to do with the way industrialization in the late nineteenth and early twentieth centuries fed consumption and created an element in the American character that equates buying with prosperity.

When security is analyzed in relation to industrialization, writers often focus on how security was used to regiment workers and to put them under greater surveillance.[17] As mentioned earlier, the regulation of workers was and remains a significant aspect of security systems. Not only have surveillance cameras and palm scanners been used, but so have software programs that are able to spot suspicious e-mail and search databases of information about employees. Consider, for example, an article in *iSecurity* magazine that discusses the importance for corporations of a well-integrated security system that archives information in order to "spot trends or detect suspicious behavior":

> Information from these [security] systems is archived in corporate databases and analyzed to spot trends or detect suspicious behavior by employees and visitors to company sites. Another trend is the growing demand for information about security ranging from actual incidents and losses to Internet chat room comments by

dismissed employees. The increasing expectation is that security information will be formatted, archived in corporate databases and made available across departments.[18]

However, in addition to employee surveillance, industrialization led to greater consumerism, especially of supplementary items that gave people a sense of being better off—such as security equipment. During the heyday of the manufacturing boom in the United States, England, and other industrializing nations, individuals were able to get jobs in factories and manufacturing plants; in addition, they could also be the truckers and freight ship operators, watchmen, telephone operators, cleanup crews, and so on for the factories and plants. Though conditions could be awful, the jobs offered many a steady income and the ability to establish themselves. But, most importantly for businesses, the workers (blue-collar floor stewards, heavy equipment operators, dock workers, mechanics, textile workers, and so on) helped the businesses to thrive since they participated in the greatest consumption of products even seen in the world. By the mid-twentieth century, buying for need was replaced by consumption for life improvement (leisure, comfort), and people turned to consumerism as a form of entertainment, as the ultimate sign of the American dream, and even as an expression of patriotism.[19]

After the attacks on New York and Washington, D.C., in September 2001, it was no coincidence that President George W. Bush urged people to go out and shop: not only in order to act as if all was normal (to show that the terrorists had not won), but also apparently as a way of minimizing the economic impact of the attacks. But who would really benefit from this or any other shopping spree? Primarily, the businesses selling the items of the spree. The security industry depends on this kind of consumerism. It has benefited from people of the middle classes who turn to commodities to make their lives nicer, more comfortable, and safer, and who have accepted the popular line of reasoning that says that shopping is good for the country and a symbol of prosperity.

Talking to a security vendor for Central One Monitoring one day on the phone, I had questioned people's reliance on "equipment" to make them safer, and the vendor had particularly strong words for me:

> That's because you think people are overboard when it comes to buying, and you're right to a point—just look at credit card debt in this country, or the national debt for that matter. But all that is good. You have a mortgage, right? Where would you be without that debt? What would happen if we all stopped shopping tomorrow, or just bought the kinds of things we need—imagine the

businesses that would go under. We owe it to our businesspeople to support them, which in turn, forces them to do right by us.

As we see in newly industrialized China—where in the early twenty-first century the largest malls in the world are being built—the middle classes expand and are boosted by industrialization. So while the Industrial Revolution contributed to the use of surveillance to achieve greater efficiency and to watch over workers, the middle classes who established themselves during this time also helped to bring luxury items into the public fold by making them an everyday part of their lives. The mass production of parts made possible by the conveyer belt and manufacturing techniques based on Taylorism and the ideas of Henry Ford also helped to make items cheaper, and with the building of roads and better forms of transportation, the items became available to a greater number of people who had the wherewithal and resources to get them. Security equipment is like appliances, cell phones, and so many other things that many of us had once done without but cannot imagine ourselves without now, for they help us to lead more comfortable lives and are our main way of showing our worth in society.

However, economic history shows us that industrialization does not last forever in most countries, and with the passing of industrialization comes other circumstances—which also affect the security industry. As the United States and much of Europe passed out of the industrial age in the latter part of the twentieth century, and as businesspeople began to steer manufacturing to Asia, India, Mexico, and other countries, the new corporate sector no longer needed industrial workers in the United States. Technology, the lifting of trade barriers, and other factors were making it less expensive and fairly easy to run manufacturing operations from thousands of miles away. In the United States, instead of workers in the industrial sense, corporate elites began to need service sector workers and low-wage or salaried toilers who care for, attend to, provide information for, defend, arrange for, and do for—in essence, "service"—the middle classes and elites.

To some extent, the security industry has arisen out of this economic transformation from an industrial economy based on manufacturing to a service economy based on information technologies. Security professionals are white-collar professionals, and their success is an example of the booming service economy and of the new businesses that have flourished as a result of it. In the 1990s, techies who were savvy were able to survive the bust of the dotcom boom by hopping on board other industries, such as the security industry, that were taking off as programming and "IT" (information technology) were petering out. As computers became simpler to use and troubleshoot and as a flood of techies hit the job market, even "IT people" began to need a new niche; many found their niche in the security industry. Along with the techies, the security industry is the home of many traveling salespeople, customer service representatives, vendors, and others who provide basic services for the middle and upper classes. They run the gamut of the service sector—from the highest levels of department managers to the lowest guards, who are like maids in hotels often scraping by on the bottom rung of the service sector. Security is essentially a service industry and has therefore benefited from the movement in the United States and other countries from a manufacturing to service economy.

The security industry also benefits from industrialization in Asian and Eastern European countries, where many components for security devices are assembled, often by women and sometimes under oppressive factory work conditions. One security professional, a woman, put it quite bluntly: "Where would we be without our Asian operations? Our Asian Pacific division is incredibly important to us." As with other technologies, security hardware—everything from basic circuitry to lasers and sensors—is assembled by people who do it cheaply, and components are brought to the United States easily, thanks in no small part to trade negotiations of the 1990s and the early twenty-first century that reduced international business and import obstacles.[20] There are a couple of things at work here that in tandem have lent a hand to the security industry and have, therefore, boosted the fortification of schools and other public places. You have materials for equipment being manufacturing and assembled more cheaply in countries newly industrialized, and you have trade barriers dismantled to bring in the equipment more easily and cheaply. You also have the benefits that come from the burgeoning middle classes in countries such as India, South Africa, and China, who invest in security equipment as they too enter the middle-class world and want the kinds of benefits and abilities that techno-security gives to other people.[21]

Businesses have always sought out the cheapest places to do business, and at one time those places were American cities and factory towns; now they are cities and towns scattered across the globe. This has helped to lower commodity prices for consumer nations like the United States and has kept the middle classes content with cheap stuff, but it has also helped to create circumstances in the United States where individuals face long-term unemployment and inevitable dead ends in their lives. Youths who would have been prepared for blue-collar work have become what some have referred to as a "superfluous population"—a population that is no longer needed.[22] They cannot make it in the service economy, and do not have the option to work in manufacturing. In some cases, some of these people become the guards, attendants, and other low-level security workers in the service economy. However, those who do not make it in the service sector often become the rationale for techno-security fortification –the people we need protection against.

Even though sheathed in utopian language about "social problems," the point made by the security consultant in the following quote highlights a basic fact of the industry: if it was not for people who are on the "edges of society," there would be no need for people in the security business:

> What we have to remember is that we have serious social problems in this country, and in the countries where our subsidiaries reside. We're not going to solve social problems right off . . . they are here at least for our lifetime. The point is to recognize that our social problems become our individual problems, that we have to fix, but also have to deal with—with our own protection. We can't wait for social problems to get fixed, we have to guard ourselves from those who live on the edges of society. We know they are there. We [the security industry] are proof that they are there.

Another security vendor got to the point much quicker, stating, "Let's face it, we got to protect ourselves from desperate people. These are the people who want to do us in."

It turns out that the people who live on the edges of society, all these "desperate people," are really important to the economy—the so-called superfluous populations are not superfluous after all. They generate immense revenues for some of the largest industries in the United States, including the prison industry and security industry, and with some training they can be molded to be part of the largest industry of all: the military industrial complex. In the United States and elsewhere, the people who cannot suit the new economy through their work provide instead their bodies: they become contained in depressed rural and urban areas and the rationale for techno-security fortification; they feed the prison system, providing the bodies to keep the prison business booming; or they provide the military muscle and know-how to fight wars abroad and to deal with dissent and crime in the United States.[23] In all cases, the security industry booms as disinvestments are made in education, social services, and the general welfare of people, and as superfluous populations increase.

The security industry has benefited greatly from disinvestments in what is sometimes called human capital. Investing in human capital through education has always been seen as a duty of capitalist America, if not for intellectual and moral reasons, then for economic reasons—as a way of maintaining a strong workforce. When work depended on manpower and some level of manual skills (and not so much on technological know-how from a more slimmed-down group of employees), investing in education and training was the means for developing human capital. But now disinvestment works equally well, for where there is public disinvestment, the private sector can come in and pick up the pieces.

These many aspects of techno-security—the making of a superfluous population, luxury consumerism, and global capitalism—have fed techno-security fortification. As the security industry becomes increasingly an international enterprise, it relies more heavily on technology production in Asia, India, and elsewhere. The industry also relies on new middle classes, which the businesses help to create, who then become the buyers of the businesses' wares. Meanwhile, the making of a superfluous population—in the United States and elsewhere—creates the dividing lines, the "us" versus "them" mentality, needed to make techno-security seem necessary. Essentially, middle-class consumerism makes it logical to spend in order to be safe; and the superfluous populations give us frightening and often racist reminders for why we must spend.

A Note on Neoliberalism

Techno-security fortification serves the economy: we see this in the use of fortification to "sell" places and to increase business and attract patrons, and we see it in the business rationale that makes schools as likely as any other place to become a market for the equipment. Fortification is not a logical response to violence. It is a response subsidized by benefactors who make the logic of security coincide with the reality that best suits their economic interests. If a company CEO is convinced that a particular market will be lucrative, then he or she will try to expand services into that market. If that market happens to be a school system, this to the CEO is just a matter of doing business and is in no way an effort to militarize schools or to undermine civil rights. Business is business, and the logic of business is what calls the shots, directly influencing the kinds of equipment available, how they look, and how and where they should be used.

But what is the logic of business? In the late twentieth and early twenty-first centuries, the logic of business has generally revolved around neoliberalism. Neoliberalism has been spread by a range of individuals and organizations, including CEOs, company board members, and international organizations such as the World Bank, Organization for Economic Cooperation and Development (OECD), and World Trade Organization (WTO). It has also been adopted by national governments and espoused in business schools at universities. While there is much that could be said about neoliberalism, the aspect of it most significant here involves its central tenets that individual choice and privatization, combined with a kind of corporate managerial system of governance, can best serve the economic interests of the greatest numbers of people and make social services and public institutions most productive. Michael Peters, James Marshall, and Patrick Fitzsimons, discussing New Zealand, described neoliberalism in relation to what is sometimes called New Public Management.[24] In New Public Management, there is nothing inherently different about a school that should make its management any different from managing an office or company (or prison, for that matter); the same kinds of systems and rules of governance—and, most specifically, technologies—should be put into place.

The use of techno-security sits well with the neoliberal way of doing things. We can see this in at least two ways. First, it fits in with efforts to streamline students, manage them better, and control and order the environment through surveillance. This is a corporate managerial system of running schools, and while totally in line with neoliberalism, it is also a logical by-product of earlier forms of school management techniques that emphasized regimentation and administrative surveillance. In another way, neoliberalism boosts privatization and expects the private sector to eventually take over many of the duties that have traditionally been in the hands of the public sector. Though not new, neoliberalism gained momentum during the 1980s, prompted by the Ronald Reagan government in the United States and the Margaret Thatcher government in England, so that by the end of the 1980s the takeover of state industries, utilities, and institutions by private enterprises exceeded sales of $185 billion; by 1992, approximately 6,800 state-run enterprises in over eighty countries had been privatized. The sale of Conrail in the United States and Margaret Thatcher's sale of the power industry in 1988 are just two examples of how public services are easily sold to private companies, who then use them to profit.[25]

In general, security professionals could be heard espousing neoliberalism when they showed their skepticism toward public services and government agencies to provide security. Often their boosting of neoliberalism was accompanied with the kind of subversive edge described earlier, as a vendor for a surveillance camera company explained:

> Who are you going to trust? Professional people who study, live, breathe, and do just about everything around security. Or our government? Our government has too much on its hands protecting. It's looking at the big picture, and so are we, but we are also looking at the little picture . . . at people like you. The government, police, FBI, whatever, they don't know you. And to be honest, they don't care about you. The government's got bigger fish to fry. They don't know you, but we do.

An engineer for a security manufacturing company had this to say about security:

> Most of us know what government-issue means. It means run-of-the-mill. There is no incentive for the government to meet our needs. We rely on governments, but what is their motivation? Just a lot of rhetoric. Now, if you put money behind it, then you are people who are genuinely invested. Who is going to meet your needs better: a flatfoot bureaucrat or a person with a contract, who wants your investment. I'm not hiding my intentions. I mean to make money, I'm in the private sector now [he used to be a police officer], and I know that I have to win you over with my services and products.

The U.S. public school system is one of the last frontiers in the neoliberal march for privatization, something the security industry knows well. We see the inroads that private companies have already made in schools not only in security, but also in food, textbook, curricula, and other services, as well as in many voucher programs, in school "takeovers" by businesses, and in the development of many charter schools. Security is integral to the boosting of a school in an open marketplace; it is used to "sell" a school. It brings the school into the twenty-first century not only technologically but also ideologically. We hear the same old neoliberal story: public officials, for various reasons, cannot provide safety, or the safety they provide is inferior to what the private sector can do, so company people have to step in, and people get down to business.

One vendor for Lenel Systems International, Inc., put it this way: "We have already seen how good school personnel can protect students—just look at Columbine." What we need, the logic says, are people in the business exclusively there to make life safer: forget the amateurs and those with bigger fish to fry. Who are you going to call—flatfoots or professionals? Professionals know how to secure facilities—it is their specialty. And it does not matter if we are talking about prisons or schools. This is the logic of neoliberalism at work.

Security Transactions

Are we to believe that school security is related to all these disparate aspects of our world—that it is so thoroughly linked to neoliberalism, militarism, and economic internationalism? Naturally, the guy using the metal detector in the school is not thinking this way: he just sees himself doing his job, trying to keep the place safe. The parents who send their children to a supersecure school do not see it this way either, except on rare occasions perhaps. They are just providing the best for their children. The person who sells the equipment does not see it this way either—she is just trying to make a sale, doing her job, as well. So who is to say that school security is really so tied into these other disparate issues?

We begin to notice these disparate issues and their influences when we look at techno-security fortification as a transaction. We notice the broader contexts within which schools "transact," and this is where we begin to see connections to such topics as the military, economic internationalism, luxury consumerism, and privatization. Security transactions involve an exchange of goods and money and services, which takes place because individuals seek to benefit in their own ways—this much is obvious. But there are also transactions among power elites that shape circumstances in the world that sometimes have bearing on security and security businesses—this can involve shifts in the economy and new policies that help to make security equipment cheaper to produce, or trade agreements that facilitate imports. There are also different kinds of transactions—there are transactions of knowledge, tactics, and equipment, as well as transactions of ideologies. Sometimes these transactions are not noticeable, happening as they do outside the purview of ordinary people—as do many business dealings. Also, they are not noticeable because, in many ways, the security industry does not want this aspect of their work to be noticed by people like you and me—it wants to sell equipment.

Security professionals convince us to buy into techno-security fortification, but the transaction depends as well on the consumer's end of the deal—that other element of capitalism that involves the actions of customers to choose to buy or not to buy. That most levels of security—from national security to personal security—have come under the purview of the private sector and therefore involve transactions is an important element of the fortification movement in schools and other public places. It is not that democratic governments are not behind it, but rather, democratic governments heralding the benefits of the private sector have continued to expect the private sector to carry out its biddings. In exchange, the private sector can expand upon the opportunities that the government gives them (by building their markets) and profit through their own business endeavors, and while doing so they can feed the economic system, which inevitably benefits the power elite.

For those living in countries that are mostly democratic and based on a constitution of human rights, surveillance is too sinister a thing when solely in the hands of the government, and officials in democratic nations know this—nobody wants to look like a tyrant. So though the end result is often the same—surveillance is accomplished—when the private sector is in on the transaction (creating an economic transaction and not just an instrument of hegemony), the government is off the hook, the needs of the market are met, and the end result—the surveillance itself—looks more like an inevitable consequence of our changing society (which, as always, we deal with by buying newer and better items) and less like an imposition of power, though of course to some extent it is. There is something appealing to the capitalist heart about a company marketing a device and a person buying it. But this does not mean that national governments do not have a stake in the fortification process. They prop up the companies that will benefit them and are pleased when the private sector takes over their responsibilities to the public. This was true during the development of railroad systems and banking systems, and is true today in the development of security systems.

In some ways, the focus on transactions is analogous to other ways of viewing techno-security fortification, in that similar issues are raised. When we view security from a perspective that highlights the role of social control, for example, we may very well end up talking about the military industrial complex—just as we do when viewing the topic with a focus on transactions. But even when people talk about the military industrial complex, often they get hung up on the military part of it and forget how much business is involved. The focus on transactions brings out the significance of the almighty dollar even when we are talking about safety, or the military for that matter. It also brings out connections between what would appear at first glance to be disparate aspects of our world. Though one is likely to see new guards in a school, one may never see what went on to get them there. But we should know. To understand even the modest use of a metal detector by the low-wage guard in a school, we should not fail to recognize the business that goes on in order to bring this guard in, the economic circumstances that create the profession, the business dealings that go into the production of the guard's equipment, and the economic logic that legitimates his or her position in the school. Transactions promote techno-security fortification in schools and elsewhere and make it seem normal and inevitable, as if people were just doing business, responding to personal needs, and doing what is logical given the circumstances. But when we look behind the transactions, we see that individuals do not just respond, but also choose. Circumstances do not just appear, but are created as a result of our interactions, policies, corporate ventures, judicial rulings, and other aspects of our world that involve a trading and dealing between individuals.

Conclusion

The Big Business of Big Brother

You are on a video camera an average of ten times a day. Are you dressed for it?

Kenneth Cole advertisement in a Los Angeles mall[1]

What does it mean when surveillance becomes a chic advertising technique for a clothing company—a flippant way of appealing to people looking for some fashionable footwear, clothes, or handbags? How about when children find great joy in seeing themselves on surveillance camera monitors? Entering a department store one time, I walked in behind a man carrying his three-year-old daughter. At the entrance of the store was a surveillance camera monitor that faced people coming in. The little girl pointed to the monitor and said with excitement, "It's Dana and daddy on tv!" The father waved to the monitor and, following his lead, so did the girl.

Increasingly, surveillance monitors are set up so people see that they are being observed—which, no doubt, delights children like Dana. This method is increasingly popular in department stores, supermarkets, and liquor stores, and is a technique that is also recommended for schools. For example, the guide *The Appropriate and Effective Use of Security Technologies in U.S. Schools* states, "Occasionally, an irate parent may threaten a school employee, but this can be mitigated if the parent sees himself being recorded on a video monitor."[2] The guide also shows two illustrations; in the first a man is seen yelling at a school employee. In the second, the same two men are facing each other, but this time the man is shown talking calmly to the school employee. This is because in the second illustration the man is on surveillance, and a monitor is set up so that he sees himself on surveillance. Security vendors claim that this style of surveillance deters crime. This may be so, but we also get used to seeing ourselves on monitors; the equipment actually brings joy to children or can be a goof for older kids who strike a pose for the cameras—but more often than not, they are just ignored. For many individuals above the age of forty or so, advanced security equipment is introduced to them as adults, and more often than not they slowly become accustomed to it. Newer generations are born into a society already outfitted with techno-security. They will not notice the high-tech security cameras in stores or their schools, no more than earlier generations noticed locks on doors, so that by the time they get to the Kenneth Cole advertisement, they are not surprised or shocked—they read the ad with a knowing smirk for its cleverness.

This acceptance of techno-security equipment, along with the forming of suburbs and housing subdivisions, and of super-secure schools, and the buying of devices that thrill us—all this and more point to the ways that individuals keep the fortification process going through their own investments in it. People purchase security and expect their store managers and social administrators (city councils, boards of education, town planners, etc.) to do the same as part of efforts to improve schools, neighborhoods, and shopping experiences; to boost the image of places; and to define places in particular ways (e.g., as orderly, safe, in control, and upscale). Even when installed in poor urban schools and housing projects, the devices are usually part of an effort to rejuvenate more well-to-do localities for business purposes and to mollify the middle classes who fear outbreaks of distant violence seeping into their everyday paths.[3] People dealing in security know these things and do all they can to satisfy their mostly professional, middle- and upper-class customers.

It has become quite commonplace in the social sciences to recognize the agency of individuals to take action, which is usually discussed in the context of powerless people asserting themselves or silenced people having a voice. But what about the agency of middle-class consumers to choose a lifestyle that requires the kinds of gizmos that security companies have for sale, and then entering into transactions to get what they want? Though security professionals can be persistent businesspeople, they are not in the business of being hegemonic bullies; they are in the business of making money, and they know that in order to make money in a capitalist, democratic country such as the United States, they need to spread their wares as far and wide as possible. The best way to do this is by urging people to be free market agents who take care of their own needs through their buying power. We already know that security can be imposed on us. But what about the security that we like, that becomes part of our personal tastes for what is new and advanced and part of our yearnings for particular houses, schools, stores, and lifestyle accessories?

What is originally created for the military and with "national security" and, more recently, "homeland security" support goes through various processes of production to get turned into everyday inventory—it is a process that transforms items from "intimidating military armament" to "sleek consumer device." There is much in place that pushes this process along: federal investments in technology development, positive meanings that we invest in technology, our fondness of trendy things, advertisements that "dress up" equipment in enticing language and images, judicial rulings that have paved the way for their use, and organizations and events that promote the equipment—each facilitating the movement of technology from research lab to sales shelf to general public. As equipment coming out of laboratories is picked up by businesses, it gets marketed with particular imagery, especially images of utopia and, perhaps most surprisingly, a progressive and sometimes subversive intent. Security professionals see themselves as businesspeople working for the betterment of society, empowering everyday people to take safety into their own hands and to protect themselves from criminals and overzealous authorities. One security vendor put it simply: "Security gives you an edge up. I don't care who you are." By the time the security equipment is marketed to schools, it already has a momentum behind it that makes it seem almost natural that some of the wealthiest, most democratic countries in the world would militarize their schools. With a rash of school shootings in the United States, Germany, and elsewhere fueling fears, with schools becoming more receptive to all kinds of business propositions, and with neoliberal school reform at full throttle, the security industry has easily stepped into the public school market.

Once we recognize that security is more about big business than Big Brother, we can better understand how techno-security has become so prominent in our society. It has become prominent in the same way that other technologies have become prominent: through mass consumption. Businesses are selling us the fortress, and we for the most part are buying it up. Even when not buying actual security devices, we buy the technology that makes the devices work. The technologies used in security equipment are often the same technologies used in cell phones, DVD players, and digital cameras. The "security" part of security technology is only the casing, the packaging—just another way of selling a technology. One casing sells us entertainment or perhaps a better means of communication. The same technology wrapped up a little differently sells us safety. It is no wonder that many companies known for their computers, appliances, cameras, and stereos, such as Polaroid, GE, Panasonic, and Texas Instruments, are also in the security business. For them, the security market is another niche; all they have to do is start a security division of the company, shift workers around to fill the new division, tweak their technologies a bit, and before you know it they are in the security business, contacting schools because they know that this market is booming, selling high-tech surveillance along with their refrigerators.

The Benefits of Techno-Security

Of course, the big question is, "Are we actually safer with the equipment?" The benefits of techno-security will be debated for years to come, and though this book is not an evaluation of techno-security, I have read a lot of research articles that have tried to answer this question. Some research indicates that security equipment helps to reduce crime and improves the public's confidence in places, making the public more likely to frequent a store, for example, and therefore improving business and the general "feel-good" character of the place. Other research indicates that techno-security does not reduce crime but rather displaces it—when criminals discover that security measures are in place, they seek out places where there is less surveillance. Also, some research indicates that though crime is reduced, the reduction reflects more general trends in crime rates, or, because techno-security is one strategy in the fight against crime, one can not be sure if the reduction is the result of techno-security or another strategy being implemented. In short, a close examination of the evaluation research on security equipment shows mixed results.[4]

So what if we were to look at benefits in another way? What if we were to look at remunerations reaped by particular groups that get perks when techno-security fortification occurs? The corporate sector benefits as new markets, such as the public school system, are laid open to private enterprises. The federal government also benefits, because it can support technological advancement for the military at the same time that it develops school and police security devices (since the devices used in schools, by police, and by the military are so similar). The federal government, in conjunction with research laboratories and security corporations, can also use schools to test new technologies and communities' responses to them, as the National Institute of Justice has done. States and the public school sector benefit from federal funding and welcome the fortification as an easy way of potentially controlling and protecting youths and adults in school. School districts also benefit when insurance premiums are reduced and through various perks they receive (funding as well as public approval) when they install the equipment. The general citizen also benefits from a tax write-off and reduced insurance premiums. Hence, there are many who benefit from techno-security fortification. Unfortunately, the one important benefit—actually making us safer—is not quite clear.

When we view techno-security fortification in relation to corporate enterprises, judicial systems, and the political will of a country's elite, we begin to come to grips with the immense power that is behind the fortification process, and the importance that the fortification has for individuals. For the middle classes who welcome its presence, a better set of promoters could not be procured—essentially, they have the most powerful people in the United States and elsewhere rallying around techno-security fortification. For those who are critical, you would have more success educating customers about the potential problems with the equipment than going up against this set of promoters. But most people with the power to make a change (if that is what they want) do not do much at all, for they understand intuitively that they too benefit from the fortification, for it protects—or gives an image of protecting—their lifestyles. Police commissioners and politicians are quick to point out that many people, including those who are poor and living in public housing, welcome security cameras, and that techno-security is installed for the protection of us all. However, in the big scheme of things, techno-security fortification benefits those with the supplementary income to afford the devices and the assets that need protection—and it always has. Techno-security was first developed to help the upper classes maintain control of people who may challenge their prosperity. Whereas dictatorships use strongarm tactics to protect the privilege of the elite, democratic countries use techno-security fortification. In many countries, legacies of segregation and exploitation have resulted in fortification—because fortification is a less tyrannical means of control, and ultimately benefits businesses and gives the middle classes peace of mind.

Techno-security fortification is part of a history of segregation and colonization in countries such as the United States, England, and South Africa, where structural inequalities and historical animosities continue even after the official dismantling of oppressive systems of government. In many cases, the devices and controlling mechanisms of techno-security fortification have replaced the devices and controlling mechanisms of colonialism, segregation, and apartheid. One of the newest developments in residential lifestyle in postapartheid South Africa is the move to create gated communities and to make public roads private; this is seen as well in the United States, especially in suburbs of major cities and in the sprawl of housing subdivisions. Suburbanization after the *Brown v. Board of Education* (1954) school desegregation ruling, and newer forms of subdivisions and gated communities, highlight to what extent individuals will go to separate themselves, this time through their buying power. Many seeking what they call "security" seem in perpetual retreat, distancing themselves from the public realm and setting up layers of barriers, monitors, and detectors to protect their assets and their image of what a happy, middle-class life should be like. But the communitarian notions of peacefulness and easy living that accompany secure neighborhoods and schools hide to what extent feeling safe relies on class and race segregation, where people partition themselves off in often homogenous and fortified microsocieties.

Since the very first days of private security in the nineteenth century, security has been used for the benefit of the middle classes and wealthy. The technology has changed, but this basic fact has not. Asset protection has always been the name of the game. Today, we also see place protection. In the past, laws, social taboos, and outright threats of violence maintained boundaries between the rich and the poor and between the racially dominant and racially oppressed. But now, in some ways techno-security is used to reinstall those boundaries, helping to replace the old segregationist systems of government with equally segregationist democracies of private enterprise.

Getting Back to School Security

When it comes to school security, we cannot forget the reasons why school staff may be fearful—we have to take their worries seriously. But we should also look at the ways that fear can overtake our common sense and drive our behaviors in an almost irrational way. Part of the fortification of schools has to do with the panic that lies just below the daily school routine but rises quickly and with the slightest provocation. I saw this happen, for example, in the main office of one city high school when the lights went out unexpectedly one day. At the time, there were three students in the office: two were waiting for something or somebody, and one was a student helper filing papers. There were four secretaries, an assistant principal going through papers in a file cabinet, and the principal in his office on the telephone. When the lights suddenly went out, the secretaries and the vice principal were the first to react, the vice principal in a near panic calling to the secretaries to get on the phone and "somehow find out what is happening." One secretary was saying that they had lost communication—"We don't have communication without the electricity." Another secretary verified this, calling out, "We lost communication." I was beginning to feel nervous, but I was not sure if it was because I feared something or because of the reactions of the school personnel.

The head of security came in, pointed out that all the guards could be in contact with each other through their walkie-talkies, and ordered one guard to trot around the school and tell the other guards to tune in to station 3 so they could communicate. The principal came out of his office looking up at the ceiling lights, then turned to the head of security and requested that all the teachers be notified that they were going into lockdown. The head of security nodded, then spoke into his walkie-talkie, ordering the guards to walk each of the hallways and to tell all of the teachers that they were going into "lockdown mode." It was obviously not a good time to talk to the principal (the reason why I was there), so I decided to leave. I left the office and was headed for the front doors of the school when somebody shouted at me, calling me by name, "You can't leave! Stop right there." It was a teacher whom I knew, who was joking around with me, playing off of the apparent nervousness in the air. I did not know at first that it was a joke and jumped when he shouted at me. He must have seen my expression because he told me to calm down and that he was only kidding. But he also told me that I was not permitted to leave the school during a lockdown, something I had forgotten. After the lockdown had been lifted, I left the school, feeling quite shaken up. We found out later that the reason for the school blackout involved a truck driver who had inadvertently backed into a utility pole, knocking out electricity for several blocks.

When such incidents occur, a rising feeling of panic often results from eye contact, nonverbal cues that show uncertainty more than fear but increasingly reveal fear, and, at least for me, images of disaster come to mind. I started out curious about the lights but ended up more than a bit nervous, although also a bit put off by what seemed to me an overreaction by school personnel—but was it an overreaction? Certainly, at the beginning of the twenty-first century there is ample cause for worry about violence in schools. What if it was a shooter or terrorist who had cut the lights? As security professionals are fond of saying, "You never know."

Most teachers and administrators who I have met and interviewed in the last several years see security technology and police as boons to schools. When I try to understand their views, these kinds of stories involving fear and panic come to mind. But there are other stories that I think of, too—these stories involve regular people who boast about the security installations and feel happy when they know that their school is using the equipment. While fear may be a part of this, their enthusiasm is also evident—they just like the stuff.

There is a typical logic that goes into effect when people talk about security, which goes something like this: an individual, group, or institution faces a threat, and people are scared, want protection, and are "desperate" and "hysterical"—as security professionals were fond of saying—so they are driven to contract with security vendors to get the equipment that will protect them. Though there are different versions of the story, each usually begins with the individual (or institution or neighborhood) who feels a threat and must therefore respond. But how about the logic laid out in this book: you have technology being developed to maintain military might, you have companies that profit when it is sold, you have people who are infatuated with the stuff, you have laws that have legitimized its use, and you have cooperation among federal, corporate, and military spheres to pull off a big sale. Fear and danger are parts of this, of course, but they take a back seat to all that is pushing the creation, production, and sale of the equipment. Fear is real, but so is the joy that Dana feels when she sees herself on "television" or the fun that Garrett Metal Detectors tells us we will have using their SuperScanners.

Security: A Boon or a Bust on Our Rights?

Will the techno-security fortification of schools end up being a boon for school safety, or will it be another way of squashing civil liberties and feeding the prison system? Will fear drive us to fortify to the point of self-imprisonment, or will our good common sense keep techno-security in check? Who are we to believe: the ACLU or security professionals? The ACLU will warn you of potential constitutional violations that can result from the devices. Security professionals will tell you that techno-security is a great step forward for safety, for social betterment, and for the general advancement of humans. But in many ways, the disagreement is outdated and based on a bygone era. It presupposes that security equipment can be extracted from a school, house, or person's life. Increasingly, though, techno-security is becoming integral to architecture and the daily business of running a place or living one's life; it is becoming a life accessory and a professional tool for people looking to get ahead. Techno-security in schools will one day be totally integrated with office databases, lighting, bookkeeping, ID'ing, and scheduling, and will be part of parking lots, hallways, classrooms, and the engineering of the buildings. Those who fear that schools will become like military states have a valid case, but they sometimes forget how cool-looking techno-security can be, and with more advanced stuff it becomes more appealing and less intrusive. With more advanced lasers, for example, we can take readings without people even knowing it. We can jack up the "flow" of metal detectors: soon people will be able to shoot through metal detectors like cars on the E-Z Pass. The swipe of a funky-looking school ID will act as a tracking and bookkeeping device and make attendance easier. There are no back-room interrogations here, just people going about their day. Schools will exude security-ness, but they will do so in a clean and quaint way. Companies are quite capable of making surveillance cameras for schools the size of an eraser so that nobody would see them. But why do we still see them? Partly to deter violence, but also because they look good. Additionally, covert cameras may seem too totalitarian; better to have people see the cameras and *like* what they see.

We have seen the benefits and disadvantages of technology, we experience them everyday, and with hardly a glance at a newspaper we can see technology's incredible potential and potentially devastating effects. If society becomes safer, if it becomes more difficult to smuggle weapons into schools, and if violence decreases, nobody will claim that these are unintended consequences—it just proves how security technology can work for us. But if we socialize every new generation to accept as a natural part of life being watched and inspected, if we allow our privacy and civil rights to be slowly eroded, and if we lose opportunities to develop human relationships, who would say that these were unintended consequences? We know, for example, that as the technology becomes more integral to the everyday running of schools—as "networks," "integration," and "scalability" increase—schools and other institutions will not be able to function without the newest stuff. It is quite possible that we will forget that there was a time when schools did not have all this military-like equipment. How do we get back to those days if we cannot even imagine them or remember them? Do we, in fact, want to get back to those days, or are such yearnings a matter of misguided nostalgia—of being old-fashioned?

Some would say that the kinds of violations that the ACLU talks about need not happen. You will hear the old saw about it being people who do harm, not the thing: it is not the metal detector that violates a student's privacy, but the guard who is using it in an unjust way. But there is a fine line between what is permitted and what is not, and the equipment is far from benign, for it is meant to find out about us, to record us, to gather information about us, and to keep us out of places or keep us in—this is what it is supposed to do. When something goes too far, it may be a guard who has gone too far, but this is very easy to do with a device that is specifically made to unearth nearly everything about us.

The issue is not how far do we let others go with techno-security; rather, how far do *we* go? You want that nice house in the suburbs or that fancy apartment in the trendy neighborhood? It has a built-in surveillance system, which you end up paying for with your mortgage, rent, or co-op fees. You want that cell phone? It comes with a GIS system that can be used to locate its bearer so that worried parents can keep tabs on their kids—a technology first developed so soldiers could hone in on a cell-phone-carrying enemy, sometimes for a missile strike. You want to attend a nice public school? You will find it well secured, with security equipment networked into the management system of the entire school—your tax dollars at work. Of course, there are times when security is put in place against our will or without us knowing about it; but the idea that it is some authoritarian organization above us that is setting up the equipment to keep down little people is a single-dimensional way of looking at techno-security fortification. In some ways, security businesses must love the Big Brother story. What better way to divert attention? While the critics are clamoring about government oppression and a surveillance society gone awry, businesspeople are trotting out their wares for thousands of willing customers. They take what the critics say, refute them—they feel insulted, they think the critics are a bunch of loonies—then take that idea of a surveillance society gone awry and turn it into a cute advertisement. You're on surveillance camera ten times a day. Are you dressed for it?

Making a Place Safe

This book does not focus on what we should do to make places safer. The focus is primarily on what has promoted the fortification, not whether it is good or bad, and if bad, what alternatives we should seek. But the research has given me a perspective on security that has changed the way I think about the equipment and what I feel should be done to make places such as schools safer. When judging the appropriateness of a particular security system, I used to want to know about the equipment and what it can do and not do. Certainly, I still want to know this, but I also want to know about the business that goes on behind the scenes—how is it that the equipment has become an option for schools, and, if the equipment is already installed, how did it get there?

Ultimately, I have become critical of *stuff*—given what I have seen, read, and heard from vendors, I worry that safety comes with a price tag. While there may always be an aspect of safety that is achieved through the use of devices by people who can afford them, it seems to me that safety is more likely to be genuine if there are not huge profits being made from it. There are ways of creating safe places that cost little money. Many of the ideas put forth in Crime Prevention through Environmental Design (CPTED) seem to make sense and do not always require large sums of money. Naturally, CPTED has its security businesses and architectural firms that profit, but the ideas and strategies in CPTED can be incorporated (and some can be ignored, if appropriate) when general facility improvements are being done or when new schools are built. Additionally, there have been numerous books and articles written about the benefits of peace education, violence prevention, and conflict resolution strategies that are worth looking at as alternatives to techno-security fortification.[5] Also, some use of techno-security can help, especially if it is combined with CPTED and efforts in the school to improve relationships and help youths with problems. Given the reality of violence, it is not reasonable to say that we must do away with all security equipment. It seems to me that minimal use of techno-security can go a long way, but the problem is that even minimal use is becoming passé. There are all kinds of incentives and aspects of techno-security that make it necessary to get a "complete package" of units that are integrated and networked into other school management mechanisms. Businesses are driving this, because they know that selling a school a single metal detector or even a few cameras is not as profitable as selling them a larger package.

In our efforts to make places safer, if we just increase the technology without improving relationships and without solving problems that make it more likely that violence will occur, then we are misguided. Making schools safe will happen when our society becomes a safer place, and that will happen when circumstances and behaviors in our world are improved so that people act peacefully. Technology cannot do this. No matter how advanced the device is, it will never be able to solve underlying causes and circumstances that lead to wrongdoing. Regardless of our social views, or whether we blame lack of self-control, poor character, poverty, lack of moral values, desperation, or socialization for violence—whatever reason we may give for why we have violence—few of those reasons will be solved with techno-stuff. Technology does not solve poverty, and it will not give us greater moral values. Even with the technology and know-how to end starvation, people still go hungry; we have the technologies to live comfortable lives in peace, but we do not do it. It takes brainpower and will to make a world safer; it takes people who commit to a life of care, in which individuals genuinely make efforts to be good to each other, not only in rhetoric but also in their actions. This does not make violence go away, but neither does techno-security. The difference is that one takes true will and clear thinking, and the other costs a bundle of money.

Security professionals do not provide us with safety; they sell fortresses. Fortresses make them money. Safety is an abstraction, and there's no money in that. What we get are fortress schools, fortress shopping malls, fortress neighborhoods, and even fortress personal zones, which we agree to assume make us safer. Those promoting the fortification, and those who buy into it, will shape how we live and what places such as schools will look like, how we will be policed, how we will fight wars, how information about us will be kept and used, and how we will go about our everyday business. It is likely that we will live in a kind of cyborg land where almost everything we do is mediated through technology and where technology becomes so much a part of us that we feel exposed, in danger, and unprepared without it.

No doubt, we are creating a system of security that will have implications for years to come—that is obvious to everyone, regardless of their positions on it. If we compare security in the early twenty-first century to transportation in the mid-twentieth century, we get a good sense of how new "systems" are put into place and with what kinds of implications. In the 1950s in the United States, businesses, federal policies, and military directives made the highway system a reality—much like what has happened with security in the early twenty-first century. In the 1950s, cars were marketed, people bought them, and the 1956 National Defense Highway Act provided funding that made highway development a matter of national security. Policies were put in place to make car culture affordable and enticing to the middle classes. Road work created jobs. People zipped along highways and liked the feel of it. Essentially, the 1950s was a juncture when transportation went in a particular direction, with clear long-term implications, and due to specific policies and transactions.

The United States (and other countries) is at a similar juncture with security, with a similar cast of characters behind it. But the juncture is quickly passing. Those with the power and resources to promote the techno-security system have kicked into high gear with policies, laws, and taxpayer money. The military and national security directives are in place. Security businesses have established themselves and people are buying like mad. The products look good. New jobs have been created; even facility engineers, architects, general contractors and techies have found a profitable niche. And the equipment: It can make you better than human, give you a leg-up in the rat race of life, increase your assets, and make your life a happy, comfortable, and efficient one—as any security professional will tell you. But this is not really about safety. What is called "safety" or "security" is the slant that is given to the technology-thing to make the sale, a way of defining an item to make it appealing and seem like a necessary accessory to any worthwhile life. The days of brutish spy devices and of henchmen in the corners are gone, having been replaced with a world of mass appeal, where even things like love and companionship and of course safety are bought on the open market and provided by professionals in the business. But where is the safety in any of this? What we are talking about here is the beauty of business—the promise of private enterprise. All we have to do is pay for it.

And where do schools fit in? What part do they have in all this? In many ways, schools are no different from other places that have fortified in recent years; they reflect the security industry's success in broadening their market beyond military and policing sectors and into public and private sectors. But schools are also unique, because the security equipment is used primarily to oversee youths (and increasingly school employees and parents) and is therefore used in a targeted way. The idea that techno-security oversees everyone, as security vendors claim, is not entirely correct when it comes to schools. Not only is the surveillance targeted, it is installed in places where people are compelled to go. To some extent, many adults can limit their part in the techno-security fortification (though this is becoming more improbable), but students cannot. Schools also socialize youths to the norms and manners of society, and in the techno-security school, they are given the impression that life should be fortified. The techno-security fortification of schools also shows us that businesses have won out in determining how we will become safer—we will do it with gizmos, the kinds of stuff they sell. More advanced technology will be developed and upgraded forms will be passed on from generation to generation; fortification will stretch through lifetimes—from schooling to elderly care. Schools also show the extent of fortification in the larger society. By the time military gear starts making its way into schools, the fortification of a society is already on its way to becoming complete.

Appendix

Overview of Research

Selling Us the Fortress is based on four years of research on the security industry and its growing relationship with schools. The research involved the following:

- Participant observations and field note taking at security industry conferences, trade shows, and training sessions
- Interviews with security industry professionals and consultants
- Analyses of security industry trade magazines, pamphlets, advertisements, and Internet postings
- Data collection through telephone discussions and e-mail exchanges with security professionals
- Reviews of law cases related to techno-security devices, as well as earlier precedents involving search and seizure, privacy, and information gathering
- Analyses of federal documents and manuals related to security and schooling

From 2000 to 2004, I attempted to immerse myself in the security industry. I did this by attending security conferences and interviewing security professionals; reading the trade magazines, newsletters, and Internet postings distributed in the business; participating in e-mail exchanges with security professionals; attending training sessions; and calling and e-mailing sales representatives about equipment and developments between schools and security businesses. Much of the research was conducted by being involved in activities that are open to the public and by having informal interviews and conversations with security professionals. Part of the strength of the research is that it was conducted by doing what anybody can do; therefore, I was able to explore the "natural environment" of the security industry and understand not only the "hard facts" but also the culture of the industry and its everyday workings. The research was systematic to the extent that I planned the procedures of the research in advance and had certain goals about how many security professionals I would interview, how many conferences I would attend, how many advertisements I would analyze, and so on. I kept detailed notes, which were analyzed according to qualitative research methods. However, the research was also less than rigid in that I did not determine in advance a completion date for the research, but waited until I reached data saturation—where data began repeating and no new information emerged—before concluding the study. I was also open to modifications in the research and changed my methods when I found them unsuitable, as discussed in the section on semistructured and informal interviews.

Observations at Conferences, Trade Shows, and Training Sessions

I attended three major security industry conferences. Two were international, and one was a national conference. Two (one international and one national) also included a trade show and training sessions. In order to preserve confidentiality, I will describe the research I conducted at each, but not name the conferences.

Conference 1

The first conference I attended was in 2001 and was organized by a security industry group that specializes in organizing international conferences. The conference lasted for two days. Each day involved a series of presentations by some of the most prominent CEOs and presidents in the security business, and many of the largest and most successful companies were represented. The conference ended with a panel discussion that included people, such as the lawyer and the police chief mentioned in Chapter 5, who were not in the private security business per se. The conference did not focus on school security in particular, but there was much discussion about schools and allusions to school security. The conference was attended by about 1,200 security professionals, most of whom were vendors, sales representatives, consultants, and other midlevel professionals in the business. There were also several informal activities that were part of the conference (dinner, tours, and a cocktail party).

I observed nearly all of the presentations at this conference. When not attending the presentations, I interviewed individuals attending the conference, especially those who dealt with schools. During the conference I took copious field notes, asked questions during the question-and-answer portion of presentations, spoke to eight presidents and CEOs after their presentations, and interviewed eight security professionals. These ranged from semistructured to informal interviews. I also spoke informally with security professionals and told them about my research in order to get feedback from them. Additionally, I collected the names and contact information of people who agreed to be interviewed at a later date. I also collected written information, including trade magazines, advertisements, notices, newsletters, and books.

Conference 2

The second international conference I attended was in 2002 and was organized by one of the largest and most esteemed associations in the industry. There were about 17,000 attendees, and presentations were given by not only company presidents and CEOs but also a general in the military and a senator. The conference also included a trade show and training sessions. The training sessions were hosted by companies that wanted to teach individuals about their equipment and how to use particular devices. The conference included over 2,200 booths representing over 800 companies. Each booth was attended by sales representatives and vendors, and had much written information. The conference was attended by all levels of security professionals: end users, vendors, sales representatives, consultants, and high-level management. The items on display included nearly all forms of security—from razor wire fencing to facial recognition technology.

I attended two presentations on institutional (including school) security and wrote field notes based on these presentations. However, I spent most of my time at the trade show and interviewing security professionals. I visited thirty booths that showed some connection to school security and attended a training session on the use of metal detectors. After visiting each booth, I wrote field notes about what I observed and learned from talking to the sales representatives. At four booths, I was able to conduct interviews with six security professionals. I also conducted three more interviews at the end of the conference. However, much of my information came from informal interviews and conversations with attendees and sales representatives at the booths. I was also able to use security devices at the booths and have them used on me. I collected information from each booth I visited and put myself on their e-mail lists in order to receive further information and to have a contact for asking questions later.

Conference 3

The last conference I attended, in 2004, was organized by a prominent national security organization. Slightly less prominent than the organization hosting Conference 2, the organization, nevertheless, is among the major security groups and includes security professionals, consultants, engineers, and those in technology and architecture fields. The organization holds two conferences each year, one in the eastern region of the United States and one in the western region. I attended the one in the East. In organization, the conference was almost identical to Conference 2, though on a smaller scale. There were presentations by prominent individuals in the security industry, a trade show, and training sessions. There were about 8,000 attendees at the conference and about 450 companies represented.

The research I conducted was similar to the research I conducted at Conference 2. However, I did not attend any conference presentations. Instead, I attended two training sessions. The first was hosted by a large security corporation that sold software for security cameras. At the training session, I watched a demonstration of the software and used the computer to program surveillance cameras. The second training session was on infrared surveillance and was hosted by a midsized security company that specialized in school surveillance (among other applications). I watched a presentation by the owner of the company, then a demonstration of the cameras. Though I did not have an opportunity to use the equipment, I participated in a question-and-answer period, and was able to ask many questions about school applications of the equipment. I also interviewed six security professionals and, again, had many opportunities to talk to and informally interview security professionals, participate in discussions, observe interactions between vendors and conference attendees, and collect written materials.

Semistructured and Informal Interviews

I conducted two forms of interviews. Early in the research, I tried to conduct formal interviews and found that this was an inappropriate means of gathering data. Whenever I tried to tape-record interviews, individuals became very guarded, and the act of tape-recording disrupted the natural environment. People were especially guarded following the 2001 attacks in New York City and Washington, D.C., so that any sign that I was prying into the security business or documenting security information caused me to be viewed as suspect.

Hence, I conducted twenty-three semistructured interviews with security professionals that were much more informal than I had originally intended. During these interviews I sometimes took notes, but often found that extensive note taking (like tape-recording) caused participants to feel self-conscious and caused a rift in our exchanges. Therefore, during interviews I kept my note taking to a minimum, often just jotting down statistics and other kinds of information that would be impossible to remember but would jog my memory later when writing more extensive notes after the interviews. Sometimes conducted in lunchrooms, sometimes at vendors' booths, and sometimes while standing at a trade show, these interviews lasted for about 20–60 minutes. The majority of individuals I interviewed were sales representatives, distributors, and vendors. However, I also interviewed five executives (CEOs and presidents of companies), two architects, and three security consultants.

In addition to these semistructured interviews, I conducted many informal interviews. These interviews were often impromptu opportunities to talk to and question a particular person in detail. Often, conversations would become informal interviews. When this occurred, I would tell the person that I was conducting research and then seek permission to ask questions. I conducted about twenty informal interviews in this way. Often, I used these opportunities to test some of my ideas and conclusions and to get clarification about topics raised in presentations and in other interviews. Additionally, I followed up some of these interviews with e-mail exchanges, sometimes immediately after a conference and in some cases months after our initial interviews. In addition to these interviews, I also communicated with security professionals through e-mail and had conversations with individuals over the phone. While the data gained through semistructured and informal interviews were valuable, some of the best information came from the countless conversations and discussions I had (in person, by e-mail, and over the phone) with security professionals.

Analyses of Advertisements and Trade Literature

I collected advertisements from about seventy-five security companies. While this is a small percentage of actual companies, it includes some of the better-known companies, a mix of large and small companies, and, most significantly, those companies that market to schools. Since 2001, I have received thousands of pages of advertisements (along with pamphlets, newsletters, videos, and press releases). These were sent to me by mail; also, I received many advertisements by e-mail. Most of the advertisements were sent to me as a result of visiting company booths at trade shows; I also went on company websites to look at advertisements and to request further information; and, finally, I called companies in order to receive their advertisements and to talk to sales representatives.

When I received advertisements, I analyzed them in three ways. First, I read through them to find references to school security. The second step was to read through the school-related advertisements for basic information about the companies, equipment, prices, and other kinds of factual information. I kept notes on each of the companies and made copies of intriguing illustrations. After getting this basic information, I read the advertisements in a more critical way in order to draw conclusions about how items were sold, how individuals were represented, how images were used, and other kinds of textual points. Sometimes I would follow up my readings of advertisements with phone calls to sales representatives in order to ask questions about particular items. Most often, though, I received phone calls from sales representatives after they had sent me advertisements. I often used these opportunities to ask questions and to seek informal interviews.

I also read several of the primary magazines in the security industry, especially *American School and University, Security Management, Access Control and Security Systems*, and *Security News*. As with the advertisements, I read these first to find references to schools, then for factual information, and then for textual points. I also read the magazines to keep informed about security events such as conferences and training sessions, and to keep in touch with industry news and developments. I also collected the advertisements that appeared in the magazines and kept a collection of articles that were about school security.

Other Research: Document Analyses and Law Reviews

In order to learn about federal policies and laws related to security, I obtained and studied many primary sources. These primary sources included policy documents, statistical reports, congressional records, and court rulings. I also examined manuals and guidebooks distributed by governmental agencies, professional organizations in the security industry, and businesses. Finally, I relied on law journals and several information databases for secondary sources.

A Note on Method

The research methods are rooted in qualitative sociology. I sought to understand the everyday workings of the security industry by being a semi-impartial observer of it. Since most data involved the collection and interpretation of field notes, interviews, and security literature, I was aware that my perspective inevitably influenced what kinds of data I collected and how I interpreted them. Therefore, I sought to gather multiple forms of data and to check my conclusions against these other data—in a manner often referred to as "continuous comparison." I also expressed my forming ideas to security professionals in order to get their feedback. The research methods were chosen because they helped me to study security equipment in schools within its economic, political, and judicial contexts. This is a political economy approach that tries to understand how lives and circumstances we experience are influenced by market forces, politics, and other overarching structural realities that often take place outside the purview of the common citizen. No doubt, the methods have their limitations—there were times when I felt there was a need to focus on school-based issues related to security and not just on the corporate, political, and judicial factors promoting it. But there has been much fine work done that has focused on schools themselves; and what much of this literature points to is the fact that schooling is linked to larger contexts that also need to be understood, which is the intention of this book.

Notes

Introduction: Getting Down to the Business of Being Safe

1. Cited in Michelle Light, "Scoop from the Loop," e-mail bulletin from the Children & Family Justice Center, Northwestern University Legal Clinic, 2002, m-light@law.northwestern.edu.
2. Though security vendors began focusing on the housing market in the 1980s, which is when equipment was becoming more affordable for the middle classes, the 1990s saw continued growth in the home security market, and, for the most part, the installation of home security equipment was more common among the wealthy. In the 1990s, the home security business grew at an annual rate of 10 percent and was a $14 billion a year business by the end of the decade; 39 percent of houses costing $300,000 or more have security systems, whereas only 9 percent costing $100,000 or less have security systems. Meanwhile, poorer households are much more likely to be burglarized than richer households. This information is found in Christian Parenti, *The Soft Cage: Surveillance in America from Slavery to the War on Terror* (New York: Basic Books, 2003), 192.
3. David Lyon, *The Electronic Eye: The Rise of Surveillance Society* (Minneapolis: University of Minnesota Press, 1994).
4. Craig D. Uchida, Edward Maguire, Shellie E. Solomon, and Megan Gantley, *Safe Kids, Safe Schools: Evaluating the Use of Iris Recognition Technology in New Egypt, NJ.* (Washington, D.C.: U.S. Department of Justice, December 2004), www.ncjrs.org.

5. In order to protect the identity of the school, police officer, and guard, I am not giving an exact citation of the article. The article appeared in *American School & University*.

6. "Reoccurring revenue" is an important aspect of selling security equipment. It refers to the fact that security equipment will require of the buyer continual payments for upgrades and maintenance of the equipment.

7. For a description of the research methods, see the appendix.

8. In 2003, video cameras documented a raid by South Carolina police on a high school in Goose Creek. During the raid, over one hundred students were detained, and many were forced to lie on the floor with their arms outstretched while police searched them for drugs. Some of the police were shown with their guns drawn. There had been reason to believe that some of the students were selling drugs in the school, but drugs were not found. In the days following the airing of the surveillance camera images on national news, there were complaints made about the aggressive raid, but not about the surveillance cameras.

9. American Civil Liberties Union, "ACLU Asks Arizona School District to Reject Face-Recognition Checkpoints," December 17, 2003, www.aclu.org.

Chapter 1: The Security Industry and the Public School Market

1. Alan Matchett, *CCTV for Security Professionals* (New York: Butterworth-Heinemann, 2002), 128.

2. Bryan Vossekuil and Robert A. Fein, codirectors, with Marisa Reddy, Randy Borum, and William Modezeleski, *The Final Report and Findings of the Safe School Initiative: Implications for the Prevention of School Attacks in the United States*, May (Washington, D.C.: U.S. Secret Service and U.S. Department of Education, 2002), www.secretservice.gov/ntac/ssi_final_report.pdf.

3. Ibid., 18.

4. Ibid., 41.

5. Bryan Vossekuil, Marisa Reddy, and Robert Fein, codirectors, *Safe School Initiative: An Interim Report on the Prevention of Targeted Violence* (Washington, D.C.: U.S. Secret Service, October 2000), www.secretservice.gov/ntac/ntac_ssi_report.pdf.

6. Robert A. Fein and Bryan Vossekuil, *Protective Intelligence Threat Assessment Investigations: A Guide for State and Local Law Enforcement Officials* (Washington, D.C.: U.S. Department of Justice, Office of Justice Programs, National Institute of Justice, 1998).

7. Mary Ellen O'Toole, *The School Shooter: A Threat Assessment Perspective* (Washington, D.C.: Federal Bureau of Investigations, U.S. Department of Justice, n.d.).

8. Ibid.

9. Gil-Patricia Fey, Ron. J. Nelson, and Maura L. Roberts, "The Perils of Profiling," *School Administrator* 57 (2000): 12–16; and Scot Lafee, "Profiling Bad Apples," *School Administrator* 57 (2000): 6–11.

10. Gayle Tronvig Carper and Steven Rittenmeyer, "In Search of Klebold's Ghost: Investigating the Legal Ambiguities of Violent Student Profiling," in *Balancing Rights: Education Law in a Brave New World*, 2002 Conference Papers, ed. Education Law Association (Dayton, Ohio: Education Law Association, November 2002), 185–98.

11. Ibid.

12. National Center for Education Statistics, U.S. Department of Education, Fast Response Survey System (FRSS), "Principal/School Disciplinary Survey on School Violence," FRSS Form no. 63 (Washington, D.C.: U.S. Department of Education, 1997), http://nces.ed.gov/programs/crime/ pdf/principal/schlViolence.pdf.

13. National Center for Education Statistics, U.S. Department of Education, "Public and Public Charter School Surveys," Schools and Staffing Survey (SASS) (Washington, D.C.: U.S. Department of Education, 1999–2000).

14. This information can be found in Christian Parenti, *The Soft Cage: Surveillance in America from Slavery to the War on Terror* (New York: Basic Books, 2003). The concerns over the "tagging" of citizens turned out to be justified: the company Addressograph Corporation did develop a prototype metal tag that it presented to the Social Security Board, though it was not approved.

15. Cited in Michelle Light, "Scoop from the Loop," e-mail bulletin from the Children & Family Justice Center, Northwestern University Legal Clinic, 2002, m-light@law.northwestern.edu.

16. "Networked Security: Analog Cameras and Video Servers Improve School Safety and Security," *American School & University* 77 (February 2004, school security suppl.): SS16.

17. All company-based publications sent via direct mail or e-mail are in the possession of the author. WebEyeAlert, "WebEyeAlert Web-Based Surveillance Technology Used in School Emergency Exercise," e-mail advertisement, Chelmsford, Massachusetts, and Littleton, Colorado, June 12 (WebEyeAlert, a division of Biscom, Inc. , 2003).

18. "Securing the Bus Ride: Digital Recording Systems Save Money and Improve Security," *American School & University* 76 (September 2003, school security suppl.): SS16.

19. Ibid.

20. IR Security & Safety, "Engineered Solutions for High-Abuse Environments," brochure (IR Security & Safety, 2001), inside front cover; and "Crosswinds Arts and Science Middle School," *American School & University* 75 (November 2002): 88.

21. Oscar Newman, *Defensive Space: Crime Prevention through Urban Design* (New York: Collier, 1976); also noted in John Fay, *Encyclopedia of Security Management: Techniques and Technology* (Boston: Butterworth-Heinemann, 1993), 200.

22. Tod Schneider, Hill Walker, and Jeffrey Sprague, *Safe School Design: A Handbook for Educational Leaders* (Eugene, Ore.: ERIC Clearinghouse on Educational Management, 2000).

23. Buck Simpers, "Safety First: Creating a Safe Environment Includes More than Just a Locked Door," *American School & University* 77 (February 2004, school security suppl.): 12

24. Both quotations are from the Architectural Portfolio distributed annually by *American School & University*. The first quotation is in the Architectural Portfolio, *American School & University* 76 (November 2003): 111; and the second is in the Architectural Portfolio, *American School & University* 75 (2002): 95.

25. Philips Communication, Security, & Imaging, "Easyline 2002/2003," advertisement booklet, inside front cover.

26. Ibid., 44.

27. IR Security & Safety, "Engineered Solutions for High-Abuse Environments," inside front cover.

28. Cited in David Lyon, *The Electronic Eye: The Rise of Surveillance Society* (Minneapolis: University of Minnesota Press, 1994).

29. Edward Blakely and Mary Gail Snyder, *Fortress America: Gated Communities in the United States* (Washington, D.C.: Brookings Institution Press, 1997); and Setha Low, *Behind the Gates: Life Security, and the Pursuit of Happiness in Fortress America* (London and New York: Routledge, 2003).

30. Bosch Security Escort Systems/Installation Success Story, "A Healthy Recipe for Senior Independence with Security," news release, www.boschsecurity.us/securityescort.

31. Ibid.

32. See Christian Parenti, *The Soft Cage: Surveillance in America from Slavery to the War on Terror* (New York: Basic Books, 2003), 173.

33. Ibid.

34. Matt Richtel, "A Student ID That Can Also Take Roll," *New York Times*, Wednesday, November 17, 2004, A24; for an interesting description of such technology, see Jennifer McCormick, *Writing in the Asylum: Student Poets in New York City Schools* (New York: Teachers College Press, 2004).

35. Chicago's security system is one of many in the United States. Other cities include Baltimore, three cities in New Jersey (Newark, South Orange, and Dover), Memphis, Tampa Bay, Virginia Beach, and San Diego. In 1993, Tacoma, Washington, became one of the first cities in the United States to install surveillance cameras in a residential neighborhood. The cameras were installed with community support and with the help of a community group who worked with the police and secured a $125,000 federal grant to install three pan-tilt-zoom cameras on light poles. In 1997, the Tacoma police reported a dramatic drop in crime in the area. From a high of 224 reported incidents in 1993, in 1994 there were 87 incidents and in 1995 only 125 reported incidents. See Marcus Nieto, *Public Video Surveillance: Is It an Effective Crime Prevention Tool?* (Sacramento: California Research Bureau, 1997).

36. Stephen Kinzer, "Chicago Moving to 'Smart' Surveillance Cameras," *New York Times*, Tuesday, September 21, 2004, A18.

37. Cited in ibid.

38. Pauline Lipman, "Making the Global City, Making Inequality: The Political Economy and Cultural Politics of Chicago School Policy," *American Educational Research Journal* 39 (2002): 379–422.

39. Pauline Lipman, "Cracking Down: Chicago School Policy and the Regulation of Black and Latino Youth," in *Education as Enforcement: The Militarization and Corporatization of Schools*, ed. K. Saltman and D. Gabbard (New York: RoutledgeFalmer, 2003), 81–102.

40. *The Effect of Closed Circuit Television on Recorded Rates and Public Concern about Crime in Glasgow*, Crime and Criminal Justice Research Findings no. 30 (Glasgow: Scottish Office Central Research Unit, 1999), 2.

41. Paul Martin, "Square Gets Hip to Protection," *Security Management* (June 2001): 42–50.

42. See Alex Molnar, *Giving Kids the Business: The Commercialization of America's Schools* (Boulder, Colo.: Westview Press, 1996); also Alex Molnar, *School Commercialism: From Democratic Ideal to Market Commodity* (New York and London: Routledge, 2005).

43. Bosch Security Escort Systems/Installation Success Story, "A Healthy Recipe for Senior Independence with Security," news release, www.boschsecurity.us/securityescort.

Chapter 2: Selling Social Betterment for One's Own Private Utopia

1. Reported by Stephen Kinzer, "Chicago Moving to 'Smart' Surveillance Cameras," *New York Times*, Tuesday, September 21, 2004, A18.

2. Montner & Associates, "Grading Your School's Safety Plan," news release accompanying "Building Security, ESSEX, Building Safer Communities" advertisement materials (Montner & Associates, 2001). In the news release, the director of ESSEX's school safety division defined school violence prevention according to three main action plans (or prongs). These involved "preventive action" (violence prevention and conflict resolution programs), "physical security" (school lockdowns and access control), and "communication" (spreading information about new security installations and initiatives).

3. Ibid.

4. ESSEX Industries, "Complete Facility Security," brochure (ESSEX Industries, 2001), front cover.

5. Ibid.

6. Security businesses depend on the equipment developed for the military and with military funding. Private security firms also depend on police who provide training, buy equipment, and sometimes retire as police officers and work for security companies. To some extent these groups lose clear divisions, especially as companies contract with police departments and the military, and work together in training sessions, and as individuals move from group to group through career changes.

7. ESSEX Industries, "Complete Facility Security," back cover.

8. The program is conducted through a partnership with Diebold. In addition to Diebold's electronic security equipment, it has produced computerized voting machines, which were controversial during the lead-up to the 2004 presidential race. After the election, the machines caused more controversy, because people complained that votes cast on these machines were not being counted.

9. See Montner & Associates, "Grading Your School's Safety Plan."

10. Raymond Murphy, *Social Closure* (Oxford: Clarendon Press, 1988), 245.

11. For a good overview of research that has focused on professionals and issues related to occupations and work, see Keith MacDonald, *The Sociology of the Professions* (London: Sage, 1995).

12. See, for example, Émile Durkheim, *Professional Ethics and Civic Morals* (New York: Free Press, 1957); also, Talcott Parsons, "Professions and Social Structure," in Talcott Parsons, *Essays in Sociological Theory*, 34–49 (Glencoe, Ill.: Free Press, 1954).

13. See Howard S. Becker, Blanche Geer, Everett C. Hughes, and Anselm L. Strauss, *Boys in White: Student Culture in Medical School* (Chicago: University of Chicago Press, 1961); also Everett Hughes, *Men and Their Work* (New York: Free Press, 1958).

14. Everett Hughes, *On Work, Race, and the Sociological Imagination*, ed. Lewis Coser (Chicago: University of Chicago Press, 1994).

15. MacDonald, *The Sociology of the Professions*.

16. Garrett Super Wand, "A Revolutionary New Design for Security Screening," single-page advertisement (Garrett Super Wand, 2001).

17. Scott Lash and John Urry, *The End of Organized Capitalism* (Madison: University of Wisconsin Press, 1988).

18. Unlike industrial society, where quantities of laborers are needed and jobs are menial and repetitive, work in the United States and other postindustrial nations now relies on a slimmed-down crew of ambitious individuals willing to work odd hours, to travel, to relocate, and to change jobs easily. Labor has been mostly replaced by service industries and professional occupations (the white-collar, midlevel salary, or temporary workers), work is often more temporal and spatially dispersed (people can work for businesses from their homes hundreds of miles away and are quick to change jobs), technology has made work more efficient (hence, less workers are needed), and corporations are less devoted to particular places and operate in a more international world that stretches job opportunities across continents.

19. John Urry, *Consuming Places* (London and New York: Routledge, 1995), 90.

20. Barbara Ehrenreich, *Fear of Falling: The Inner Life of the Middle Class* (New York: Pantheon Books, 1989).

21. C. Wright Mills, *White Collar* (New York: Oxford University Press, 1951).

22. Suburban development has a long utopian history that can be seen in the bucolic names given to the earliest developments (Forest Hills, Riverside, etc.) and in the ideas of famous planners and visionaries, including Robert Owens and Charles Fourier, and more recently Frank Lloyd Wright and Oscar Newsman, who attempted to create the perfect life through planned

communities and architecture, and who profited from middle-class fears of crime, racial integration, and the deteriorating state of cities in the twentieth century. See Edward Blakely and Mary Gail Snyder, *Fortress America: Gated Communities in the United States* (Washington, D.C.: Brookings Institution Press, 1997).

23. See, for example, Barry Glassner, *The Culture of Fear* (New York: Basic Books, 1999).

24. Anthony Giddens, *The Consequences of Modernity* (Stanford, Calif.: Stanford University Press, 1990).

25. Joel Best, *Random Violence: How We Talk about New Crimes and New Victims* (Berkeley: University of California Press, 1999); and Glassner, *The Culture of Fear.*

26. Glassner, *The Culture of Fear,* xi.

27. Setha Low, *Behind the Gates: Life, Security, and the Pursuit of Happiness in Fortress America* (London and New York: Routledge, 2003).

28. Setha Low, "The Edge and the Center: Gated Communities and the Discourse of Urban Fear," *American Anthropologis* 103 (2001): 45–58.

29. Michael Davis, *City of Quartz: Excavating the Future of Los Angeles* (London: Verso, 1990); and Dennis Judd, "The Rise of New Walled Cities," in *Spatial Practices,* ed. H. Ligget and D.C. Perry (Thousand Oaks, Calif.: Sage, 1995), 144–65.

30. David Sibley, *Geographies of Exclusion* (London and New York: Routledge, 1995).

Chapter 3: The Safest Society That Technology Can Create and Money Can Buy

1. Sandia National Laboratories, "Funding for a School Security Center at Sandia Looking Brighter," news release, October 28, 1999, www.sandia.gov/media/NewsRel/NR.

2. The word "utopia," which many claim that Thomas More coined, has been translated from Greek to mean "no place" (u-topia) as well as "a good place" (eu-topia).

3. Cited in Constantine Hadjilambrinos, "Technological Regimes: An Analytical Framework for the Evaluation of Technological Systems," *Technology in Society* 20 (1998): 179–94, 181.

4. Hadjilambrinos, "Technological Regimes."

5. H.G. Wells, *A Modern Utopia* (1905; reprint, Lincoln: University of Nebraska Press, 1967); see especially the introduction by Mark Hillegas.

6. Nell Eurich, *Science in Utopia* (Cambridge, Mass.: Harvard University Press, 1967), 231–34.

7. Thomas More, *Utopia* (1516; reprint, New York: Penguin Books, 2003). See the introduction in Charles Andrews, *Famous Utopias* (New York: Tudor Publishing, 1937), for further information about the circumstance in England during the time when Thomas More was writing *Utopia.*

8. Joel Nelson and David Cooperman, "Out of Utopia: The Paradox of Postin-dustrialization," *Sociological Quarterly* 39 (1998): 584.

9. Lewis Mumford pointed out that the development of glass has had a profound effect on technological innovations, such as microscopes, mirrors, and telescopes, and has altered not only society but also the way people view and understand the world and themselves. Glass has also been integral to security technology in terms of bulletproof glass, one-way mirrors, and lenses for security cameras and lasers. Lewis Mumford, *Technics and Civilization* (New York: Harcourt Brace Jovanovich, 1934).

10. Max Weber, *The Theory of Social and Economic Organization* (New York: Oxford University Press, 1947), 251.

11. No author, "Integrated Technologies Spell Improved School Safety," *School & University Security*, October 2004, 10–14.

12. Julie K. Petersen, *Understanding Surveillance Technologies: Spy Devices, Their Origins & Applications*, ed. Saba Zamir (New York: CRC Press, 2000).

13. See Erik Robelen, "Unsafe Label Will Trigger School Choice," *Education Week*, October 23, 2002, 1.

14. See Tim Weiner, "Lockheed and the Future of Warfare," *New York Times*, November 28, 2004, C1.

15. Located in Albuquerque, New Mexico, Sandia employs more than 8,000 scientists, engineers, mathematicians, technicians, and support personnel.

16. Mike Kennedy, "Security: Making Contact," *American School & University* 74 (February 2001): 1–3.

17. Jake Wagman, "District Will Use Eye Scanning," *Philadelphia Inquirer*, October 24, 2002, www.philly.com. The U.S. Department of Justice funded the program on the condition that the school allow a third party to document the effectiveness of the system and people's attitude toward it; see also Craig D. Uchida, Edward Maguire, Shellie E. Solomon, and Megan Gantley, *Safe Kids, Safe Schools: Evaluating the Use of Iris Recognition Technology in New Egypt, NJ.* (Washington, D.C.: U.S. Department of Justice, December 2004), www.ncjrs.org.

18. Mary Green, *The Appropriate and Effective Use of Security Technologies in U.S. Schools* (Washington, D.C.: U.S. Department of Justice, Office of Justice Programs and National Institute of Justice with Sandia National Laboratories, 1999), exhibit 4.4 visual, p. 111; exhibit 3.10 visual, p. 88.

19. "Homeland Security Grants and Funding FY03," May 28, 2003, www.grantwriting.com/hsu2.html.

20. Securing America Investment Act of 2001, HR 2970 IH, 107th Congress, 1st sess.

21. Michelle Light, "Scoop from the Loop," e-mail bulletin from the Children & Family Justice Center, Northwestern University Legal Clinic, 2002, m-light@law.northwestern.edu.

22. P.J. Huffstutter, "A High School Where the Sensorship Is Pervasive," *Los Angeles Times*, September 8, 2002, A1.

23. Phil Sweeney, "With WebEye, Biscom Puts Video Security on the Web," *Boston Business Journal*, August 24–30, 2001, 1; and J. McVeigh, "School

Officials Hope Cameras Will Stop Threats," *Derry (New Hampshire) News* (n.d.). Both sources found in WebEyeAlert, a division of Biscom, "Professional Internet Live Video Monitoring and Intrusion Detection/Notification," brochure (WebEyeAlert, 2001), inside handout.

24. WebEyeAlert advertisement, "Professional Internet Live Video Monitoring and Intrusion Detection/Notification," inside pamphlet spread, 2003.

25. LG Electronics U.S.A., Inc., Iris Technology Division (LG Electronics U.S.A., Inc., 2002), single-page brochure.

26. Quoted in an address to attendees of the Securing New Ground Sixth Annual Conference, "The New World of Security," New York City, November 7–8, 2001.

27. See Dan Weisberg, "Scalable Hype: Old Persuasions for New Technology," in *Critical Studies in Media Commercialism*, ed. R. Anderson and L. Strate (Oxford: Oxford University Press, 2000), 186–200; and David Collingridge, *The Social Control of Technology* (New York: St. Martin's Press, 1980).

28. IR Interflex, InterAccess, a division of Ingersoll-Rand Company, advertisement pamphlet (IR Interflex, InterAccess, 2002), inside front cover.

29. CEIA USA Ltd., an ISO 9001 Company, single-page brochure (CEIA USA Ltd., 2002).

30. IR Interflex, InterAccess, advertisement pamphlet, inside front cover.

31. Arnold Pacey, *Meaning in Technology* (Cambridge, Mass.: MIT Press, 1999), 82.

32. Roland Barthes, *Mythologies* (New York: Farrar, Straus and Giroux, 1972).

33. Grocery stores are using finger scanners in order to verify customers who pay with checks, credit cards, or debit cards. The Pick 'n Save Metro Market, for example, uses finger scanners that were provided by the San Francisco-based company Pay By Touch. Before customers can pay by using the finger scanners, they complete an enrollment procedure, which requires them to have their fingers scanned, to have these scans saved in a database, and to give financial information. See Elizabeth Beaulieu, "Grocery Store Picks Biometrics," *Security Director News*, October 2004, 16.

34. Rhea Borja, "Finger-Scanning Technology Monitors School Employees," *Education Week*, October 23, 2002, 8.

35. Ibid.

36. Jane Wakefield, "A Face in the Crowd," *Mother Jones*, November–December 2001.

37. Ibid.

38 Samuel Nunn, "Police Technology in Cities: Changes and Challenges," *Technology in Society* 23 (2001): 11–27.

39. Howard Safir, *Security: Policing Your Homeland, Your State, Your City* (New York: St. Martin's Press, 2003).

40. The surveillance cameras on police cruisers are activated by a procedure (such as turning on the police car's headlights). The systems cost several thousand dollars per cruiser to install. The Cook County (Illinois) Sheriff's Department spent $4,400 for each car outfitted.

41. Nunn, "Police Technology in Cities: Changes and Challenges."

42. Marcus Nieto, *Public Video Surveillance: Is It an Effective Crime Prevention Tool?* (Sacramento, Calif.: California Research Bureau, 1997).

43. "Security Industry Requests Federal Surveillance Law," *Presstime Bulletin*, September 2001.

44. M. L. Elrick, "Cops Tap Database to Harass, Intimidate," *Detroit Free Press*, July 31, 2001, 1; and Avis Thomas-Lester and Toni Locy, "Chief's Friend Accused of Extortion," *Washington Post*, November 26, 1997, A01.

45. Justice Brown, "Maricopa County Tests Facial Recognition Technology in Schools," Center for Digital Education, May 2004, p. 1, www.centerdigitaled.com.

46. Mark Monmonier, *Spying with Maps: Surveillance Technologies and the Future of Privacy* (Chicago: University of Chicago Press, 2002), 172.

47. No Child Left Behind Act of 2001, HR 1, SEC. 9528, Armed Forces Recruiter Access to Students and Student Recruiting Information, www.ed.gov

48. Edward Tenner, *Why Things Bite Back: Technology and the Revenge of Unintended Consequences* (New York: Alfred Knopf, 1996); see also Paul Durbin, *Philosophy of Technology* (Boston: Kluwer Academic Publishers, 1989); and Harry Scarbrough and J. Martin Corbett, *Technology and Organization: Power, Meaning, and Design* (London and New York: Routledge, 1992).

49. Robert Romanyshyn, *Technology as Symptom and Dream* (London and New York: Routledge, 1989).

50. Anne Roe, "A Study of Imagery in Research Scientists," *Journal of Personality* 19 (1951): 459–70.

51. Arnold Pacey, *Meaning in Technology* (Cambridge, Mass.: MIT Press, 1999).

Chapter 4: The Promises of Techno-Security Fortification

1. Quotation is from a presentation that he gave at the Securing New Ground Sixth Annual Conference, "The New World of Security," November 2001, New York City.

2. This episode also occurred at the Securing New Ground Sixth Annual Conference, "The New World of Security," November 2001, New York City.

3. Ingersoll-Rand, the parent company of IR Interflex, is a multinational corporation serving customers in climate control, industrial productivity, infrastructure design, and security. Of its $9.7 billion worldwide annual sales, security and safety account for about $2 billion.

4. IR Interflex, "Interflex Product Overview: Technologies to Manage People, Openings, and Assets" (IR Interflex, 2002), 17.

5. Donna Haraway, *Simians, Cyborgs, and Women: The Reinvention of Nature* (London and New York: Routledge, 1991).

6. Denis O'Sullivan, "Sharing the Wealth: Spreading Security Information— and Its Value—across the Organization," *iSecurity*, August 2001, 12.

7. See School Buyers Online, "Londonderry School System: WebEyeAlert Makes the Grade," December 3, 2001, www.schoolbuyersonline.com.

8. Vigilos Avanta™, "Preliminary Documentation," submitted December 13, 2001, written and compiled by Brenda Snowden, end user liaison.

9. Lewis Mumford, *Technics and Civilization* (New York: Harcourt Brace & Company, 1934); see also Ronnie Casella, "The False Allure of Security Technologies," *Social Justice* 30 (2003): 82–93.

10. George Basalla, *The Evolution of Technology* (Cambridge: Cambridge University Press, 1988), 7–11.

11. Arnold Pacey, *Meaning in Technology* (Cambridge, Mass.: MIT Press, 1999).

12. SimplexGrinnell, a trademark of Tyco International Services AG, "Integrated Security: The Architects of a Secure World," brochure (SimplexGrinnell, 2002), inside back cover.

13. The following two company descriptions (for PacketVideo and Evolution Software, Inc.) are from the conference program for Securing New Ground Sixth Annual Conference, "The New World of Security," November 2001, New York City.

14. See, for example, Oscar Gandy, *The Panoptic Sort: A Political Economy of Personal Information* (Boulder, Colo.: Westview, 1993); David Lyon and E. Zureik, eds., *Surveillance, Computers, and Privacy* (Minneapolis: University of Minnesota Press, 1996); and Michel Foucault, *Discipline and Punish: The Birth of the Prison* (New York: Vintage Books, 1977).

15. Northern Computers, Inc., advertisement, *iSecurity*, August 2001, 7.

16. Ronnie Casella, "Security, Schooling, and the Consumer's Choice to Segregate," *Urban Review* 35 (2003): 129–48.

17. For a very good short overview of the development of private security, see Milton Lipson, "Private Security: A Retrospective," in *The Private Security Industry: Issues and Trends*, Annals of the American Academy of Political and Social Science, vol. 498, ed. Ira Lipman (Newbury Park, Calif.: Sage, 1988), 11–22.

18. Cited in Christian Parenti, *The Soft Cage: Surveillance in America from Slavery to the War on Terror* (New York: Basic Books, 2003), 145.

19. Ibid.

20. IR Interflex, "Interflex Product Overview," 1.

21. Videolarm, advertisement, *Security Magazine* 41, no. 10 (October 2004): 17.

22. Larry Cuban, *Oversold and Underused: Computers in the Classroom* (Cambridge, Mass. Harvard University Press, 2003).

23. Larry Cuban, *Teachers and Machines: The Classroom Use of Technology Since 1920* (New York: Teachers College Press, 1986).

Chapter 5: Horror Stories That Sell

1. Cited in Tyson Lewis, "The Surveillance Economy of Post-Columbine Schools," *Review of Education, Pedagogy, and Cultural Studies* 25 (2003): 335–55.

2. From "Datelines," *Access Control & Security Systems* 45 (December 2002): 4.

3. Reported by Andrea Gural, "Security Industry Ramps Up Suppliers," *Security Systems News* 4 (November 2001): 1.

4. For analyses of professional culture, see Eliot Freidson, *Professionalism Reborn* (Chicago: University of Chicago Press, 1994); Keith MacDonald, *The Sociology of the Professions* (London: Sage Publications, 1995); and Jeff Schmidt, *Disciplined Minds* (New York: Rowman & Littlefield Publishers, 2000).

5. Orson Welles, *The War of the Worlds*, radio broadcast, 1938, www.members. aol.com/jeff1070/wotw.html.

6. Hadley Cantril, *The Invasion from Mars* (New York: Harper & Row, 1940).

7. Barry Glassner, *The Culture of Fear* (New York: Basic Books, 1999), 208.

8. Silent Witness, "Camera Line-Up, Silent Witness Enterprises, Ltd.," brochure (Silent Witness, 2002), single-page ad.

9. Press Release, "The Protection Bureau Helps Increase School Bus Safety with Chaperone TV Monitoring Systems," November 17, 2003, www.security-net.com. Though its name is misleading, The Protection Bureau is a company that partnered with Silent Witness to install the cameras.

10. ADT, "Are You Still Relying on Traditional Security?" *Access Control & Security Systems* 45 (December 2002): 7.

11. Integral Technologies, "FirstLine Digital Surveillance," *American School & University* 75 (April 2002): 87.

12. CEIA, cover letter accompanying advertisements, September 18, 2002.

13. Garrett Metal Detectors, Garrett School Safety, "Walk-through & Hand-held Application: Washington D.C. Public Schools Motto: 'Children First,' Means Zero Tolerance for Weapons," advertisement flyer (Garrett Metal Detectors, 2002).

14. Garrett Metal Detectors, *Safe Schools*, videotape, 1999.

15. This scene was depicted in Michael Moore's movie *Bowling for Columbine*, 2002.

16. Metor, Metorex Security Products, "Metor Customer Reference List," June 4, 2002, sent with accompanying advertisements.

17. Metorex Security Products, An OSI Systems, Inc. Company, "RE: METOR Walk Through and Hand Held Metal Detectors As Advertised in School Construction News," cover letter, June 4 (Metorex Security Products, 2002).

18. Accessories for the Metorex metal detectors also included a wheel kit ($150), traffic counter ($440), and battery backup ($688).

19. See, for example, Judith Browne, *Derailed: The School to Jailhouse Track* (Washington, D.C.: Advancement Project, 2003); Ronnie Casella, "Punishing Dangerousness through Preventative Detention: Illustrating the Institutional Link between School and Prison," *New Directions for Youth Development: Research, Theory, and Practice* 99 (2003): 55–70; Jennifer McCormick, *Writing in the Asylum: Student Poets in City Schools* (New York: Teachers College Press, 2004); and Garrett Duncan, "Urban Pedagogies and the Celling of Adolescents of Color," *Social Justice* 27 (2000), 29–42.

20. See Elissa Gootman, "City Faces Criticism after Bronx Principal's Arrest," *New York Times*, February 9, 2005, www.nytimes.com.

21. WizKid OptoTech, "Extreme CCTV Surveillance Systems," information packet (WizKid OptoTech, 2001), 9.

22. Alan Matchett, *CCTV for Security Professionals* (New York: Butterworth-Heinemann, 2003).

23. WizKid OptoTech, "Extreme CCTV: ABC's of a WizKid Design," brochure (WizKid OptoTech, 2002), 1.

24. WizKid OptoTech, "Extreme CCTV Surveillance Systems," d3.

25. Press release by *TechBeat*, "SCORMAP Gets High Marks," National Law Enforcement and Corrections Technology Center, Spring 2004, www.nlectc.org/techbeat/spring 2004.

26. Jeff Lupinacci, "A Safe Haven," *American School & University* 75 (December 2002): 36–38.

27. Matchett, *CCTV for Security Professionals*.

28. The Technical Assistance Response Unit (TARU) has worked with the housing authority in New York City to install surveillance cameras in public housing units. The NYPD captain and director of TARU said that their priority was "to make the move into biometrics" and that they, like other police departments in the United States and in places such as the UK and Europe, were experimenting with microcameras on police uniforms outfitted with facial recognition technology.

29. The conference did not include a trade show, and most of the presenters were CEOs, company presidents, or senior managers, so the attorney and the police captain were ancillary presenters. At other conferences, ancillary presenters included generals in the military and Washington politicians, especially those associated with the U.S. Department of Defense. Usually they gave keynote addresses or, as in the case of this attorney and police captain, presented on a panel. Sometimes these ancillary presentations were meant to provide information to security equipment dealers and company owners about laws and pending legislation affecting private security. At other times, they were meant to raise the profile of the association sponsoring the event, as when high-ranking politicians and military officers spoke; under these circumstances, very little information was given, but instead the talks were more inspirational than informative, and were meant to highlight the importance and stature of the group. When this attorney spoke, however, he provided information about laws. He did not exactly raise the profile of the conference, but added to it a sense of self-reflection and awareness.

Chapter 6: Security, the Law, and Federal Policy

1. Both quotations are from "Video Monitoring Rekindles Privacy Debate," *Security Sales & Integration* 26 (October 2004): 44.

2. Ibid.

3. *Hester v. United States*, 265 U.S. 67 (1924).

4. *Olmstead v. United States*, 277 U.S. 438 (1928).

5. *Goldman v. United States*, 316 U.S. 129 (1942).
6. *Silverman v. United States*, 365 U.S. 505 (1961).
7. *Berger v. United States*, 288 U.S. 41 (1967).
8. *Katz v. United States*, 389 U.S. 347 (1967).
9. Scott Sher, "Continuous Video Surveillance and Its Legal Consequences," Public Law Research Institute, Working Papers Series, University of California Hastings College of the Law (San Francisco: Public Law Research Institute, 1996), 3.
10. Title III of the Omnibus Crime Control and Safe Streets Act of 1968, 82 Stat. 211, 18 U.S.C. Sec. 2510–20. In 1998, the Omnibus Crime Control and Safe Streets Act was amended to provide the first funding specified to support police officers in schools, thereby boosting the establishment of school resource officers.
11. Julie K. Petersen, *Understanding Surveillance Technologies: Spy Devices, Their Origins & Applications*, ed. Saba Zamir (New York: CRC Press, 2001).
12. *United States v. Torres*, 751 F. 2d 875, 876, Court of Appeals for the Seventh Circuit (1984).
13. *United States v. Knotts*, 468 U.S. 276 (1983).
14. *United States v. Sherman*, 990 F.2d. 1265, Court of Appeals for the Ninth Circuit (1993).
15. *United States v. Taketa*, 923 F.2d 665, 677, Court of Appeals for the Ninth Circuit (1991).
16. *United States v. Knotts*, 468 U.S. 276 (1983).
17. *Vega-Rodriguez v. Puerto Rico Tel. Co.*, 110 F.3d 174, Court of Appeals for the First Circuit (1997).
18. Even a case in 1999 (*C'Debaca v. Commonwealth* , 1999 Va. App. LEXIS 72 (Ct. of Appeals of Virginia, 1999) involving a man who used a spy camera to film underneath the skirt of a woman was excused on the basis that "although the appellant aimed his camera so that the lens pointed up the victim's dress, the victim had no reasonable expectation of privacy while standing on the public fairgrounds."
19. *Thompson v. Johnson City Community College*, 930 F. Supp. 501 (D. Kan. 1996), aff'd, 103 F. 3d 1388 (10th Cir. 1997); see also Colin Hatcher, "Silent Video Surveillance in the Absence of Probable Cause: A Brief Legal Checklist," 2001, www.Findlaw.com.
20. President Bill Clinton also signed the Gun-Free Schools Act of 1994, which mandated the expulsion of students for one school year if caught with a firearm, paving the way for broader zero tolerance policies in schools. He also signed the Safe Schools Act of 1994, which provided funds for violence prevention programs and some security measures.
21. In 2003, the U.S. Department of Justice, Federal Bureau of Investigation, and Drug Enforcement Administration began lobbying the Federal Communications Commission to propose that the Communications Assistance for Law Enforcement Act be expanded in order to require technology companies to install hardware on the latest telecommunication devices that would enable law enforcement personnel to wiretap the devices easily, and

that the costs associated with this be paid by companies that would be free to pass on the costs to consumers. The Communications Assistance for Law Enforcement Act of 1994 already requires companies to build into their devices items that would make it possible for authorities to wiretap, and the new amendment updated the law to include the newest technologies.

22. *In re Randy G.* (2001) 26 Cal.4th 556 [110 Cal.Rptr.2d 516]; see also Christopher Milligan, "Facial Recognition Technology, Video Surveillance, and Privacy," *Southern California Interdisciplinary Law Journal* 9 (1999): 295–333.

23. *New Jersey v. T.L.O.*, 469 U.S. 325 (1985).

24. Cases involving searches have also dealt with the use of drug-sniffing dogs and strip searches. In these cases, the powers of school authorities to conduct searches are limited. In 2003, the use of drug-sniffing dogs to search seventeen Native American students caused a public outcry and a lawsuit by the American Civil Liberties Union (*Shenona Banks et al. v. Wagner School Board*). The raid with the drug-sniffing dogs occurred in an elementary school and was conducted by the Bureau of Indian Affairs in the Wagner School District in South Dakota. Some of the students were in kindergarten, but authorities felt that this would be a good lesson for even the youngest and most innocent. The students were told to put their hands on their desks and to not touch the dogs. Then the dogs were led down the aisles of classrooms, sniffing at the students' legs, hips, and feet. Some of the students were so scared that they urinated in their pants. Ultimately, the school district agreed to not use the dogs in this way again. See American Civil Liberties Union press release, "South Dakota School Officials Terrorized Kindergarten Classes with Drug-Sniffing Dogs, ACLU Charges," July 25, 2002, www.aclu.org/DrugPolicy/.

25. Alana Keynes, "Security Guards Can Question Students Even in the Absence of Reasonable Suspicion," *Legal Update* 6 (2001): 9–10.

26. *Thomas v. Roberts*, 2003 WL 934249 (11th Cir. March 10, 2003).

27. Myrna Baskin and Laura Thomas, "School Metal Detector Searches and the 4th Amendment," *University of Michigan Journal of Law Reform* 19 (1986): 1037–1106.

28. Ibid., 1073.

29. *People v. Dukes*, 580 N.Y.S. 2d 850, New York Criminal Court (1992).

30. *State v. J.A.*, 679 So.2d 316 (Fla. 3rd DCA 1996); see also Lawrence Rossow and Jacqueline Stefkovich, *Search and Seizure in the Public Schools*, 2nd ed. (Topeka, Kans.: National Organization on Legal Problems of Education, 1995).

31. *People v. Pruitt*, 278 Ill. App. 3d 194, 208 (1996); other cases discussed in this paragraph include, *In the Interest of S.S.* 680 A.2d 1172 (Pa. Super. Ct. 1996); *The People of the State of California v. Latasha W.*, Super. Ct. No. YJ 12201 (1998), Court of Appeal of the State of California Second Appellate District; *In re F.B.*, 555 Pa. 661, 726 A.2d 361 (Pa. 1999); see also Jacqueline Stefkovich, "Search and Seizure of Students in Public Schools: 2002 Update of Fourth Amendment Cases," in *Balancing Rights: Education Law in a*

Brave New World, Conference Papers 2002, ed. Education Law Association, (Dayton, Ohio: Education Law Association, November 2002), 301–13.

32. *The People of the State of California v. Latasha W.*, Super. Ct. No. YJ 12201 (1998), Court of Appeal of the State of California Second Appellate District.

33. *Cason v. Cook*, 810 F. 2d 188, 192 (8th Cir. 1987); see also Stefkovich, "Search and Seizure of Students in Public Schools.".

34. Cited in Rossow and Stefkovich, *Search and Seizure in the Public Schools*, 41, referring to *United States v. Calandra*, 414 U.S. 338 (1974).

35. Cited in ibid., 42, referring to *Jones v. Latexo Independent School District*, 499 F. Supp. 223 (E.D. Tex. 1980).

36. Sara Doyle, "FERPA: What Exactly Is an Educational Record?" in *Balancing Rights: Education Law in a Brave New World*, Conference Papers 2002, ed. Education Law Association, (Dayton, Ohio: Education Law Association, November 2002), 271–78.

37. USA PATRIOT Act of 2001, HR 3162 RDS; No Child Left Behind Act of 2001, HR1, 20 USC 6301.

38. Doyle, "FERPA."

39. Lynn Daggett, "FERPA Update 2002: The Two New Supreme Court FERPA Cases, and Post 9/11 Congressional Balancing of Student Privacy and Safety Interests," in *Balancing Rights: Education Law in a Brave New World*, Conference Papers 2002, ed. Education Law Association (Dayton, Ohio: Education Law Association, November 2002), 255–69.

40. No Child Left Behind Act of 2001, HR 1, SEC. 9528, Armed Forces Recruiter Access to Students and Student Recruiting Information, www.ed.gov/policy/elsec/leg.

41. Daggett, "FERPA Update 2002."

Chapter 7: Transactions on the Open Market

1. Dwight D. Eisenhower, "Military-Industrial Complex Speech," January 17, 1961, Public Papers of the Presidents, Dwight D. Eisenhower, 1960, 1035–40, www.coursesa.matrix.msu.edu.

2. Steven Herbert, "Police Subculture Reconsidered," *Criminology* 36 (1998): 343–69.

3. See, for example, John Devine, *Maximum Security: The Culture of Violence in Inner-City Schools* (Chicago: University of Chicago Press, 1996); and Ronnie Casella, *Being Down: Challenging Violence in Urban Schools* (New York: Teachers College Press, 2001).

4. The Rudolph Giuliani claim that Howard Safir was the "greatest police commissioner in New York City's history," is stated on the front cover of Safir's book, *Security: Policing Your Homeland, Your State, Your City* (New York: St. Martin's Press, 2003); the quotation is from Safir's book, p. 27.

5. School resource officers and police officers working in schools were often trained to follow the principles of "community policing." One school resource officer described community policing as "a philosophy of law

enforcement in which police officers and private citizens work together in creative ways to help solve contemporary community problems, including crime, fear of crime, social and physical disorder, and neighborhood decay." See Michael Skelly, "The School Beat," *American School Board Journal* 184 (1997): 25–27.

6. Safir, *Security*, 33.

7. Reauthorization of Matching Grant Program for School Security, October 7, 2003, H.R. 2685.

8. See "Alarm Industry Coalition to Educate Law Enforcement Leaders," *Security Sales & Integration* 26 (October 2004): 16.

9. Samuel Nunn, "Police Technology in Cities: Changes and Challenges," *Technology in Society* 23 (2001): 12.

10. Nunn, "Police Technology in Cities," 13.

11. This information and statement by Jerry Dobson are in Mark Monmonier, *Spying with Maps: Surveillance Technologies and the Future of Privacy* (Chicago: University of Chicago Press, 2002). Jerry Dobson was critical of such devices and told the hypothetical story partly as a warning.

12. For an interesting analysis of JROTC, see Marvin Berlowitz and Nathan Long, "The Proliferation of JROTC: Education Reform or Militarization," in *Education as Enforcement: The Militarization and Corporatization of Schools*, ed. K. Saltman and David Gabbard (London and New York: Routledge, 2003), 163–76.

13. U.S. Department of Defense, "Today's Military—Life-Stories" (n.d.), www. todaysmilitary.com.

14. Tim Weiner, "A New Model Army Soldier Rolls Closer to the Battlefield," *New York Times*, February 16, 2005, A1.

15. C. Wright Mills, *The Power Elite* (Oxford: University of Oxford Press, 1956).

16. For a discussion of London's "ring of steel," see Jon Coaffee, *Terrorism, Risk and the City: The Making of a Contemporary Urban Landscape* (Aldershot, UK: Ashgate Publishing Company, 2003).

17. See Robert McCrie, "The Development of the U.S. Security Industry," in *The Private Security Industry: Issues and Trends*, Annals of the American Academy of Political and Social Science, vol. 498, ed. Ira Lipman (Newbury Park, Calif.: Sage, 1988), 23–33.

18. Denis O'Sullivan, "Sharing the Wealth: Spreading Security Information— and Its Value—across the Organization," *iSecurity*, August 2001, 1.

19. See, for example, John Urry, *Consuming Places* (London and New York: Routledge, 1995).

20. Some countries and some populations have benefited heartily while others have suffered from policies adapted often through economic organizations such as the World Bank and World Trade Organization that have pushed neoliberalism and the mantras of free trade and privatization. Increased travel and ease of communication have also bolstered economic internationalism, but so have policies that have reduced obstacles for businesses to make foreign direct investments, reduced tariffs and quotas on imports,

helped to privatize state-owned utilities, and relaxed border controls for goods.

21. For information about issues related to globalization as it relates to education, see David Bloom, "Globalization and Education: An Economic Perspective," in *Globalization: Culture and Education in the New Millennium*, ed. Marcelo M. Suarez-Orozco and Desiree Baolian Qin-Hilliard (Berkeley: University of California Press, 2004); P. Brown and H. Lauder, "Education, Globalization, and Economic Development," *Journal of Education Policy* 11 (1996): 1–25; and Carlos Alberto Torres, "Globalization, Education, and Citizenship: Solidarity versus Markets? *American Educational Research Journal* 39 (2002): 363–78.

22. Garrett Duncan, "Urban Pedagogies and the Celling of Adolescents of Color," *Social Justice* 27 (2000): 29–42.

23. This is a simplification of reality, of course, for it is too easy to say that the old blue-collar class is now driven to be the grunts for military exploits; but there is something to be said for the economic changes that have created circumstances where the only option for many young people with ambition is the military, which is, after all, advertised to them as an adventure, a means to an education and a career, and a way to get ahead in life (just as college is advertised to middle-class youths).

24. Michael Peters, James Marshall, and Patrick Fitzsimons, "Managerialism and Educational Policy in a Global Context: Foucault, Neoliberalism, and the Doctrine of Self-Management," in *Globalization and Education: Critical Perspectives*, ed. N. Burbules and C.A. Torres (London and New York: Routledge, 2000), 109–32.

25. This information is in Alex Molnar, *Giving Kids the Business: The Commercialization of America's Schools* (Boulder, Colo.: Westview, 1996).

Conclusion: The Big Business of Big Brother

1. Christopher Milligan, "Facial Recognition Technology, Video Surveillance, and Privacy," *Southern California Interdisciplinary Law Journal* 9 (1999): 295–333.

2. Mary Green, *The Appropriate and Effective Use of Security Technologies in U.S. Schools* (Washington, D.C.: U.S. Department of Justice, Office of Justice Programs and National Institute of Justice with Sandia National Laboratories, 1999).

3. See, for example, Cameron McCarthy, A.P. Rodriguez, E. Buendia, S. Meacham, S. David, H. Godina, K.E. Supriya, and C. Wilson-Brown, "Danger in the Safety Zone: Notes on Race, Resentment, and the Discourses of Crime, Violence and Suburban Security," *Cultural Studies* 11 (1997): 274–95; and Greg Dimitriadis and Cameron McCarthy, "Violence in Theory and Practice: Popular Culture, Schooling, and the Boundaries of Pedagogy," *Educational Theory* 29 (1999): 125–38.

4. Some of the evaluation research addressing these outcomes includes *The Effect of Closed Circuit Television on Recorded Rates and Public Concern*

about Crime in Glasgow, Crime and Criminal Justice Research Findings no. 30 (Glasgow: Scottish Office Central Research Unit, 1999); Jason Ditton and Emma Short, "Yes, It Works—No, It Doesn't: Comparing the Effects of Open-Street CCTV in Two Adjacent Town Centres," *Crime Prevention Studies* 10 (1999): 201–23; Marcus Nieto, *Public Video Surveillance: Is It an Effective Crime Prevention Tool?* (Sacramento: California Research Bureau, 1997); Dean Wilson and Adam Sutton, *Open-Street CCTV in Australia,* a report to the Criminology Research Council (Melbourne, Australia: Criminology Research Council, 2003); Clive Norris and Gary Armstrong, "CCTV and the Social Structuring of Surveillance," *Crime Prevention Studies* 10 (1999): 157–78; and Kate Painter and Nick Tilley, *Surveillance of Public Space: CCTV, Street Lighting and Crime Prevention* (New York: Criminal Justice Press, 1999).

5. See, for example, Ian Harris and Mary Lee Morrison, *Peace Education,* 2nd ed. (Jefferson, N.C.: McFarland Press, 2003); Pedro Noguera, *City Schools and the American Dream* (New York: Teachers College Press, 2003); Tianlong Yu, *In the Name of Morality* (New York: Peter Lang Publishing, 2004); Nan Stein, *Classrooms and Courtrooms: Facing Sexual Harassment in K–12 Schools* (New York: Teachers College Press, 1999); and Johanna Wald and Michal Kurlaender, "Connected in Seattle? An Exploratory Study of Student Perceptions of Discipline and Attachments to Teachers," *New Directions for Youth Development* 99 (2003): 35–54.

References

ADT. "Are You Still Relying on Traditional Security?" *Access Control & Security Systems* 45 (December 2002): 7.

"Alarm Industry Coalition to Educate Law Enforcement Leaders." *Security Sales & Integration* 26 (October 2004): 16.

American Civil Liberties Union. "ACLU Asks Arizona School District to Reject Face-Recognition Checkpoints." December 17, 2003. www.aclu.org.

Barthes, Roland. *Mythologies*. New York: Farrar, Straus and Giroux, 1972.

Basalla, George. *The Evolution of Technology*. Cambridge: Cambridge University Press, 1988.

Baskin, Myrna, and Laura Thomas. "School Metal Detector Searches and the 4th Amendment." *University of Michigan Journal of Law Reform* 19 (1986): 1037–1106.

Beaulieu, Elizabeth. "Grocery Store Picks Biometrics." *Security Director News*, October 2004, 16.

Becker, Howard S., Blanche Geer, Everett C. Hughes, and Anselm L. Strauss. *Boys in White: Student Culture in Medical School*. Chicago: University of Chicago Press, 1961.

Berlowitz, Marvin, and Nathan Long. "The Proliferation of JROTC: Education Reform or Militarization." In *Education as Enforcement: The Militarization and Corporatization of Schools*, edited by K. Saltman and David Gabbard, 163–76. London and New York: Routledge, 2003.

Best, Joel. *Random Violence: How We Talk about New Crimes and New Victims*. Berkeley: University of California Press, 1999.

Blakely, Edward, and Mary Gail Snyder. *Fortress America: Gated Communities in the United States*. Washington, D.C.: Brookings Institution Press, 1997.

Bloom, David. "Globalization and Education: An Economic Perspective." In *Globalization: Culture and Education in the New Millennium*, edited by Marcelo M. Suarez-Orozco and Desiree Baolian Qin-Hilliard. Berkeley: University of California Press, 2004.

Borja, Rhea. "Finger-Scanning Technology Monitors School Employees." *Education Week*, October 23, 2002, 8.

Bosch Security Escort Systems/Installation Success Story. "A Healthy Recipe for Senior Independence with Security." News release. www.boschsecurity. us/securityescort.

Brown, P., and H. Lauder. "Education, Globalization, and Economic Development." *Journal of Education Policy* 11 (1996): 1–25.

Browne, Judith. *Derailed: The School to Jailhouse Track*. Washington, D.C.: Advancement Project, 2003

Cantril, Hadley. *The Invasion from Mars*. New York: Harper & Row, 1940.

Carper, Gayle Tronvig, and Steven Rittenmeyer. "In Search of Klebold's Ghost: Investigating the Legal Ambiguities of Violent Student Profiling." In *Balancing Rights: Education Law in a Brave New World*, 2002 Conference Papers, edited by the Education Law Association, November, 185–98. Dayton, Ohio: Education Law Association, 2002.

Casella, Ronnie. *Being Down: Challenging Violence in Urban Schools*. New York: Teachers College Press, 2001.

———. "The False Allure of Security Technologies." *Social Justice* 30 (2003): 82–93.

———. "Punishing Dangerousness through Preventative Detention: Illustrating the Institutional Link between School and Prison." *New Directions for Youth Development: Research, Theory, and Practice* 99 (2003): 55–70.

———. "Security, Schooling, and the Consumer's Choice to Segregate." *Urban Review* 35 (2003): 129–48.

Coaffee, Jon. *Terrorism, Risk and the City: The Making of a Contemporary Urban Landscape*. Aldershot, UK: Ashgate Publishing, 2003.

Collingridge, David. *The Social Control of Technology*. New York: St. Martin's Press, 1980.

"Crosswinds Arts and Science Middle School." *American School & University* 75 (November 2002): 88.

Cuban, Larry. *Oversold and Underused: Computers in the Classroom*. Cambridge, Mass: Harvard University Press, 2003.

Cuban, Larry. *Teachers and Machines: The Classroom Use of Technology Since 1920*. New York: Teachers College Press, 1986.

Daggett, Lynn. "FERPA Update 2002: The Two New Supreme Court FERPA Cases, and Post 9/11 Congressional Balancing of Student Privacy and Safety Interests." In *Balancing Rights: Education Law in a Brave New World*, 2002 Conference Papers, edited by the Education Law Association, November, 255–69. Dayton, Ohio: Education Law Association, 2002.

"Datelines." *Access Control & Security Systems* 45 (December 2002): 4.

Davis, Michael. *City of Quartz: Excavating the Future of Los Angeles*. London: Verso, 1990.

Devine, John. *Maximum Security: The Culture of Violence in Inner-City Schools*. Chicago: University of Chicago Press, 1996.

Dimitriadis, Greg, and Cameron McCarthy. "Violence in Theory and Practice: Popular Culture, Schooling, and the Boundaries of Pedagogy." *Educational Theory* 29 (1999): 125–38.

Ditton, Jason, and Emma Short. "Yes, It Works—No, It Doesn't: Comparing the Effects of Open-Street CCTV in Two Adjacent Town Centres." *Crime Prevention Studies* 10 (1999): 201–23.

Doyle, Sara. "FERPA: What Exactly Is an Educational Record?" In *Balancing Rights: Education Law in a Brave New World*, 2002 Conference Papers, edited by the Education Law Association, November, 271–78. Dayton, Ohio: Education Law Association, 2002.

Duncan, Garrett. "Urban Pedagogies and the Celling of Adolescents of Color." *Social Justice* 27 (2000): 29–42.

Durbin, Paul. *Philosophy of Technology.* Boston: Kluwer Academic Publishers, 1989.

Durkheim, Émile. *Professional Ethics and Civic Morals.* New York: Free Press, 1957.

The Effect of Closed Circuit Television on Recorded Rates and Public Concern about Crime in Glasgow, Crime and Criminal Justice Research Findings no. 30. Glasgow: Scottish Office Central Research Unit, 1999.

Ehrenreich, Barbara. *Fear of Falling: The Inner Life of the Middle Class.* New York: Pantheon Books, 1989.

Eisenhower, Dwight D. "Military-Industrial Complex Speech." January 17, 1961. Public Papers of the Presidents, Dwight D. Eisenhower, 1960, 1035–40. www.coursesa.matrix.msu.edu.

Elrick, M. L. "Cops Tap Database to Harass, Intimidate." *Detroit Free Press*, July 31, 2001, 1.

Eurich, Nell. *Science in Utopia.* Cambridge, Mass.: Harvard University Press, 1967.

Fay, John. *Encyclopedia of Security Management: Techniques and Technology.* Boston: Butterworth-Heinemann, 1993.

Fein, Robert, and Bryan Vossekuil. *Protective Intelligence Threat Assessment Investigations: A Guide for State and Local Law Enforcement Officials.* Washington, D.C.: U.S. Department of Justice, Office of Justice Programs, National Institute of Justice, 1998.

Fey, Gil-Patricia, Ron Nelson, and Maura Roberts. "The Perils of Profiling." *School Administrator* 57 (2000): 12–16.

Foucault, Michel. *Discipline and Punish: The Birth of the Prison.* New York: Vintage Books, 1977.

Freidson, Eliot. *Professionalism Reborn.* Chicago: University of Chicago Press, 1994.

Gandy, Oscar. *The Panoptic Sort: A Political Economy of Personal Information.* Boulder, Colo.: Westview, 1993.

Giddens, Anthony. *The Consequences of Modernity.* Stanford, Calif.: Stanford University Press, 1990.

Glassner, Barry. *The Culture of Fear.* New York: Basic Books, 1999.

Gootman, Elissa. "City Faces Criticism after Bronx Principal's Arrest." *New York Times*, February 9, 2005. www.nytimes.com.

Green, Mary. *The Appropriate and Effective Use of Security Technologies in U.S. Schools.* Washington, D.C.: U.S. Department of Justice, Office of Justice Programs and National Institute of Justice with Sandia National Laboratories, 1999.

Gural, Andrea. "Security Industry Ramps Up Suppliers." *Security Systems News* 4 (November 2001): 1.

Hadjilambrinos, Constantine. "Technological Regimes: An Analytical Framework for the Evaluation of Technological Systems." *Technology in Society* 20 (1998): 179–94.

Haraway, Donna. *Simians, Cyborgs, and Women: The Reinvention of Nature*. London and New York: Routledge, 1991.

Harris, Ian, and Mary Lee Morrison. *Peace Education*, 2nd ed. Jefferson, N.C.: McFarland Press, 2003.

Hatcher, Colin. "Silent Video Surveillance in the Absence of Probable Cause: A Brief Legal Checklist." 2001. www.Findlaw.com.

Herbert, Steven. "Police Subculture Reconsidered." *Criminology* 36 (1998): 343–69.

"Homeland Security Grants and Funding FY03." May 28, 2003. www.grantwriting.com/hsu2.html.

Hughes, Everett. *Men and Their Work*. New York: Free Press, 1958.

———. *On Work, Race, and the Sociological Imagination*, edited by Lewis Coser. Chicago: University of Chicago Press, 1994.

Judd, Dennis. "The Rise of New Walled Cities." In *Spatial Practices*, edited by H. Ligget and D. C. Perry, 144–65. Thousand Oaks, Calif.: Sage, 1995.

Kennedy, Mike. "Security: Making Contact." *American School & University* 74 (February 2001): 1–3.

Keynes, Alana. "Security Guards Can Question Students Even in the Absence of Reasonable Suspicion." *Legal Update* 6 (2001): 9–10.

Kinzer, Stephen. "Chicago Moving to 'Smart' Surveillance Cameras." *New York Times*, Tuesday, September 21, 2004, A18.

Lafee, Scot. "Profiling Bad Apples." *School Administrator* 57 (2000): 6–11.

Lash, Scott, and John Urry. *The End of Organized Capitalism*. Madison: University of Wisconsin Press, 1988.

Lewis, Tyson. "The Surveillance Economy of Post-Columbine Schools." *Review of Education, Pedagogy, and Cultural Studies* 25 (2003): 335–55.

Light, Michelle. "Scoop from the Loop." E-mail bulletin from the Children & Family Justice Center, Northwestern University Legal Clinic, 2002. m-light@law.northwestern.edu.

Lipman, Pauline. "Making the Global City, Making Inequality: The Political Economy and Cultural Politics of Chicago School Policy." *American Educational Research Journal* 39 (2002): 379–422.

———. "Cracking Down: Chicago School Policy and the Regulation of Black and Latino Youth." In *Education as Enforcement: The Militarization and Corporatization of Schools*, edited by K. Saltman and D. Gabbard, 81–102. London and New York: RoutledgeFalmer, 2003.

Lipson, Mark. "Private Security: A Retrospective." In *The Private Security Industry: Issues and Trends*, Annals of the American Academy of Political and Social Science, vol. 498, edited by Ira Lipman, 11–22. Newbury Park, Calif.: Sage, 1988.

Low, Setha. "The Edge and the Center: Gated Communities and the Discourse of Urban Fear." *American Anthropologist* 103 (2001): 45–58.

———. *Behind the Gates: Life Security, and the Pursuit of Happiness in Fortress America*. London and New York: Routledge, 2003.

Lupinacci, Jeff. "A Safe Haven." *American School & University* 75 (December 2002): 36–38.

Lyon, David. *The Electronic Eye: The Rise of Surveillance Society*. Minneapolis: University of Minnesota Press, 1994.

Lyon, David, and E. Zureik (eds.). *Surveillance, Computers, and Privacy*. Minneapolis: University of Minnesota Press, 1996.

MacDonald, Keith. *The Sociology of the Professions*. London: Sage, 1995.

Martin, Paul. "Square Gets Hip to Protection." *Security Management* (June 2001): 42–50.

Matchett, Alan. *CCTV for Security Professionals*. New York: Butterworth-Heinemann, 2002.

McCarthy, Cameron, A. P. Rodriguez, E. Buendia, S. Meacham, S. David, H. Godina, K. E. Supriya, and C. Wilson-Brown. "Danger in the Safety Zone: Notes on Race, Resentment, and the Discourses of Crime, Violence and Suburban Security." *Cultural Studies* 11 (1997): 274–95.

McCormick, Jennifer. *Writing in the Asylum: Student Poets in New York City Schools*. New York: Teachers College Press, 2004.

McCrie, Robert. "The Development of the U.S. Security Industry." In *The Private Security Industry: Issues and Trends*, Annals of the American Academy of Political and Social Science, vol. 498, edited by Ira Lipman, 23–33. Newbury Park, Calif.: Sage, 1988.

McVeigh, J. "School Officials Hope Cameras Will Stop Threats." *Derry News*, New Hampshire (n.d.)

Milligan, Christopher. "Facial Recognition Technology, Video Surveillance, and Privacy." *Southern California Interdisciplinary Law Journal* 9 (1999): 295–333.

Mills, C. Wright. *White Collar*. Oxford: Oxford University Press, 1951.

———. *The Power Elite*. Oxford: Oxford University Press, 1956.

Molnar, Alex. *Giving Kids the Business: The Commercialization of America's Schools*. Boulder, Colo.: Westview, 1996.

———. *School Commercialism: From Democratic Ideal to Market Commodity*. New York and London: Routledge, 2005.

Monmonier, Mark. *Spying with Maps: Surveillance Technologies and the Future of Privacy*. Chicago: University of Chicago Press, 2002.

More, Thomas. *Utopia*. 1516. Reprint, New York: Penguin Books, 2003.

Mumford, Lewis. *Technics and Civilization*. New York: Harcourt Brace Jovanovich, 1934.

Murphy, Raymond. *Social Closure*. Oxford: Clarendon Press, 1988.

National Center for Education Statistics, U.S. Department of Education, Fast Response Survey System (FRSS)."Principal/School Disciplinary Survey on School Violence." FRSS Form no. 63. Washington, D.C.: U.S. Department of Education, 1997. http://nces.ed.gov/programs/crime/ pdf/principal/schlViolence.pdf.

National Center for Education Statistics, U.S. Department of Education. "Public and Public Charter School Surveys." Schools and Staffing Survey (SASS). Washington, D.C.: U.S. Department of Education, 1999–2000.

Nelson, Joel, and David Cooperman. "Out of Utopia: The Paradox of Postindustrialization." *Sociological Quarterly* 39 (1998): 583–96.

"Networked Security: Analog Cameras and Video Servers Improve School Safety and Security." *American School & University* 77 (February 2004, school security suppl.): SS16.

Newman, Oscar. *Defensive Space: Crime Prevention through Urban Design.* New York: Collier, 1976.

Nieto, Marcus. *Public Video Surveillance: Is It an Effective Crime Prevention Tool?* Sacramento: California Research Bureau, 1997.

Noguera, Pedro. *City Schools and the American Dream.* New York: Teachers College Press, 2003.

Norris, Clive, and Gary Armstrong. "CCTV and the Social Structuring of Surveillance." *Crime Prevention Studies* 10 (1999): 157–78.

Northern Computers, Inc. Advertisement. *iSecurity,* August 2001, 7.

Nunn, Samuel. "Police Technology in Cities: Changes and Challenges." *Technology in Society* 23 (2001): 11–27.

O'Sullivan, Denis. "Sharing the Wealth: Spreading Security Information—and Its Value—across the Organization." *iSecurity,* August 2001, 12.

O'Toole, Mary Ellen. *The School Shooter: A Threat Assessment Perspective.* Washington, D.C.: Federal Bureau of Investigations, U.S. Department of Justice, n.d.

Pacey, Arnold. *Meaning in Technology.* Cambridge, Mass.: MIT Press, 1999.

Painter, Kate, and Nick Tilley. *Surveillance of Public Space: CCTV, Street Lighting and Crime Prevention.* New York: Criminal Justice Press, 1999.

Parenti, Christian. *The Soft Cage: Surveillance in America from Slavery to the War on Terror.* New York: Basic Books, 2003.

Parsons, Talcott. "Professions and Social Structure." In Talcott Parsons, *Essays in Sociological Theory,* 34–49. Glencoe, Ill.: Free Press, 1954.

Peters, Michael, James Marshall, and Patrick Fitzsimons. "Managerialism and Educational Policy in a Global Context: Foucault, Neoliberalism, and the Doctrine of Self-Management." In *Globalization and Education: Critical Perspectives,* edited by N. Burbules and C. A. Torres, 109–32. London and New York: Routledge, 2000.

Petersen, Julie K. *Understanding Surveillance Technologies: Spy Devices, Their Origins & Applications,* edited by Saba Zamir. New York: CRC Press, 2000.

Richtel, Matt. "A Student ID That Can Also Take Roll." *New York Times,* Wednesday, November 17, 2004, A24 .

Robelen, Erik. "Unsafe Label Will Trigger School Choice." *Education Week,* October 23, 2002, 1.

Roe, Anne. "A Study of Imagery in Research Scientists." *Journal of Personality* 19 (1951): 459–70.

Romanyshyn, Robert. *Technology as Symptom and Dream.* London and New York: Routledge, 1989.

Rossow, Lawrence, and Jacqueline Stefkovich. *Search and Seizure in the Public Schools*, 2nd ed. Topeka, Kans.: National Organization on Legal Problems of Education, 1995.

Safir, Howard. *Security: Policing Your Homeland, Your State, Your City*. New York: St. Martin's Press, 2003.

Saltman, Kenneth, and David Gabbard. *Education as Enforcement: The Militarization and Corporatization of Schools*. London and New York: Routledge, 2003.

Sandia National Laboratories. "Funding for a School Security Center at Sandia Looking Brighter." News release, October 28, 1999. www.sandia. gov/media/NewsRel/NR.

Scarbrough, Harry, and J. Martin Corbett. *Technology and Organization: Power, Meaning, and Design*. London and New York: Routledge, 1992.

Schmidt, Jeff. *Disciplined Minds*. New York: Rowman & Littlefield Publishers, 2000.

Schneider, Tod, Hill Walker, and Jeffrey Sprague. *Safe School Design: A Handbook for Educational Leaders*. Eugene, Ore.: ERIC Clearinghouse on Educational Management, 2000.

School Buyers Online. "Londonderry School System: WebEyeAlert Makes the Grade." December 3, 2001. www.schoolbuyersonline.com.

"Securing the Bus Ride: Digital Recording Systems Save Money and Improve Security." *American School & University* 76 (September 2003, school security suppl.): SS16.

"Security Industry Requests Federal Surveillance Law." *Presstime Bulletin*, September 2001.

Sher, Scott. "Continuous Video Surveillance and Its Legal Consequences." Public Law Research Institute, Working Papers Series, University of California Hastings College of the Law. San Francisco: Public Law Research Institute, 1996.

Sibley, David. *Geographies of Exclusion*. London and New York: Routledge, 1995.

Simpers, Buck. "Safety First: Creating a Safe Environment Includes More than Just a Locked Door." *American School & University* 77 (school security suppl., February 2004): SS12.

Skelly, Michael. "The School Beat." *American School Board Journal* 184 (1997): 25–27.

Stefkovich, Jacqueline. "Search and Seizure of Students in Public Schools: 2002 Update of Fourth Amendment Cases." In *Balancing Rights: Education Law in a Brave New World*, 2002 Conference Papers, edited by the Education Law Association, November. Dayton, Ohio: Education Law Association, 2002, 301–13.

Stein, Nan. *Classrooms and Courtrooms: Facing Sexual Harassment in K–12 Schools*. New York: Teachers College Press, 1999.

Sweeney, Phil. "With WebEye, Biscom Puts Video Security on the Web." *Boston Business Journal*, August 24–30, 2001, 1

Tenner, Edward. *Why Things Bite Back: Technology and the Revenge of Unintended Consequences*. New York: Alfred Knopf, 1996.

Thomas-Lester, Avis, and Toni Locy. "Chief's Friend Accused of Extortion." *Washington Post*, November 26, 1997, A01.

Torres, Carlos Alberto. "Globalization, Education, and Citizenship: Solidarity versus Markets?" *American Educational Research Journal* 39 (2002): 363–78.

Uchida, Craig, Edward Maguire, Shellie E. Solomon, and Megan Gantley. *Safe Kids, Safe Schools: Evaluating the Use of Iris Recognition Technology in New Egypt, NJ.* Washington, D.C.: U.S. Department of Justice, December 2004. www.ncjrs.org.

Urry, John. *Consuming Places.* London and New York: Routledge, 1995.

U.S. Department of Defense. "Today's Military—Life-Stories." N.d. www.today-smilitary.com.

Videolarm. Advertisement. *Security Magazine* 41, no. 10 (October 2004): 17.

"Video Monitoring Rekindles Privacy Debate." *Security Sales & Integration* 26 (October 2004): 44.

Vossekuil, Bryan, and Robert A. Fein, codirectors, with Marisa Reddy, Randy Borum, and William Modezeleski. *The Final Report and Findings of the Safe School Initiative: Implications for the Prevention of School Attacks in the United States.* May. Washington, D.C.: U.S. Secret Service and U.S. Department of Education, 2002. www.secretservice.gov/ntac/ssi_final_report.pdf.

Vossekuil, Bryan, Marisa Reddy, and Robert Fein, codirectors. *Safe School Initiative: An Interim Report on the Prevention of Targeted Violence.* . Washington, D.C.: U.S. Secret Service, October 2000. www.secretservice.gov/ntac/ntac_ssi_report.pdf.

Wagman, Jake. "District Will Use Eye Scanning." *Philadelphia Inquirer,* October 24, 2002. www.philly.com.

Wakefield, Jane. "A Face in the Crowd." *Mother Jones,* November–December 2001, 24.

Wald, Johanna, and Michal Kurlaender. "Connected in Seattle? An Exploratory Study of Student Perceptions of Discipline and Attachments to Teachers." *New Directions for Youth Development* 99 (2003): 35–54.

Weber, Max. *The Theory of Social and Economic Organization.* New York: Oxford University Press, 1947.

Weiner, Tim. "Lockheed and the Future of Warfare." *New York Times,* November 28, 2004, C1.

———. "A New Model Army Soldier Rolls Closer to the Battlefield." *New York Times,* February 16, 2005, A1.

Weisberg, Dan. "Scalable Hype: Old Persuasions for New Technology." In *Critical Studies in Media Commercialism,* edited by R. Anderson and L. Strate, 186–200. Oxford: Oxford University Press, 2000.

Welles, Orson. *The War of the Worlds.* Radio broadcast, 1938. www.members.aol.com/jeff1070/wotw.html.

Wells, H. G. *A Modern Utopia.* Lincoln: University of Nebraska Press, 1967.

Wilson, Dean, and Adam Sutton. *Open-Street CCTV in Australia.* A report to the Criminology Research Council. Melbourne, Australia: Criminology Research Council, 2003.

Yu, Tianlong. *In the Name of Morality.* New York: Peter Lang Publishing, 2004.

Glossary and List of Organizations

The research for this book required that I learn a professional and technological language, and though I tried to minimize the use of esoteric "techno-security-speak," some use of it could not be helped, for the language is central to the selling of the equipment. The following is a glossary of words and phrases used in the book, as well as a list of organizations involved in school security.

Glossary

abilities—reference to new powers and possibilities that technology can bestow on individuals. Also reference to technology's capabilities to adapt to all facilities and needs of customers. *See also* configurability, scalable (and scalability), and survivability.

analog—technology based on continuous streams of information; unlike digital, which is based on distinct bits of information.

anomaly detection—security equipment, software, and law enforcement activities that recognize and alert authorities to odd behavior, such as hesitant walking in a parking lot or loitering behind a building.

authentication framework—security systems that match individual characteristics to information in a database to check for identity.

biometrics—a form of security technology based on systems that process genetic or physical characteristics (such as fingerprints, eye structures, intonation and voice patterns, and hand geometry) through scans and lasers; used in conjunction with database information for identification purposes.

browser-enabled—security equipment that is capable of being operated through the Internet.

camcorder—visual- and audio-recording device with playback abilities.

CCTV—closed-circuit television; filmed with video surveillance cameras.

compliant software—software that can be adjusted and modified to meet the needs of specific users.

configurability—the ability to adjust hardware and software to make them compatible with existing systems or particular needs.

CPU—central processing unit; the main body of a computer housing its programming units.

cryptology—the study of codes and ciphers.

digital—the transfer of information in distinct bits of data; unlike analog, which transfers in a continuous stream of information.

DVMR—digital video multiplexers and recorders.

DVR—digital video recording.

end users—those who use the products; customers.

flow—reference to efficiency in checking or searching people at security points. Also, reference to the integration of technology and digital communication.

GIS—geographical information system or "satellites;" referring to a security system that collects, organizes, and analyzes spatial information.

high discrimination—referring to technology, such as a metal detector, that is able to detect many kinds of illicit items, with capabilities to tell the difference between legal and illegal items.

high frequency, low volume—using security equipment frequently but on less people at one time.

information architecture—security technology that processes multiple forms of information obtained from different security equipment; reference to the compilation of information for security purposes.

integrated—similar to scalable. A system that functions well with many attachments and networks. Also, a system that links many forms of security equipment.

IP (multicast) technology—Internet protocol; referring to an IP address.

LAN—local area network.

live streaming—like "real-time" streaming. Referring to instantaneous surveillance images of incidents as they occur.

monocle screen—miniature computer screen that can attach to a visor or head strap for viewing.

motion tracking system—a security system capable of charting motion and determining speed and abnormal movements.

multimedia applications—reference to security equipment that conveys information in multiple ways, including the use of visuals, sound, charts, and maps. Also, reference to software that can be used for security as well as information and entertainment purposes.

multiplexer—a device that enables several digital signals to transmit simultaneously, making integrated systems possible.

nanotechnology—the development of microscopic technologies through the manipulation of atoms and molecules.

network architecture—the creation and integration of a multifaceted security system; referring to the composition of its infrastructure.

neuronal algorithms—referring to the patterning and sequencing of neurons for identification purposes.

PDA—personal digital assistant; a handheld computer with capabilities for communication, scheduling, and other organizing needs.

"point and click"—reference to a form of portable security device that enables individuals to view or hear through barriers.

protective wear—security equipment that is attached to clothing or is developed in the form of clothing.

PSD—personal security device; reference to security equipment used to protect oneself, often handheld or attached to clothing.

real time—live recording and video projection, so individuals can watch activities and manipulate video cameras from an outside source as they occur.

RFID—radio frequency identification; reference to transmissions of information through radio frequencies, used in ID tracking and scan cards.

scalable (and scalability)—security equipment that is capable of being modified for various systems and needs, and is easily updated with newer systems.

streaming—processes related to the transmission of audio and visual data in a network infrastructure.

survivability—referring to durable equipment capable of withstanding abuse and attempted destruction.

technology convergence—unifying multiple services such as voice, data, and video on one network.

telephony (also IP telephony)—referring to the transmission of sound over great distances.

3-D augmented systems—security systems that can present to a user a 3-D image of an environment.

total connectivity—connecting software to hardware. Also, connecting technology to humans.

voice recognition technology—technology that can record voice patterns and check matches between a particular voice pattern and a database of voice patterns for identification purposes.

Organizations

American Institute of Architects (AIA)
American Society for Industrial Security (ASIS)
Campus Safety Association
Center for the Prevention of School Violence
Council of Educational Facility Planners (CEFP
Council of the Great City Schools
Education Commission of the States (ECS)
International Association of Campus Law Enforcement Officers (IACLEO)
International Association of Professional Security Consultants (IAPSC)
National Alliance for Safe Schools (NASS)
National Association of School Resource Officers (NASRO)
National Association of School Safety and Law Enforcement Officers
National Program for Playground Safety (NPPS)
National School Plant Management Association (NSPMA)
National School Safety and Security Services (NSSSS)
National School Supply and Equipment Association

Index